Contemporary Political Sociology

Contemporary Political Sociology

Globalization, Politics, and Power

Second Edition

Kate Nash

A John Wiley & Sons, Ltd., Publication

Edition history: Blackwell Publishers Ltd (1e, 2000)

Blackwell Publishing was acquired by John Wiley & Sons in February 2007. Blackwell's publishing program has been merged with Wiley's global Scientific, Technical, and Medical business to form Wiley-Blackwell.

Registered Office
John Wiley & Sons Ltd, The Atrium, Southern Gate, Chichester, West Sussex, PO19 8SQ, United Kingdom

Editorial Offices
350 Main Street, Malden, MA 02148-5020, USA
9600 Garsington Road, Oxford, OX4 2DQ, UK
The Atrium, Southern Gate, Chichester, West Sussex, PO19 8SQ, UK

For details of our global editorial offices, for customer services, and for information about how to apply for permission to reuse the copyright material in this book please see our website at www.wiley.com/wiley-blackwell.

Library of Congress Cataloging-in-Publication Data
Nash, Kate, 1958–
    Contemporary political sociology : globalization, politics, and power / Kate Nash. – 2nd ed.
        p. cm.
    Rev. ed. of: Readings in contemporary political sociology, c2000.
    Includes bibliographical references and index.
    ISBN 978-1-4443-3074-8 (hardcover : alk. paper) – ISBN 978-1-4443-3075-5 (pbk. : alk. paper)
1. Political sociology. I. Readings in contemporary political sociology. II. Title.
    JA76.R4 2010
    306.2–dc22
                                    2009039199

A catalogue record for this book is available from the British Library.

Set in 11 on 13.5 Sabon by Toppan Best-set Premedia Limited
Printed in Singapore by Ho Printing Singapore Pte Ltd

01   2010

To Minky

Contents

Preface to the Second Edition

The first edition of this book, published ten years ago, was written before the "Battle for Seattle" brought issues of global justice into mainstream public awareness; before the World Social Forum; before global climate change moved from scientific controversy to undeniable fact; before the world watched incredulously as one plane and then another hit the Twin Towers in New York; before the invasion of Iraq in the name, first, of global security, and then, when the threat of "weapons of mass destruction" proved to be a fiction, of liberation and human rights; and before the global financial crisis which has led to the nationalization of banks in the UK and elsewhere, and talk of the dangers of free markets everywhere.

In many respects, the framework provided by the first edition has held up well. There has been a resurgence of social movements, in a new global cycle of protest. Citizenship is well established as a branch of sociological study in its own right. And questions of democracy and globalization have become more pressing than ever before, nationally and internationally. The book has been relatively easily updated within this framework, with topical discussions of the internationalizing state; neo-liberalism, wealth, and poverty; the continuing viability of multiculturalism; ongoing questions of post-national citizenship; and the concrete strategies adopted by global social movements to democratize global governance. In addition, I have tried to address some topics I did not look at in the first edition, especially new possibilities of global media, including activist uses of new media technologies and the popular humanitarian imagination; and the growing importance of human rights.

I have also made extensive revisions. To add material, I have had to remove some. One of the main ways I have made room is to leave aside debates over modernity, post-modernity, and postmodernism, which no longer engage sociologists as they did ten years ago. In part, no doubt, this is due to the resurgence of what seem very modern questions, concerning capitalism and imperialism, inequalities and redistribution, state sovereignty and universal human rights. It is also related to a sense that learning to *think* in radically different ways, though exciting, is no longer enough if does not offer the tools for "positive" political visions. Of course, dreaming up abstract and idealist political programs is not an appropriate task for sociology, but it is important to be able to study how social actors are trying to bring about social change, and the challenging movements, events and projects of globalization are not easily mapped in terms of resistance/deconstruction or radical multiplicity. I have completely altered chapter 5 in order to discuss the concrete projects of democratization I see emerging out of current political practice.

I have also modified somewhat my understanding of cultural politics and the state. Although I thought, and still think, of "cultural politics" as involving the contestation and redefinition of meanings in all ongoing social structures and settings, I now realize that I under-estimated the importance of the state as an especially significant site and target of cultural politics. Writing in the 1990s, I was perhaps more influenced than I supposed by ideas that the state was no longer relevant, by Foucauldian and other approaches, by new social movement theorists, and also by the rather loose ideas about globalization that were in the air (though not in sociology, where they were very much challenged). Although I certainly did not see the state as irrelevant, the theory of cultural politics I suggested as a way of studying the deep-rooted and far-reaching effects of social movements tended, I think now, to neglect the particular privileges of states with regard to force, which enables them to make and enforce law, to collect and re-distribute wealth, and to go to war. It would be much more difficult with the rise of the "security state" and human rights issues today, not to mention wars in Afghanistan and Iraq, to neglect the importance of force to the exercise of state power; and I also have a better understanding of the role of the state as actively involved in projects of in neo-liberal globalization. I have consequently revised the theory of cultural politics to include an understanding of the use of force that is defined and used "in the name of the state" in chapter 1. I have also become interested in a wider range of ways of understanding cultural politics, and I have learned a lot from writings in American cultural sociology, especially those of Jeffrey Alexander. I have found his ideas of the civil sphere especially useful as a way of understanding the informal, and yet bounded, aspects of citizenship. I have also added a section in chapter 1 on the

Durkheimian tradition of political sociology which I now see as a very important contribution to contemporary sociological understandings of culture.

This second edition retains the focus of the first on the advanced capitalist liberal-democracies of North America, Europe, and Australasia (which I sometimes refer to in short-hand as "the West"). It is not possible to write a book from nowhere. I am not well equipped to write a book that would "provincialize Europe" by using theoretical frameworks developed elsewhere, though I am certainly in favor of the intellectual and political aims of the project (Chakrabarty 2007). It is important to avoid over-generalization, and all sorts of issues and questions – perhaps especially those of citizenship, but also the form and ideas of social movements – develop in relation to particular states. The perspective I take in the book is that of progressive global social movements: feminism, environmentalism, and the global justice movement all share a sense of transnational responsibility, and build networks to address structures of social life that connect and affect people across borders. In addition, I have tried to consider the limits of the perspectives outlined here, and to be sensitive to the geo-politics they imply; writing, reading, studying, and discussing are, themselves, a kind of cultural politics. I have especially thought about geo-politics in chapters 2 and 5, which have been completely rewritten for the second edition, and I have tried to pay attention to the interconnections and interdependencies of movements, structures, actions and events across wider geographical areas throughout the book. There may be a growing sense of political responsibility for the way in which "people here participate in the production and reproduction of structural processes that condition the lives of people far away" (Young, 2004: 371). One of the tasks of political sociologists is surely to understand the difficulties of developing and acting on that sense.

I would like to thank the following people from whom I've learned directly about the ideas in this book over the last ten years: Suki Ali, Jeffrey Alexander, Les Back, Clive Barnett, Alice Bloch, Kirsten Campbell, Lilie Chouliaraki, Nick Couldry, Nonica Datta, Marie Dembour, Natalie Fenton, Elisa Fiaccadori, Anne-Marie Fortier, Nancy Fraser, Monica Greco, David Hansen-Miller, Clare Hemmings, Madeleine Kennedy-McFoy, George Lawson, Kevin McDonald, Jennie Munday, Lawrence Pawley, Shanta Pillai, Unni Pillai, Noortje Marres, Manoranjan Mohanty, Zee Nash, Anne Phillips, Alan Scott, Anna Marie Smith, Nick Stevenson, John Street, Roberta Sassatelli, Alberto Toscano, Fran Tonkiss, and Neil Washbourne.

Kate Nash

Chapter 1

Changing Definitions of Politics and Power

The election of Barack Obama as President of the United States was a global media event, anticipated, analyzed, and celebrated around the world. In the run up to the election, even his most ardent supporters feared it would not be possible because although Americans seemed to agree they were in the midst of an economic and political crisis and shared a desire for change, many white Americans would not be able to bring themselves to vote for a black man with a foreign name that sounded suspiciously like that of public enemy number one, Osama Bin Laden. The long-term politicization of racist social relations, the growth and consolidation of black pride and solidarity since the civil rights movement of the 1950s, and the contestation of the "naturalization" of white domination in the US played a crucial role in the conditions under which his election was possible; as well as Obama's cool, "post-racial" self-presentation as sophisticated, urbane, smart, and yet, "of the people." The meaning of the event for those – many more – of us who will never be in a position to elect a US president is perhaps even more interesting. The election of Obama was a chance for Americans to confirm, largely to themselves, that the ideal of America as the land of opportunity for everyone and the guardian of democracy for the world, while it might have become somewhat tarnished as a result of bankers' greed and the excesses of the "war on terror," was still a cause for hope. But the incredible joy and relief with which Obama's presidency was greeted across the world was also about hope. In Europe, the reputation of America rose immediately, even amongst social movement activists, along with the expectation that American foreign policy would now become fairer and more cooperative. Shortly after the election, I saw

graffiti in an East London park that I interpret as a tribute to the new
beginning offered by Obama's presidency: "Anti-Americanism is a con-
spiracy against radicalism."

Obama's election cannot properly be understood without addressing
how culture and politics are intertwined. Contemporary political sociology is concerned with cultural politics as what we might call the "politics
of politics." From this perspective, what events *mean* to those who interpret and act on them is what matters. What counts as "political" in terms
of content and style must first be made political; it must be made visible
and relevant to visions of how social relations are and could be organized.
Processes of politicization in this respect are very far from under the
control of professional politicians and public relations experts, however
hard they try to set the agenda. But contemporary political sociology is
also concerned with cultural politics in a wider sense: what is made
"political" is not simply confined to what takes place within government,
political parties, and the state. The perspective of cultural politics also
helps us make sense of how the meanings of social relations and identities
are consistently challenged wherever they are framed as unjust, exclusionary, and destructive of the capacities of individuals and groups.

Understanding "politicization" across the social field has not typically
been the subject matter of political sociology until fairly recently. Political
sociology has never been easily distinguishable as a field of research from
others in the discipline of sociology. In general terms, however, it has been
seen as concerned, above all, with relations between state and society.
Most practitioners would probably agree with Orum's broad definition:
political sociology directs attention toward "the social circumstances of
politics, that is, to how politics both is shaped by and shapes other events
in societies. Instead of treating the political arena and its actors as independent from other happenings in a society, [political sociology] treats
that arena as intimately related to all social institutions" (Orum, 1983:
1). In principle, given the wide range of this definition, it might be
expected that political sociologists would be interested in power as at least
a potentiality in all social relations, and to have elaborated a conception
of politics as an activity conducted across a range of social institutions.
In practice, however, although they have sometimes gestured toward such
an approach, the focus of political sociology has been politics at the level
of the nation-state. It has shared what may be seen as the prejudice of
modern sociology for taking "society" as the unit of analysis and treating
it as a distinct, internally coherent, and self-regulating entity, organized
around the nation-state. The most influential definition of power in sociology is that of Max Weber: power is "the chance of a man or a number

of men to realize their own will in a communal action even against the resistance of others who are participating in the action" (Weber, 1948a: 180).[1] On this definition, power could be a dimension of any social relation, and politics need not be seen as a highly specialized activity exercised only in relation to a specific institution. In fact, however, Weber, like others, focused his attention on the state as a special kind of institution that successfully possesses a monopoly of the legitimate use of force within a given territory (Weber, 1948b: 78). As Dowse and Hughes argue in their introduction to political sociology, although there seems to be no compelling *analytic* argument why the discipline should have focused its attention on state institutions, *as a matter of fact*, political sociologists have concerned themselves principally with the ways in which society has affected the state (Dowse and Hughes, 1972: 7).[2]

Over the last couple of decades, however, political sociology has shifted away from this focus on how society affects the state. From the point of view of contemporary political sociology, such an approach is fundamentally flawed. In the first place, economic, political, and cultural globalization means that what the state is and does is now itself in question. Though action taken in the "name of the state" is often very effective, and with the "war on terror" following 9/11, state violence has become more visible in some respects, state action must now almost invariably take into account institutions, processes, and actors in relation to which states were previously considered sovereign and autonomous. At the same time, the class formations around which national political parties were organized have become fragmented and the political concerns associated with class-based political parties problematized. The structure of the workforce has changed and with it, the expectation of stable, secure working lives for many people. The fragmentation and pluralization of values and lifestyles, with the growth of the mass media and consumerism and the decline of stable occupations and communities, all mean that previously taken-for-granted social identities have become politicized. In this context, the rise of social movements and networks organized differently from parties, and representing non-class identities such as gender, ethnicity, and sexuality, have changed both the form and the content of politics. Wider definitions of power and politics are needed to encompass the formation, contestation, and transformation of identities and institutions across the social field, if fluid, fragmented, and fast-changing contemporary social relations are to be understood.

Empirical changes would not be sufficient, however, to create a new approach to political sociology if there were not also new theoretical tools with which to make sense of them. There has been a paradigm shift in political sociology away from state-centered, class-based models of political participation, or non-participation, toward an understanding of politics as a potentiality of all social experience. It is in this sense that contemporary political sociology is concerned with cultural politics, understood in the broadest possible sense as the contestation and transformation of social identities and structures.

In the following three sections of this chapter, we will begin our discussion of political sociology with a look back at how it developed through the study of the work of the "founding fathers," Marx, Weber, and Durkheim. We will then go on to consider the "analytics of power" developed by Michel Foucault, the single most influential thinker on the development of contemporary political sociology, and the work on "governmentality" that directly draws inspiration from his writings on politics and power. I will then introduce the most important theoretical themes of contemporary political sociology and explain why the concept of "cultural politics" is so useful to understanding "politics of politics" today. Finally, there will be an outline of the chapters to follow, indicating how each one deals with a particular theme in contemporary political sociology.

1.1   The Marxist Tradition of Political Sociology

In many respects, it is far from evident that the state should have a central place in Marxist analyses of capitalism, given their overwhelming theoretical commitment to the view that it is economic relations which ultimately determine all social and political life. Marx himself, concerned primarily as he was with capitalism as a mode of production, concentrated on the economic level, and had relatively underdeveloped and tentative views on the state. In fact, Adam Przeworski goes so far as to suggest that, given his theory of capitalism as a self-perpetuating economic system of production and exchange, there was no room in it for theorizing the state as contributing to its reproduction (Przeworski, 1990: 6970). Although this is an extreme view, based on Marx's later work, it is true that it has proved very difficult for neo-Marxists to give due weight to ideology and politics without giving up the central theoretical Marxist commitment to economic class struggle as the motor of history.

The roots of later Marxist theorizations of political power as a translation of economic power concentrated in the modern state are there already in Marx's writings. Although Marx had no fully developed theory of the state, he did discuss it in various ways throughout his writings. Here we shall follow Dunleavy and O'Leary's (1987) classification of Marx's analyses of the state into three distinct and somewhat contradictory positions on how it contributes to the reproduction of the capitalist system and the economic power of the bourgeoisie. All of them have been followed up in different ways by neo-Marxist theorists (Dunleavy and O'Leary, 1987: 209). First, in the instrumental model, the coercive aspect of the state is emphasized; it is seen above all as repressive of working-class resistance to exploitation. The "executive of the modern state" is "but a committee for managing the affairs of the whole bourgeoisie" (Marx, 1977: 223). On this model, economic power is quite simply translated into political power, by which means the dominant bourgeoisie rules over subordinate classes through the liberal state. Second, in his later, more empirical writings, Marx suggested a different model of the state – the arbiter model (Dunleavy and O'Leary, 1987: 210). In "The Eighteenth Brumaire of Louis Bonaparte," he sketches the modern state in such a way as to suggest its relative autonomy from the interests of the bourgeoisie. The modern state has grown so strong that in exceptional moments, when the bourgeoisie cannot completely dominate the other classes against which it must struggle, it may become an arena for competing interests, an ostensible mediator, and may even act independently to limit the power of the bourgeoisie (Marx, 1992). However, "state power does not hover in mid-air"; it is only class interests that are represented at the political level and, ultimately, economic power will determine how state power is to be used (Marx, 1992: 237). Despite the relative autonomy of the modern state, then, economic power is translated into political power since it needs the material support of the historically ascendant class, and it therefore works ultimately to ensure the economic advantage of the bourgeoisie. Third, in his mature economic work, Marx suggested a third model of the state: the functionalist version. In this view, developed in *Capital*, volume 3, the state is "superstructural," determined entirely by changes in the economic "base" of society. The state apparatus, government, and legal forms operate in order to optimize the conditions for capital accumulation, regardless of how directly the bourgeoisie manages state institutions and irrespective of the balance of forces in society (Dunleavy and O'Leary, 1987: 21011). In this understanding of the state, political power is irrelevant; the state is but an epiphenomenon of the economic logic of the capitalist system which reproduces itself in every social and political institution to the advantage of the dominant economic class.

For some time after Marx's death, this economistic model of capitalist reproduction was Marxist orthodoxy. Although early Marxists gave some consideration to the role of the state in sustaining capitalism, theorists such as Kautsky and Plekhanov, concerned above all to establish Marxism as a rigorous science, worked to discover the historical laws by which the economy developed. They, therefore, reduced the superstructure – the political, ideological, and cultural – to emanations of the economic base (Taylor, 1995: 24952). It is the neo-Marxist rejection of this simplistic economism which in recent years has led theorists to consider political power at the level of the state as relatively autonomous of economic power.

Neo-Marxism

Writing in the 1920s, Antonio Gramsci was the first Marxist to theorize the ideological and political superstructures as relatively autonomous of the economic base. As such, he was a major influence on other neo-Marxists such as Louis Althusser. The key term for Gramsci is "hegemony" which means the way in which the dominant class gains consent for its rule through compromises and alliances with some class fractions and the disorganization of others, and also the way in which it maintains that rule in a stable social formation (Gramsci, 1971; Simon, 1982). In terms of Dunleavy and O'Leary's typology, Gramsci's is an arbiter theory of the state: the state is formed by the balance of forces achieved in the struggle for hegemony. For Gramsci, a class does not take state power; it becomes the state (Laclau and Mouffe, 1985: 69). However, Gramsci is innovative in Marxism in not thinking of the state as the institution in which politics takes place. According to Gramsci, hegemony is gained in the first place in civil society where ideology is embodied in communal forms of life in such a way that it becomes the taken-for-granted common sense of the people. All relations of civil society involve issues of power and struggle, not just class relations. Politics is more a cultural sensibility than an institutional activity for Gramsci. In this respect, he has been an important influence on the political sociology of cultural politics, especially through the work of Stuart Hall in cultural studies (Morley and Chen, 1996).

Gramsci's thought in this respect was limited, however, by his commitment to economism. Gramsci, like Althusser, saw ideology as practices that form subjects; for both thinkers, our experience and our relationship to the world are mediated through ideology. In Gramsci's view, subjects are not necessarily class subjects, but rather collective political wills formed by articulating ideas and values in different combinations in order to draw different groups into the hegemonic project. However, as a

Marxist, Gramsci was committed to the belief that ideological struggle is grounded in class struggle; he, therefore, argued that there must always be a single unifying principle in every hegemonic formation and that this can only be given by a fundamental economic class. As Laclau and Mouffe (1985: 69) point out, this is not just to say that, ultimately, the economy determines politics, but also to see the economy itself as outside hegemony, as somehow naturally given and non-political. As they argue, this means that there is nothing for Marxists to do but identify the direction in which the economy is heading; there is no possibility of political intervention, or even of effective class struggle, in the domain that really matters to Marxists, the economy. In their view, Gramsci limited the scope of politics in that it should be seen as fundamental to the founding and contestation of any social order whatsoever. Gramsci's model is also limited in that, seeing politics as ultimately rooted in class struggle, it cannot give sufficient weight to social movements organized around gender, race, sexual politics, the environment, and so on. However, to reject economic determinism and the centrality of the class struggle is to go beyond Marxism altogether.

Similar issues arise in the work of Althusser. Although his project was to rescue Marxism from economism, insofar as it remains within the Marxist framework, economism cannot be avoided. Althusser maintained that the state should be seen as relatively autonomous of the economic base. However, his theory of the state is better described as "functionalist," rather than in terms of Dunleavy and O'Leary's arbiter model. Although he insists that political structures have their own laws of development, there is no discussion of class conflict at this level; the state is fully implicated in the logic of capitalism, where it functions to reproduce the mode of production (Dunleavy and O'Leary, 1987: 255). As Althusser sees it, the state is relatively autonomous of the economic base because, although the economy determines "in the last instance," it does so by determining another level of the mode of production as dominant according to the specificity of the mode of production: in feudalism, religion is dominant; in capitalism, the state. Furthermore, since the capitalist mode of production requires the state to reproduce its conditions of existence, there is a reciprocal determination between the economic and political levels; the last instance of economic determination never arrives since the economy is itself formed by the political (Althusser, 1971).

Insofar as Althusser's theory of the state is functionalist, it has been criticized as involving a sophisticated form of economic reductionism. The problem is that, if the economy is determining in the last instance, then whatever the form and dynamic of contingent, actually existing capitalist states, ultimately they are irrelevant in relation to the necessity of the reproduction of capitalism itself. In fact, the term "relative autonomy" is oxymoronic; if autonomy is relative, then ultimately it is not autonomy at all. As Paul Hirst argues, Althusser is trapped by his own question – "how is it possible for capitalist social relations to exist?" – since there is no general answer to this question which would not involve him in the teleological logic of functionalist explanations. Althusser is searching for the causes of an existing state of affairs which the explanation then takes to be necessary for their existence; in effect, the consequences make the causes necessary (Hirst, 1979: 435). The conclusion that Hirst draws from this is that, if the relative autonomy of the state is to be taken seriously, there can be no reduction of the political to the economic: the form of social classes produced as effects of politics must be analyzed as such.

In fact, the most influential aspect of Althusser's work has been the importance he gave to issues of ideology and subjectivity. Althusser saw the state as working through the repressive institutions of the police and the army, but also through ideology embedded in state institutions – for him, a mixture of public and private institutions, including those of education, the family, trade unions, and religion. Althusser saw society as a complex of structures, each with its own dynamic, linked into a totality by the ultimate determination of the economy. The function of ideology is to make individuals into subjects who will fit the positions provided by those structures. Although it is described as consisting of "representations" – "images, myths, ideas, or concepts" – ideology does not work through the conscious mind, but in an unconscious relation to the world which is lived in social practices, such as religious rituals, political meetings, and so on (Althusser, 1971: 3944). Althusser's theory of ideology avoids the pitfalls of the Marxist notion of "false consciousness," in which people are seen as dupes of the capitalist system, since he does not see ideology as consciousness at all; in his view, ideology is itself material, involving experiences lived in real social practices. However, ideology does involve a degree of mystification in that subjects necessarily live an imaginary relation to their real conditions of existence (Barrett, 1991: chapter 5).

Althusser's lasting influence lies in the way in which he situated ideology as a matter of *practices* rather than conscious ideas and beliefs and the emphasis he gave to subjectivity as a means of social control. We will return to this point in section 1.5, where we discuss cultural politics. However, the Marxist epistemology that gave him the assurance to assert that subjects systematically misrepresent reality is problematic. Althusser maintained that Marxism is scientific because it is "open" and "counter-intuitive," where ideology is "closed," and that it draws its problems from politics and practice rather than from critical theory (Benton, 1994: 45–9). This is problematic since Marxism has invariably seemed extremely dogmatic to non-believers, and at the same time, it has been riven by factional disputes. Furthermore, it is difficult to draw a distinction between science and ideology according to the "openness" of science given that, following Thomas Kuhn's (1970) very influential work on science; it is generally acknowledged that even the natural sciences are less concerned with genuinely testing theories than with confirming them.

1.2 The Weberian Tradition of Political Sociology

The autonomy of the political at the level of the state is central to Weber's political sociology. In fact, Weber's work stands at the beginning of a tradition of thought that is explicitly anti-Marxist on just this issue of the autonomy of the state and the importance of liberal democratic politics. As a liberal committed to the defense of individual freedom, which he saw threatened in modernity, Weber opposed his work to Marx's economic determinism. He took the concentration of the means of administration in the nation-state to be as important as the concentration of the means of production in capitalism theorized by Marx (Bottomore, 1993: 1011).

As we saw above, Weber defined power in such a way as to suggest that it may be present in all social relations, so that politics need not be seen as confined to the single arena of the state. In fact, his definition of politics is also very broad: "[it] comprises any kind of *independent* leadership in action" (Weber, 1948a: 77). Despite these definitions, however, Weber immediately narrowed the field of his analysis to the power and politics of the nation-state. He saw the state as the most powerful institution in modern society since it has gained the legitimate monopoly of force over a given territory, and, therefore, took politics to involve "striving to share power or striving to influence the distribution of power, either among states or among groups within a state" (Weber, 1948a: 78). As David Held points out, Weber's emphasis on territoriality is crucial; the modern state is a nation-state in competitive relation to other nation-states, rather than with armed segments of its own population (Held, 1987: 150). Weberian sociology, therefore, explicitly shares the propensity of sociology in general, and included Marxism in the ways we have discussed, for taking total societies organized around nation-states as the object of its analysis.

Weber describes the state as gaining its power in modernity by concentrating the means of administration in the hands of an absolute monarch, expropriating the "ownership of the means of administration," in a way similar to that described by Marx in the case of workers who are deprived of control of the means of production (Weber, 1948b: 812). Officials in modern, rational bureaucracies have little or no control over what they do since the rules and procedures of bureaucracies take on a life of their own, restricting the activities and decisions of those who work in them to the functions of the offices they fill. In this way, bureaucracy forms a "steel-hard housing" within which most individuals in modern societies must live and work, since its effects are felt not only by those who work in administration, but also by those who are administered.[3] According to Weber, this form of life is the price that must be paid for living in a highly complex and technically advanced society. Bureaucratic administration is the only rational way of managing economically and politically differentiated societies since economic enterprises need predictability above all; without it, they cannot calculate in order to ensure profitability. This is why the socialist dream that the state will wither away once the dominant class has been deprived of its power in the ownership of the means of production is more like a nightmare for Weber: to abolish private property would increase the power of the state since there would be no countervailing power of the market, and management of the economy would come entirely under the control of bureaucrats (Held, 1987: 1504).

Although Weber saw himself as a neutral social scientist, his political sociology has a normative dimension. He is concerned to analyze representative democracy as it actually works in modern societies, arguing that the ideal of participatory democracy cannot be practiced in large-scale, complex societies. On the other hand, however, he is also concerned that democracy may be the only way in which the "steel-hard housing" of modern bureaucratic power can be broken. Clearly, the elite administration that must run modern societies cannot be directly accountable to the masses; this would make for inefficiency and unpredictability, especially given what Weber sees as the irrationality and ignorance of the general population. Democracy is important, nevertheless, primarily because elections provide testing grounds for charismatic leaders who are then given the mandate of the people and who can establish the goals the bureaucrats are to realize. Such leaders offer the only chance of overriding the bureaucratic machinery (Giddens, 1972: 389). More conventionally, democracy is important because, even if it only offers the opportunity to dismiss the ineffective from office, it thereby provides a certain degree of protection for the people (Held, 1987: 15460). In Weber's view, democracy is less the rule of the people than the rule of an elite which combines exceptional leaders and bureaucratic experts.

Political sociologists have been inspired by Weber's view of liberal democratic politics. Elite theorists tend to see democracy as working along the lines proposed by Weber (Marsh, 1995: 285) and, although the history of its intellectual development has not been thoroughly traced, there are affinities between pluralist theories and Weber's view that there are many sources of power, not just the economy, and that elites do not rule supreme but can be challenged by organized groups in the political process (Held, 1987: 187). However, it may be that Weber's view of power and politics is problematic in terms of his own sociological theory. Despite his belief in democracy as a way of mitigating the power of bureaucracy, Weber was generally pessimistic, seeing the "polar night of icy darkness" in which individual freedom is highly constrained by impersonal administration as a likely outcome of the development of modern societies (Weber, 1948a: 128). But this pessimism is linked to his view that the majority of the population is uninterested in, and ignorant of, political matters. There are undoubtedly long-term trends towards lack of interest in and apathy concerning party political matters; the proportion of the population in Western liberal democracies who use their vote is in steady decline. On the other hand, if politics is defined more widely, we may see individuals as much more actively engaged in re-making social relations than he was able to discern from within the terms of the political sociology he founded.

Elite theorists

Elite theorists are concerned with the question of how and why it is that a minority must always rule over a majority, which they see as inevitable in any society. Political elite theorists are, above all, concerned with the decision-makers in society, those they see as holding power as a cohesive, relatively self-conscious group (Parry, 1969: 134). Modern elite theorists have been extremely influential in political sociology. Joseph Schumpeter, in particular, has been an important figure as a popularizer of Roberto Michels's ideas on political parties and Weber's theory of democracy. He influenced the generation of sociologists and political scientists involved in the professionalization of the discipline in the 1950s, especially in the US. According to Bottomore (1993: 28), so great was this influence that, for some time afterwards, political scientists in particular took electoral politics and voting behavior as the only worthwhile topic of study, to the exclusion of the substance of political conflicts.

Michels took the concentration of power in the hands of an elite to be a necessary outcome of complex organizations. He is responsible for the emphasis in empirical political sociology on analyzing the dynamics of party politics. His famous "iron law of oligarchy" states that, in modern societies, parties need to be highly organized and so, inevitably, become oligarchic, being hierarchically run by party leaders and bureaucracy such that the bulk of members are excluded from decision-making (Michels, 1962). Michels was critical of this process, although he saw it as tragically inevitable. As a socialist, he was disappointed that socialist parties would be unable to realize their democratic ideals, unlike Weber and Schumpeter for whom bureaucratic and hierarchical parties are the only means by which political leadership in large-scale societies can emerge (Scott, 1996a: 317–18).

Developing Michels's thesis, Schumpeter saw democracy as nothing but competition between political parties whose elite members deal in votes, just as businessmen deal in commodities. It does not, and should not, mean rule by the people; it is rather a method for arriving at political decisions by means of a competitive struggle for the people's vote. Once elected, professional politicians must be allowed to rule, assisted by a strong, independent bureaucracy of expert administrators, since the stability of the political system requires respect for the judgment of elected representatives (Schumpeter, 1943).

A radical version of Weberian elite theory is the institutional elite theory proposed by C. W. Mills. In Mills's view, the elitism of the US in the twentieth century is a serious hindrance to democracy rather than the factor that makes it possible and viable. As he sees it, power has become concentrated and unified in the elites of three institutions in the US: the military, the corporate, and the political; the connections between them having been strengthened by the growth of a permanent war establishment in a privatized incorporated economy since World War II. This concentration, combined with the one-way communication of the mass media as it is organized by elites, makes ordinary citizens ignorant and rather complacent, although fitfully miserable, about the extent to which they lack control over their lives (Mills, 1956).

Mills's argument is similar to that of Marxist elite theorists, notably Ralph Miliband, for whom the capitalist class assures its reproduction by means of the close links it enjoys with the leaders of such powerful institutions as political parties, the civil service, the media, and the military (Miliband, 1969). They differ, however, in that Mills refuses to see the power elite as necessarily unified by virtue of its economic class position and social background, arguing that the shared interests and perspectives of its members are the contingent product of particular historical developments. Marxists, of course, explain the unity of the elite in terms of the interests of capitalism (Bottomore, 1964: 34). However, a comparison of Miliband's and Mills's studies clearly reveals the convergence of Weberians and Marxists on the issue of the relative autonomy of the state. For Miliband, like other neo-Marxists, the state must be able to separate itself from the immediate interests of ruling-class factions if it is to be effective in ensuring the interests of capitalism in the long run (Held, 1987: 207). For Mills, as for other Weberians, however much it is conditioned by elite decisions taken elsewhere, the political elite of the state has its own effectivity.

Elite theory has tended to approach studies of democratic processes from a conservative perspective, radical and Marxist elite theorists notwithstanding. Schumpeter's work has not only focused attention on electoral politics as if they were politics *tout court*, it has also led to "actually existing" democracy being taken as a more or less perfect instrument of rule, with scope for only minor, technical improvements (Bottomore, 1993: 28). In effect, for empirical political sociologists – the charge is less valid in the case of more conceptual and normative work (Held, 1987: 178–85) – a limited view of what politics involves has been strongly linked to a limited view of what democracy must be if it is to be practicable and to allow for stable government. The state-centric view of power and politics held by elite theorists is linked to their understanding of mass society consisting of a passive, ignorant, and apathetic population: technically incompetent to participate fully in politics, according to competitive elitists; and continually deceived as to its real interests, according to more critical versions. Once politics is seen as a matter of everyday life, however, the emphasis changes completely. Contemporary political sociologists see society itself as cut across with inequities of power, any of which may be politicized and, therefore, become the focus of contestation. Far from being passive, social agents are seen as engaged in remaking their own identities and the institutions of their everyday lives.

Pluralism

Unlike elite theory, theorists of pluralism do tend to see citizens as actively involved in politics.[4] As pluralists see it, politics is a matter of competing interest groups, none of which can dominate completely over any of the others since all have access to resources of different kinds. Furthermore, they see the state itself as a set of competing and conflicting institutions, rather than a monolithic entity which exerts its power over the rest of society (Smith, 1995: 211). For this reason, they avoid the term, preferring to think in terms of government. Similarly, the "people" in a democracy is not a unified whole with a single will to be exerted, far less an apathetic, incompetent mass which needs to be ruled by an elite. Democratic politics involves endless bargaining in order to influence government policy, which is nothing more than a compromise between the differing interest groups involved in the political process (Dowse and Hughes, 1972: 135).

In response to their critics, pluralists have revised what has been taken as naïve view of the openness of liberal democratic politics. Neo-pluralists see elites, and especially corporate elites, as having a greater degree of influence than other groups on government policy; they take it that this may not be openly and visibly exerted in the political process and that it may constrain the effective influence of other interest groups (Held, 1987: 202). In this respect, in neo-pluralism, there is a convergence between neo-Marxism, pluralism, and radical elite theory (Marsh, 1995). However, neo-pluralists do not fully endorse the presuppositions of elite theory; instead, they argue that the elite are not unified, nor are they capable of manipulating and deceiving the citizens into accepting elite rule. On the pluralist view, elites must be seen as existing only insofar as they are genuinely responsive to the interest groups they purport to serve (Dowse and Hughes, 1972: 138). Neo-pluralists also depart from the assumptions of neo-Marxists: although business may on occasion subvert the democratic process, this is a contingent matter; politics at the level of the state is primary and so it cannot be the case that the state is ultimately driven by the interests of any particular group, including the capitalist class.

Although pluralists take a wide view of politics as central to social life and independent of the state, ultimately they share the definition of politics held by classical political sociologists. Pluralists are interested in the plurality of interest groups which form and re-form in the social only insofar as they orient their demands to governmental institutions. Although the state is seen as little more than the arena in which social groups engage in political conflict, it is only insofar as these conflicts take place at the level of the state that they are treated *as* political (McClure, 1992: 118–19). By definition, for pluralists there is no politics outside the state.

This limited pluralist definition of politics is linked to a restricted definition of power which, although wider than that of other schools in traditional political sociology, nevertheless makes it impossible to see the construction and contestation of social identities as political. Famously, Dahl (1956: 13) defines power as "a realistic ... relationship, such as A's capacity for acting in such a manner as to control B's responses." This presupposes an already constituted social actor who is in possession of power such that he or she is able to control the effects produced. As critics of pluralism have pointed out, the emphasis on observable effects means that they neglect ideas and the way in which the political agenda may be shaped in such a way that direct manipulation of the outcome of the political process is unnecessary (Lukes, 1974). Indeed, we must understand the very formation of the identities, capacities, and concerns of social groups as effects of power. The formation of identities and the construction of political perspectives are much more fundamental ways in which the politics of politics is structured than by decisions taken in a centralized bureaucracy.

Although pluralists do not take the interests of the social groups they study as given, their definitions of power and politics prevent them from understanding the formation and contestation of political identities in the social field and lead them to focus only on the way in which individuals try to maximize their interests at the level of government. In this respect, the pluralist perspective remains within the framework of traditional political sociology. A theory of politics of this kind cannot begin to grasp the asymmetries of power between groups in civil society that have been politicized by the activities of new social movements since the 1960s; pluralists were, in fact, extremely surprised by this development (Held, 1987: 199–200).

1.3   The Durkheimian Tradition of Political Sociology

Durkheim's work has not had the same degree of status and influence as that of Marx and Weber in political sociology. For Durkheim, the state was of relatively little significance in creating and maintaining social order, which is for him the key problematic of sociology. Durkheim's interests lay rather in questions of social solidarity, and especially with the possibility that the rise of individualism might give members of modern societies a sense of belonging together rather than resulting in a war of all against all. The state does have an important role to play in securing social order, but it can only do so by means of a moral consciousness shared by all members of society – even if the state must sometimes take the lead in formulating it (Giddens, 1971: 102; Lukes, 1973: 668–74). For Durkheim, the state is an outcome of the division of labor that creates modern societies, whilst at the same time it contributes to the expansion of individual freedom. Most importantly, it takes on the function of reflecting on and refining society's "collective representations," the social symbols that express beliefs and values in public rituals and ceremonies, and which guide individuals and constrain their behavior. Durkheim famously, and strikingly, likens the state to the brain: "its principal function is to think" (Durkheim, 1992: 51). Modern societies can only be bound by "organic solidarity," which is experienced by those who find themselves interdependent because they occupy different but equally essential roles in the collective endeavor that is society, and who are bound by common respect for the rights of the individual. This is compared to the mechanical solidarity experienced in simpler pre-modern societies where a strong sense of community is generated out of the similarities of members' lives. The state fosters solidarity by creating and transforming collective representations into binding decisions in law and policy for the good of all (Vogt, 1993).

Although Durkheim generally writes as if what is functional for social order will inevitably come to pass, according to Hans-Peter Muller, his political sociology is intended to show how organic solidarity *might* be achieved. Durkheim actually lived through times of great conflict in nineteenth century France, which he attributed to the difficult transition from an agrarian-corporatist to an industrial-capitalist society (Muller, 1993: 95; see also Lukes, 1973). Unlike Marx or Weber, however, Durkheim did not see conflict as intrinsic to modern societies. On the contrary, where there is conflict, this is attributable to lack of proper social and normative integration. According to Durkheim, it was necessary to reform French society, to prevent egoism triumphing over moral individualism, by coordinating the democratic state, occupational groups, and the individualistic ideal. This meant reform to create a meritocratic society: Durkheim saw inherited wealth as undermining basic levels of trust in the legal contracts on which modern economies depend (Parkin, 1992: chapter 4). It also involved the fostering of occupational associations, or guilds, to mediate between the state and the individual, to protect the individual from the state if it should become too strong, but above all to foster moral consciousness for the common good. For example, Durkheim believed that individuals should vote as members of their professional associations rather than according to where they happen to live, in order to encourage each person to reflect on their shared interests with others in their group and, by extension, with others in the society. Associations are moral communities intended to reshape self-interest for the good of all rather than to further the aims of their members; though linked to occupation, Durkheim seems to have imagined a guild as more like a civil rights organization than like a trade union. This makes him something of a pluralist, though in a rather limited sense, given his overarching concern with harmony between members of society rather than conflict (see Cladis, 2005). Durkheim also seems to have something in common with elite theorists of democracy insofar as he sees "certain personages or classes in society" employed in the state as particularly well suited to interpret society's moral consciousness on behalf of everyone else (Parkin, 1992: 39).

Insofar as he regarded a high degree of substantive equality to be absolutely essential to well-functioning modern societies, Durkheim was not as conservative as he is often seen (Turner, 1992). It is in the more fundamental aspects of Durkheimian sociology that we see his conservatism. Despite his proposals for democratic reform, Durkheim's conceptualization of society actually has no place for politics at all. For Durkheim, social conflicts are inherently pathological, because he makes no allowance for valid disagreements over the interpretation of "collective representations": not only must there be consensus on cultural norms for society to work harmoniously, to be morally healthy, but the right norms for a particular form of society are identifiable by the sociologist. The social conflict Marx and Weber see as intrinsic to modern societies, Durkheim sees as "pathological," at best a result of difficult transition to a properly functioning new society in which the science of sociology, which Durkheim saw himself as discovering, has a special legislative role. There is no place for politics in Durkheim's sociology, only for scientifically informed social reform; politics is contingent and partial, fundamentally unnecessary to a properly functioning society, and actually inherently immoral.

Neo-Durkheimian political sociology

Neo-Durkheimian political sociology is inspired by Durkheim's work on the importance of collective representations as both constraining and enabling, and the way in which they are reinforced and elaborated in rituals, performances, and solidaristic passions. This work takes Durkheim's problematic of the moral basis of social cohesion as its object of study, and especially the cultural conditions of democracy and social justice. Where the optimism of Durkheimian functionalism ultimately denies the importance of politics (as Lukes puts it, in his early work at least, Durkheim tends to assume "an identity between the 'normal,' the ideal, and the about-to-happen" [Lukes, 1973: 177]), neo-Durkheimian studies focus on the *difficulties* of achieving and maintaining solidarity, and on the way in which the very definitions of social justice may be expanded in complex contemporary societies.

In his work *The Civil Sphere*, Jeffrey Alexander builds on the later work of Durkheim on religion to argue that, although contemporary societies have been transformed by secular humanism, spiritual dimensions are vital to the construction of social solidarity.[5] He argues that there is an underlying consensus in American society that democracy is sacred, and that it must be protected from profane counter-democratic persons, events, and activities. The civil sphere is organized around cultural codes that maintain this fundamental binary opposition and which are available, and invariably drawn on, when concrete political disputes arise. The civil sphere exists alongside other spheres in differentiated societies, as a "solidary sphere, in which a certain kind of universalizing community comes to be culturally defined and to some degree institutionally enforced" (Alexander, 2006: 31). Membership in the civil sphere depends on accounting for oneself as motivated and as acting democratically (rationally, reasonably, and realistically, and not irrationally, hysterically, or unrealistically) to support democratic social relationships (which are open, trusting, truthful) and institutions (which are rule-regulated, not arbitrary, promote equality not hierarchy and inclusion not exclusion). Whatever or whoever comes to be defined as profane is seen as polluting, "to be isolated and marginalized at the boundaries of civil society, and sometimes even destroyed" (Alexander and Smith, 1993: 164). The civil sphere may be expanded to include class and status groups previously excluded from its terms where those stigmatized as counter-democratic are able to claim, and to institutionalize, their membership through its cultural codes. The codes of the civil sphere may also be used to "invade" the non-civil spheres of the economy, the state, the family, and religious interaction. Alexander gives detailed attention to the social movements that have successfully used the language of the ideal community of the civil sphere to bring black Americans, women, and Jews into the democratic mainstream. Ultimately, this is possible because the civil sphere is premised on moral individualism; it is the rights of the person that are sacred in contemporary societies. The civil sphere therefore contains within it the possibility of expanding terms of democratic and social justice.

Alexander's "strong programme" of cultural sociology, of which *The Civil Sphere* is the most highly developed exemplar, involves a sophisticated account of how culture, structure, and social action fit together. We will draw on some of the insights of this program later in the chapter to develop the theoretical framework for analyzing cultural politics. In terms of political sociology, however, *The Civil Sphere*, whilst it brilliantly updates Durkheim's work for the twenty-first century, also shares some of the difficulties of that work with regard to politics.

Alexander's theorization of *The Civil Sphere* does not neglect political agents. There is nothing necessary or functional about the expansion of the cultural codes of the civil sphere to include those persons and situations previously excluded. Successful use of democratic symbols is contingent; it depends on the mobilization of social movements to "repair" solidarity. Nevertheless, there is a sense in Alexander's work that American society (the concrete example he analyses) is inherently just; some groups have found themselves excluded from the civil sphere, but this is the result of a mistaken attribution on the part of historically located political actors who, with the benefit of hindsight, the sociologist identifies as themselves profane, counter-democratic. Alexander presents his account as sociologically neutral, but, actually, it favors egalitarian social reform rather than authoritarian interpretations of characteristics of belonging and social organization. Like Durkheim's own theory of social reform, however, it is an account which does not acknowledge its own political position. What justifies treating the historical examples from which Alexander extrapolates the deep structure of society as more than just that – singular, successful, examples of how the use of progressive terms have been deployed on a number of separate occasions? In fact, Alexander's understanding of the way in which the deep cultural structure of society tends towards justice for all in the civil sphere makes politics oddly peripheral to his sociology. Although conflicts over interpretations of democratic codes are intrinsic to Alexander's view of society in a way that they are not part of Durkheim's, because respect for individual rights is "hardwired" into the sacred democratic codes, in a very fundamental sense no human being is ever completely excluded from the civil sphere. While a particular group may be historically and contingently excluded as "polluting," the universalizing codes of the civil sphere themselves promote a logic that inherently resists the interpretation of any individual as "outside" democratic society. In enabling, even requiring, the "outsider" position to be challenged, the cultural codes themselves therefore work against the "absolute" binary opposition between sacred and profane: the "polluted" outsider is in some way always already sacred. It is important to note that, for Alexander, definitions of counter-democratic "evil" are theoretically as fundamental to that binary structure as definitions of the sacred, but it is surely not by chance that his analyses of concrete events and social movements are invariably progressive. The problem here is reminiscent of the problem with Durkheim's functionalism: what is functional must in some way be normal and ideal. Similarly, the civil sphere is already really, deeply just, and therefore any contingent historical injustices not only do not alter that but will be, must be, eradicated. Though they may involve blood, tears, even questions of life and death, political disputes are rather superficial and ephemeral viewed in the light of the deep and necessary tendencies towards justice of the civil sphere itself.

Durkheim's foundational work should be seen alongside that of Marx and Weber as influential on political sociology. In fact, it gains in importance in contemporary political sociology because of the importance Durkheim gave to how symbolic meaning is implicated in the constitution of social relations. There is evidence, for example, that Ferdinand de Saussure, a crucial figure in the formation of contemporary political sociology – we will consider the significance of his work towards theorizing cultural politics in section 1.5 below – was directly influenced by Durkheim. As Alexander points out, even if there was no direct influence, the resonances of Durkheim's ideas about symbols in Sassure's "semiotics" are substantial (Alexander, 1998: 4–5). Just as important as a good grasp of symbolic meanings to contemporary political sociology, however, are workable definitions of power and politics that enable us to map how meanings are contested by concrete social actors and with what effects in constituting identities and perspectives across the social field. For this, we turn to the work of Michel Foucault. As we shall see, Foucault does not give us everything we need to conceptualize cultural politics: in particular, he neglects the importance of cultural meanings. Nevertheless, his radical break with previous sociological conceptions of power and politics takes us some way towards a framework for thinking about cultural politics.

1.4   Focauldian Definitions of Power and Politics

Foucault's definition of power is the single most important theoretical contribution to rethinking contemporary political sociology. Foucault himself has rather a paradoxical relationship to contemporary political sociology: although he is the theorist whose work has been most influential in its development, and although he was actively engaged in various political activities, including campaigns for prisoners' rights and gay activism, he professed himself to be much more interested in ethics than in politics (Foucault, 1984a). This preference for ethics, which he saw as a matter of self-creation rather than of principles of right and wrong, is related to his distaste for systematic theorizing. Foucault refused to provide a map of social and political institutions with which to understand contemporary politics, but his work can be used to analyze the working of power in unexpected places and unexpected ways.

In this section, we will first look at an outline of Foucault's "analytics of power," and then at work on "governmentality" that has been influenced by his later work. Although the study of neo-liberal governmentality is an important and influential strand of contemporary political sociology in itself, it does not exhaust Foucault's influence on contemporary political sociology, which has been both broader and deeper than this body of work alone. We will look at this wider influence on "cultural politics" in the final section of the chapter.

Foucault's analytics of power

Foucault explicitly denies that he has constructed a *theory* of power, arguing that power must be analyzed in its operations and effects and cannot be captured in a systematic set of related concepts conceived in advance of its application (Foucault, 1984b: 82). He prefers, therefore, to think in terms of an "analytics of power" in which power is identified only in the instances of its exercise. It is, nevertheless, possible to make some general points about this "analytics."

Power for Foucault is, above all, productive. His analyses are opposed to what he calls the "juridico-discursive" model in which power is seen as possessed by the state, especially the law, and is used to impose order on society. According to this theory, power involves legitimate prohibition modeled on the legal contract, according to liberals, or repressive legislation and policing to preserve class domination, according to radicals. It is, at any rate, essentially negative, restrictive, and inhibitory (Foucault, 1980a). According to Foucault, to think of power in this way is to miss how it works in institutions and discourses across the social field. Foucault is concerned to analyze power in the details of social practices, at the points at which it produces effects, as a fluid, reversible, and invisible "microphysics" of power. In Foucault's model, power is productive in the sense that it is constitutive, working to produce particular types of bodies and minds in practices which remain invisible from the point of view of the older model of power as sovereignty. Power is pluralist: it is exercised from innumerable points, rather than from a single political center. It is not the possession of an elite, and it is not governed by a single overarching project. However, seeing power as productive is not to see it as good. On the contrary, in most of his work at least, Foucault's use of the term "power" implies a critical perspective on social practices. It is productive of regulated and disciplined social relations and identities which are to be resisted.

The most general sense in which power is productive for Foucault is through knowledge. Knowledge, especially that of the social sciences, is closely implicated in the production of docile bodies and subjected minds. "Discourses" is the term Foucault uses for these systems of quasi-scientific knowledge. Knowledge as discourse is not knowledge of the "real" world as it exists prior to that knowledge. Although it presents itself as *representing* objective reality, in fact, discourses *construct* and make "real" the objects of knowledge they "represent." Knowledge is distinguished from other ways of apprehending the world and considered to be "knowledge" of the objective world because it is supported by practices of power. As Foucault sees it, knowledge involves statements uttered in institutional sites in which it is gained according to certain rules and procedures, by speakers who are authorized to say what counts as "truth" in that particular context. For Foucault, the analysis of discourse requires the determination of how new objects of knowledge emerge, under what discursive and non-discursive conditions, and especially, what effects of power they produce. As he puts it, "Truth is linked in a circular relation with systems of power which produce and sustain it, and to effects of power which it induces and which extend it" (Foucault, 1980b: 133).

Foucault's analysis of knowledge as constitutive and implicated in power breaks, then, with the "official" view the social sciences would like to have of themselves as disinterested, neutral, and, as such, contributing to human progress. It also breaks with the radical view that knowledge produced in elite institutions is inherently mystificatory, concealing real relations of power. As Foucault sees it, it is not so much that discourses *conceal* power, but rather that they *contribute* to its exercise in the production of social relations of authority and conformity.

Power produces individuals both as objects and as subjects. In *Discipline and Punish*, Foucault describes how docile bodies are produced by organizing individuals in practices of surveillance that train comportment according to classifications of normal and abnormal. This takes place in different ways in different institutions across the social field, including the military, factories, schools, hospitals, and so on (Foucault, 1979). In *The History of Sexuality*, volume I, he analyzes the production of sexualized bodies in practices of confession (Foucault, 1984b). According to Foucault's analysis, far from being natural, "sexuality" has been developed over a long historical period. We in the West have learned to experience ourselves as desiring in particular ways, initially through the Christian confession and now, in contemporary society, in settings which use therapeutic techniques – in psychotherapy proper, but also in counseling, social work, education, even "phone-ins" about personal problems, confessional

TV shows, and so on. In Foucault's view, the body is imprinted in history; its capacities are historically specific and produced in practices of power.

According to Foucault, power also produces subjectivity. In this respect, Foucault famously breaks with the humanist idea that the subject is the source of intentional meaning, self-reflexive, unified, and rational which has been dominant in modern Western thought (McNay, 1994: 4). For Foucault, subjects are always *subjected*, produced in discourses and practices of power which *position* them as speakers who are in possession of self-consciousness and, most importantly in the twentieth century, of an unconscious that determines desire. In *The History of Sexuality*, volume I, Foucault discusses at length the irony that in trying to liberate him or herself in therapy, the analysand is actually subjecting him or herself to a strategy of normalization which *produces* the very subject who should free him or herself in this way (Foucault, 1984a). In positioning oneself as the "I," the subject of speech in the discourse of psychoanalysis, one is produced, and experiences oneself, as an individual with secret desires which must be uncovered in analysis if one is to be free and healthy. The self of psychoanalysis is *produced*, not *discovered*. Furthermore, the production of self takes place in a relationship of power insofar as the analysand's speech, thoughts, and dreams must be interpreted by the analyst, positioned as an authority by the discourse of psychoanalysis. What the case of psychoanalysis illustrates, according to Foucault, is that subjectivity itself, the very possibility of having a self of which one is aware, of saying "I" with some degree of self-knowledge, is conditional on the exercise of power.

It is clear that Foucault could not have identified the effects of power on the body and on subjectivity using a totalizing theory of power. His analysis depends on examining the precise details of historically specific knowledges and practices as they operate differently in different institutions to produce constraining and subordinate identities. Nevertheless, his studies have been quite extensively criticized as tending to fall back into the negative view of power to which he is opposed, portraying it as a monolithic, unmitigated force of domination. Certainly, as previously noted, his use of the term "power" suggests a *critical* perspective on existing practices of subjection and objectification. In this respect, it has undoubtedly been highly effective in denaturalizing reified social constructions. However, critics argue that if *all* social relations and identities are the product of power, this critical perspective is actually redundant. There are two related points here. First, it is argued that the concept of power suggests that something is overcome, or dominated, in its exercise. If, however, all human capacities are produced in power, why call it power at all? If power is productive rather than repressive, Foucault could have said that everything is socially constructed rather than that everything is produced in relations of power, without losing the sense of his analysis (Fraser, 1989). Secondly, it is argued that, if power is productive of all capacities, it follows that individuals are nothing more than "place-fillers," without resources to resist it: they have no capacities for autonomous self-creation or the generation of meanings and values which they could use against the effects of power (McNay, 1994: 102–4). On this understanding of Foucault's work, far from freeing us from the limitations of seeing power as negative, he actually portrays it as absolutely repressive, allowing no possibility of resistance.

In Foucault's early work on power, there does seem to be an inconsistency between his theoretical commitment to an "analytics of power" as positive and the overwhelmingly negative tone of the historical analyses he carried out. He implies, and sometimes states blankly, that power is everywhere, as in this notorious statement from *The History of Sexuality*, volume I: "Power is everywhere; not because it embraces everything, but because it comes from everywhere … Power is not an institution, nor a structure, not a possession. It is the name we give to a complex strategic situation" (Foucault, 1984b: 93). Critics are undoubtedly right to point out that if power is everywhere, it becomes a metaphysical principle and loses all normative and explanatory content. As Peter Dews (1984: 21) puts it: "[O]nly if we can produce a counterfactual, specifying how a situation would change if an operation of power were cancelled … can [this] concept be empirically applied."

In his later work, however, Foucault's ideas about power developed in ways which meet these objections, at least to some extent. The most significant developments in this respect are his ideas on domination, power, and resistance. The question of whether these new ideas mean that he actually breaks with his previous ideas is controversial. There are those who see this work as a radical new departure, or at least a change of direction (McNay, 1994; Hindess, 1996: 19), while others argue that Foucault's work is "at root *ad hoc*, fragmentary and incomplete," and should not be interpreted as developing according to an ideal of unity at all (Gutting, 1994: 2). It is indisputable, however, that his later thoughts on power are a good deal more complex than those used in the earlier analyses.

In "The Subject and Power," Foucault discusses the relationship between power, domination, and resistance in contemporary society. He argues that, as a matter of definition, where there is power there must be resistance. He had sketched out this idea in his earlier work, but here he develops it further, arguing that power necessarily works on what he calls "free subjects." It is only where there is the possibility of resistance, where subjects are not fully determined but may realize different possibilities from the range with which they are faced, that it is meaningful to think in terms of power. Slavery does not involve a relationship of power where the slave is in chains, but rather a relation of violence. Apparently in opposition to his previous assertions that "power is everywhere" and that subjects are discursively constructed, Foucault is here committing himself to the view that the "free subject" necessarily exists prior to discourse. However, he retains the view that subjects are constructed in practices of power insofar as he maintains that subjects are *subjected* where they are controlled by others, and also insofar as they are tied to their own identity by conscience or self-knowledge (Foucault, 1982).

Foucault links his analyses of power directly with the antagonistic struggles of social movements, arguing that one of the most important aspects of these struggles in contemporary society is the way in which they challenge subjectification. To some extent, social movements are based on the assertion of existing identities, and so on the acceptance of categorizations of normal/not normal produced in discourses and practices of power. On the other hand, however, they sometimes involve the refusal of existing identities:

> on the one hand, they assert the right to be different and they underline everything which makes individuals truly individual. On the other hand, they attack everything which separates the individual, breaks his links with others, splits up his community life, forces the individual back on himself and ties him to his own identity in a constraining way. (Foucault, 1982: 211–12)

The examples he gives are struggles against the power of men over women, of parents over children, of psychiatry over the mentally ill, of medicine over the population, and of administration over the ways in which people live. Foucault makes the point that it is in part a result of the way in which social movements resist power that it is possible to analyze it as such. Resistance is necessary to the definition of power, and it is also methodologically important to the study of power in that it brings power relations and the methods by which it is exercised into view.

Foucault also refines his analytics of power with the concepts of domination and government in his later work. In fact, according to Barry Hindess (1996), he increasingly uses domination as a term to analyze what is more commonly thought of as power, replacing the term power with government. According to Hindess's reading, Foucault used more precise terms in order to distinguish between power as a feature of all human interactions and domination as a particular structure of power in which antagonisms are consolidated in hierarchical and stable relations. Power, then, is not denounced as such, the implication of the critical perspective of Foucault's earlier work. On the contrary, it now represents the potential fluidity of social relations. Since power only acts on those who may resist, and who may in turn act on others, there is always the possibility of reversals of power. In domination, however, those who are dominated have such little room for maneuver that reversals of power become impracticable, though they are never, strictly speaking, impossible (Foucault, 1982; Hindess, 1996). Again, the activities of social movements may be used methodologically to understand how far a particular set of social relationships should be seen as domination or as relations of power, according to the degree of freedom they enable or allow for the politics of identity and solidarity.

Governmentality

In Foucault's later work, although he remained critical of the "juridico-discursive" model of power as possessed by the state, and also of general theories of power and the state, he nevertheless began to build up something like an "analytics of power" concerning state formation and reproduction in the West. These studies concern what he called "governmentality."

Foucault defines "government" as "the conduct of conduct," the attempt to influence the actions of free subjects. It concerns how we govern ourselves as free subjects, how we govern "things," and how we are governed. In this way, Foucault's ideas on governmentality encompass his previous work on discipline and the production of docile bodies, and on the production of subjects who rely on authorities for confirmation of their "normality." What is new in this work, however, is how these disciplinary practices are now related to the historical formation of the modern state and to the way power is exercised through practices that maintain it as such.

Foucault sees governmentality as a modern form of power, which first arose in opposition to its competitor, the Machiavellian idea of sovereignty, in the sixteenth century. Machiavellianism was a doctrine developed to guide the sovereign leaders of the early modern state, advising them how to maintain peace and security. According to the advice set out in *The Prince*, the principal object of government is the maintenance of the sovereign's rule over the territory and subjects of the state. For its opponents, however, this type of rule is too external to the society and, therefore, too fragile to be successful. The practices of government should rather be *immanent* to society, exercised over "men and things" to promote wealth and well-being. It was from the eighteenth century onwards, however, according to Foucault, that governmentality was increasingly established with the development of capitalist agriculture and the redefinition of the "economy," which became associated with "population" rather than the family, and with a range of knowledges and techniques concerned with managing its expansion, health, and productivity. Through the expansion of these knowledges and techniques, including the gathering and manipulation of large bodies of statistical data, "government" itself became a science, the science of managing the welfare of the population. At the same time, the modern state, already somewhat centralized territorially as an administrative and military apparatus around the sovereign in early modernity, becomes increasingly "governmentalised." It is increasingly dispersed through disciplinary practices and "micro-politics," concerned with the "conduct of conduct," with increasing the productivity of people and things rather than with imposing order and security from above (Foucault, 1991).

The idea of governmentality clearly develops Foucault's "analytics of power" beyond the earlier critique of the "juridico-discursive" model of power as sovereignty. But Foucault does not seem to be entirely clear or consistent on how we should understand state formation and development in modernity in relation to disciplinary power. On some occasions, he continued to write in his later work as if he understood the state as largely irrelevant to disciplinary power. For example, in his lecture on "Governmentality" in 1978, Foucault argues that "maybe, after all, the State is not more than a composite reality and a mythical abstraction whose importance is more limited than we think" (Foucault, 1991: 103). This seems close to his earlier position on the study of power: it is necessary to "cut off the King's head" to avoid getting caught up in overestimating the importance of the state and related ideas like sovereignty and law at the expense of understanding how disciplinary power actually works. Indeed, in language reminiscent of Marxism, Foucault went so far as to insist that, "The State is superstructural in relation to ... power networks that invest the body, sexuality, the family, kinship, knowledge, technology and so forth" (Foucault, 1980b: 122). On other occasions, however, Foucault seems to suggest that the state is not irrelevant to the exercise of disciplinary power; government through state institutions is an important aspect of strategies of "governmentality" (see the discussion in Dean, 1994: chapter 8; also Rose and Miller, 1992; Curtis, 1995; Rose and Miller, 1995). The "conduct of conduct" is plural, attempted in different ways in institutions and practices across the social field. As such, governmentality is constructive of centralized state power, strengthening and extending it; at the same time, state institutions further disciplinary power through activities in which states specialize, such as passing legislation or raising taxes to support large-scale knowledge production with which to manage the "population."

One of the most influential developments of Foucauldian ideas of "governmentality" has been the analysis of neo-liberalism. For Foucauldians, liberalism is not a political theory, or an ideology, but rather a practice: "a "way of doing things" oriented towards objectives and regulating itself by means of a sustained reflection" (Foucault, 1997: 73–4). Neo-liberalism, by extension, is a practice, dominant in the West by the end of the twentieth century and to a certain extent spread across the world that is informed by the aim of "rolling back the frontiers of the state," which neo-liberals theorize as having intruded too far into the private sphere of the economy. For neo-liberals, the scope of state activities must be reduced in order to stimulate and maintain markets to create more wealth, but also for the sake of individual freedom, which is undermined by the extension of law and bureaucracy into private lives. "Rolling back the frontiers of the state" involves not just stimulating markets for goods and services by reducing regulation, but also creating markets where there were none before, especially within the public sector and organizations previously governed by bureaucratic hierarchies. It has gone far beyond the marketization of welfare, education, and health associated with attempts to cut public spending, the sale of public assets, and the deregulation of labor markets. Neo-liberal practice has, for example, gone so far as to marketize the prison service, turning over practices of punishment which, as Nikolas Rose points out, were previously considered essential to state sovereignty (Rose, 1999: 146). Inevitably, of course, the creation of such quasi-markets out of what were previously taken-for-granted as state practices actually requires a great deal of state activity, to set targets, regulate standards, and monitor outputs. Insofar as markets cannot do without state regulation, neo-liberalism is incoherent (Tonkiss, 2001). In practice, Foucauldians argue that neo-liberalism has resulted in the creation of a certain kind of individual, an entrepreneurial self who understands her/himself to be free to choose in the market, but who must then exercise choice continuously and correctly if s/he is not to suffer the stigma and material consequences of failing to make use of market forces, whether in education, personal development, work, or any other "life-style choice." The entrepreneurial self is free in that s/he understands her/himself to be self-governing and oriented towards self-realization, but s/he is under the imperative to manage her/himself correctly, according to increasingly fine-tuned standards that are set by economic and social management practices over which s/he has no control (Rose, 1990, 1999).

The direct influence Foucault's work has had on contemporary political sociology cannot be over-estimated. His ideas on discipline, the interrelation of knowledge and power, and more recently on governmentality, have directed attention toward the exercise of power in practices and the formation of identities across the social field. Once we begin to look at the world through the lenses Foucault provides for us, conventional politics at the level of the state is displaced to the periphery of vision and other forms of politics come into focus.

However, a Foucauldian analytics of power is not all that is needed to understand the range of engagements with hierarchy and exclusion that concern contemporary political sociologists. And the way in which contemporary political sociology sees power and politics as significant across the social field is not solely due to the influence of Foucault's work. Indeed Foucault's "analytics of power" is limited with respect to what we might call "positive" political projects, those that make demands for equality, whether of redistribution, recognition, or representation (see Fraser, 1997, 2008). Whilst, as we noted above, Foucault's critique of power may have became more nuanced as he introduced the idea of the "free subject," reflexive in relation to concrete possibilities of action, it is very difficult to envisage any kind of worthwhile politics other than resistance from within a Foucauldian framework. Successful demands for a bigger share of collective resources, more respect for particular groups, or a different democratic system, necessarily involve closing down other social possibilities, whether by state regulation or something "softer," like disallowing certain ways of talking and acting. But it is just such demands that have been so important to social movements and to challenges to extend citizenship and democracy with which contemporary political sociology is concerned. In the Foucauldian framework, all "positive" demands that are realized through collective enforcement involve the solidifying of power into domination to a greater or lesser extent; it is only through resistance that power remains fluid. It is unsurprising in this respect that Foucault himself became more interested in ethics than in politics.

1.5   Cultural Politics

Although the Foucauldian analytics of power has been an important influence on contemporary political sociology, more is needed to properly understand how politics works today. In addition to theoretical debates around Foucault's work, contemporary political sociology has also been influenced from three other main sources. The first is the intellectual work carried out within and on behalf of social movements. Sociologists from the 1970s onwards have been active participants in movements, especially in feminism and anti-racism, and have therefore been directly called on to think about politics in new ways (see Eyerman and Jamison, 1991). We will explore the politics of social movements more fully in chapter 3, and how they have been translated into struggles over definitions of citizenship rights and identities in chapter 4. The second influence, itself related both to the significance of Foucault's work and to that of social movements, was the rise of the "anti-disciplinary" discipline of cultural studies. The story of the relationship between cultural studies and sociology is long and complex, and I do not have space to do it justice here (see Denzin, 1992; Hall and du Gay, 1996; Long, 1997; Oswell, 2006). Perhaps the chief effect cultural studies has had on sociologists is to renew interest in the importance of symbolic meanings in social life. This interest has a long history in sociology (from Weber and Durkheim through to phenomenology and ethnomethodology), but it has always been somewhat marginalized in the macro-theorizing of society which has dominated the discipline, and especially the sub-discipline of political sociology. In this respect, contemporary political sociology is closely linked to the "cultural turn" that is still ongoing in sociology. Thirdly, and more recently, given how the prominence of the state has been called into question in globalization, sociologists working on this topic have also had to rethink power and politics. We look at globalization more fully in chapter 2. Here we consider Manuel Castells's theorization of power and politics, which draws on, but goes beyond Foucault's influential "analytics of power."

There are two main ways of understanding "culture" currently in the social sciences. According to one version, the "epistemological variant," culture is implicated in all social practices because, as human beings, we have access to reality, we know it and manipulate it, only through social classifications. This variant has been very much influenced by Foucault's theory of discourse. Culture is "constitutive"; it is not reflective or expressive of other social practices; it is not determined by them, nor can it be used simply as a tool or instrument to bring about change. Culture is constitutive in the sense that it is only through symbolic representations that humans experience, sense, access, and manipulate reality, whether created by human beings or not. This is not to say, of course, that culture *creates* reality as such: clearly, symbols do not create mountains out of stone or trees out of wood. It is rather that culture is constitutive of *our* reality, and this is crucial to how our social world (including its material artifacts – buildings, borders, irrigation systems, and all the rest) is reproduced and transformed. We only know the effects of material artifacts, as well as of existing social structures that exist "outside" our heads, through our own understanding and use.

On the other hand, others see the significance of culture as historically specific. As we shall see in chapter 2, this view is particularly associated with the idea that we are now moving into a new era, that of "postmodernism." Whereas in modernity, culture occupied a separate sphere of society as high art, it is argued that in postmodernism there has been an expansion of culture into other realms of society. Culture has been commodified as the value of art is increasingly closely linked to its market price and, at the same time, the economy itself is increasingly dependent on culture, in research and design, advertising, niche marketing according to lifestyle, and leisure and service industries. Politicians perform to their audiences through the media, and personalities count more than policies. And in the social realm, distinctions of status depend to an even greater extent than before on the display of cultural credentials, rather than on economic or political power (see Crook et al., 1992; Kumar, 1995). According to this version of the "cultural turn," the historical importance of culture has been determined by changes in social structure.

Whether culture is seen as universally or historically preeminent, however, cultural politics now takes on an unprecedented importance. The term "culture" is notoriously difficult to define. As a working definition, we will adopt that of Raymond Williams: culture is "the signifying system through which necessarily (though among other means) a social order is communicated, reproduced, experienced and explored" (Williams, 1981: 13). This definition includes the more commonly used conception of culture as "the works and practices of intellectuals, and especially artistic activity" (Williams, 1976: 80), and also the still narrower understanding of popular and media culture. In this most general sense, culture, as Jeffrey Alexander puts it, "is not a thing but a dimension, not an object to be studied as a dependent variable but a thread that runs through, one that can be teased out of, every conceivable social form" (Alexander, 2003: 7).

Foucault's theory of "discourse," whilst it certainly helped sociologists to understand the importance of *language* to social life, is something of a limitation with regard to understanding the importance of *meanings*. As we have seen, Foucault was concerned with what discourses do, with the effects they have on bodies and minds as a result of the authoritative way they are put into practice in institutions formed around knowledges. He was not concerned with how situated social actors interpret what discourses mean to them; only with how they are circulated and with what effects in practice. For Foucault, signs are *functions*, organized not on the basis of meaning but of *use* (see Oswell, 2006: 33). It is for this reason that his understanding of politics is limited to resistance to authority, rather than enabling anything more creative. Foucault literally does not see politics as meaningful activity.

What do contemporary sociologists mean by "meaning"? As we noted in the introduction to this section, many answers to this question have been proposed in the history of social thought. The most influential on contemporary political sociology is that of the linguist Ferdinand de Saussure. According to Saussure, meaning in language is produced in a differential play of signs, rather than by representing objects in the world. Words are *symbols* of the world, not pictures or mirrors. There is no intrinsic link between objects and words; what joins them is the way in which *words* are linked together in chains of meaning that are learned as social conventions. In fact, without language, we would be unable to identify objects and concepts with any degree of consistency (Saussure, 1966). Language does not simply *name* the world; it makes sense of it and orders it for us. Jonathan Culler gives a good example of Saussure's analysis of language as a "system of differences without positive terms." He asks us to imagine teaching a non-English speaker what the word "brown" means. To show him or her nothing but brown objects would be useless; he or she would have to learn to distinguish brown from other colors. The word "brown" does not simply label objects that are already given; it constructs "brown" things as different from gray, orange, red, and so on (Culler, 1976: 246). Furthermore, it is entirely possible to imagine a world in which such "brown" things were not distinguished at all. They are only meaningful for us because we have learned through social interactions with others to recognize them in this way. Meaning structures the world for us, then, through classifications; it exists only for us insofar as we make distinctions that have value and interest to us, and we are continually learning how others make and use socially relevant classifications.

Most importantly for our understanding of cultural politics, social meanings are not fixed; differences are not closed and final, once and for all. They cannot be fixed because social actors must continually interpret and make use of meanings in the company of other people in different situations. In fact, social meanings are continually changing simply through repeated use: symbols are meaningful only insofar as they are used regularly, and a sign that is repeated is always somewhat novel with respect to the context in which it appears (Derrida, 1978). Continuities are vital to culture; culture is the reproduction of traditions, habits, perceptions, and understandings. But culture is inherently fluid and dynamic, a continually moving and "changing same" (Gilroy, 1993: 101), which makes it open to political contestation and at the same time somewhat resistant to political invention.

On the other hand, meanings may become *relatively* solidified and fixed. At the extreme, they may become "hegemonic": taken-for-granted as if they simply reflect how things are and must be. This is problematic because settled meanings invariably enable possibilities of action that favor the projects and dreams of some at the expense of others. Collective action is needed to challenge and change meanings that have been relatively fixed. To give an example, as married women began to move into the labor force in greater numbers in the 1960s and '70s, a new term became current: "working mother." This apparently neutral definition of what was taken to be a new phenomenon became fashionable, used routinely in the media and everyday life. In the 1980s, however, with the rise of the feminist movement, it became much more controversial. It was seen as contributing to the "knowledge" that women were naturally designed for the care of home, husband, and children, that they were primarily housewives who happened to work outside the home. As such, it both described and legitimated the "double burden" of household tasks and paid work which increasing numbers of women were taking on, whilst at the same time calling into question any commitment some might have, or want to have, to career advancement, more responsibility, or higher pay at work. "Working mother" limited the aspirations of those women who identified as such, and it limited all women by treating them alike as primarily, and naturally, mothers whose first concern was their duties at home. Feminists in the 1970s and '80s challenged the term "working mother," discrediting it as a neutral description, and at the same time calling into question a whole set of assumptions which had very real effects on how women could shape their lives.

What this example also shows is the importance of symbolic meaning in structuring social life. Cultural politics is not just about words. Indeed, it need not be about words at all. Bodily gestures, fashion, flags, global brands – these are all examples of sets of meaningful signs within which we understand particular gestures and movements, what an item of clothing says about the person wearing it, and so on (see Barthes, 1972). Nor is cultural politics restricted to the manipulation of symbols in texts and images. In order for signs to be politically relevant, they must become part of routine use in *practice*.

Although Anthony Giddens does not use the term "culture," (which is surely related to the fact that he takes little interest in the *content* of social actors' interpretations), his influential theory of social practice helps us understand how social life is reproduced, and altered, through the use of meanings in a way that is close to the model of cultural politics we are discussing here (see Ortener, 2006; Sewell, 1992: 7). Giddens's structuration theory is an attempt to overcome the duality of "structure" and "agency" which he sees as a perennial motif in sociology. He argues that social reproduction should be seen as stabilizing relationships across time and space through the knowledgeable use of rules and resources on the part of social agents (Giddens, 1984). In face-to-face or mediated interactions, social actors more or less consciously sustain, re-make, or challenge structures whilst, at the same time, their interpretations and actions are themselves constrained by existing distributions of resources and ways of making sense of the world. What Giddens calls "structures" are consistent patterns of social interaction that both emerge from situated practices and provide the frameworks within which those interactions take place. To return to our example of the "working mother," it is not difficult to imagine how her daily practices at home and in paid work would be routinized in quite different ways compared with those of women who expect to negotiate with managers, colleagues, teachers, people employed to care for babies and young children, family, and friends to sustain what is currently described in the UK as "work-life balance."

Finally, what this example also shows is the importance of identities to the reproduction and modification of social structures. Although what is important in a general way in cultural politics is how symbols are interpreted and re-interpreted in social life, it is important not to lose sight of the fact that it is embodied people with emotional ties to others and individual biographies who are making social reality (see Turner, 1996). It is in the creation of identities which may then be very hard to dislodge – perhaps especially where people are barely conscious of their strong attachments to particular ways of thinking and feeling – that structures are reproduced. Gender and sexual identities may be particularly important in this respect, not just in reproducing intimate relations in private, but also in securing hierarchical relations across the social field. For example, formal politics in the state has traditionally been a very masculine activity: we have only to consider photographs of "world leaders" at, for example, G8 summit meetings to see that this is the case. On the other hand, if we think of the carnivalesque protests against neo-liberal globalization that take place at these same events, except for the small number who actively seek violent confrontation, we have a very differently gendered picture in mind. This is not to say that men and women are inherently different. It is rather that the gendered division between male and female is one that appears to be very well-established and stable – the queer politics we will consider in chapter 4 notwithstanding – and identities across the social field that are tied to masculinity and femininity may be particularly difficult to challenge and shift (see Butler, 1993, 1997).

Having outlined, then, the importance of *culture* to politics, let us turn now to *politics* itself. No easier to pin down than "culture," in very general terms, politics involves struggles over power. Political struggles are always, in some of their dimensions at least, "negative." They are always *against* existing social relations, concerned with challenging or resisting power as it is exercised by some over others. As I have suggested above, Foucault's analytics of power as productive of compliant minds and docile bodies is concerned above all with this dimension of politics. On the other hand, politics may also be "positive," carrying forward what we sometimes call "political vision," a sense of how social relations should or could be re-arranged.

The sociologist of globalization Manuel Castells has suggested a two-dimensional definition of power that usefully complements Foucault's understanding of power as productive. Defining power generally in Weberian terms as the probability of an individual or group being able to exercise its will despite resistance, Castells sees the Foucauldian understanding of power as shaping the mind – and, we should add, bodily practices too – as its most important aspect (Castells, 2009: 15–16). Power shapes understandings of reality, of "how to go on" with social routines, and the establishing of standards and norms with which social actors are expected to comply in social practices. The exercise of power always involves the successful construction of meaning that is routinized. In addition, however, Castells also argues that it is important to understand how power may, on occasion, involve force, or the threat of force. As we have seen, Foucault viewed the use of force as involving a relationship of violence rather than of power, and he suggested it was becoming less relevant as societies became more concerned with fostering disciplinary power over populations rather than with controlling and eliminating those who seemed to pose a threat to sovereign state power. For Castells, it is important to understand that the state is the ultimate guarantor of micro-powers exercised across the social field, a position it maintains because of its privileges with regard to the legitimate use of force – even if these privileges are relatively rarely exercised (Castells, 2009: 15). As the ultimate guarantor of micro-powers because of its special privileges with regard to force, action "in the name of the state" – the state itself is not unified, and "it" cannot act – does have particular importance in contemporary societies. It is not that force trumps in the exercise of power. On the contrary, state violence, the regulation of civil society, and the collection and distribution of wealth are all shaped, rationalized, and legitimated by the meanings such actions are given in ongoing practices of state formation and reproduction. The crucial point here is that the state is itself an especially significant site of cultural politics.

In this respect, it is also important to note how power and force both contribute to the economic importance of states. There are two main dimensions to the threat of state force with regard to markets. Firstly, the state is involved in the regulation and de-regulation of economic exchanges and contracts. For example, state actors have the final authority over the conditions under which multinational corporations operate within their territory. Even if communications and transport infrastructures now make it much easier than ever before to send labor, ideas for research, design and advertising, money, components and final products across borders, ultimately states still retain the authority to regulate cross-border flows. Whether or not national economies are "open" or "protected" remains a matter for political decision. Secondly, the state itself exercises significant economic power. In wealthy liberal-democracies, large amounts of money are collected as taxes and distributed to state employees employed in bureaucracy, education, healthcare, and so on, as well as in welfare to those most in need. When support for Keynesian managed capitalism was more or less hegemonic in the mid-twentieth century, state legitimacy depended on its capacity to ameliorate the effects of markets on citizens. Welfare rights are just as important as ever to many citizens, as neo-liberalizing economies are increasingly oriented towards providing low wage and insecure employment (in the US and UK, for example), while, where neo-liberalism has been strongly resisted, rates of structural unemployment tend to be high (as in, for example, France and Germany). Because money is the means by which the necessities of life – shelter, warmth, and food – are met in our societies, the threat of its complete withdrawal is a form of force. It is exercised where states do not meet obligations to ensure at least minimal levels of well-being for citizens.

Castells argues that instead of thinking in terms of the relations between "state and society," as in classical political sociology, we should rather understand social life as made up of networks. Unlike states, networks do not have clear boundaries: they do not remain within national territories, nor do they restrict themselves to a strict division between state and society. They are sets of interconnected nodes, which organize flows of information. For Castells, networks in globalization are multilayered structures: economic (involving production, consumption, and exchange), technological, environmental, political, and military. They are also multiscalar: global, national, local, and individual (Castells, 2009: 14–15; see also Castells, 2000a, 2000b, 2003, 2009). Castells sees states as nodes in networks, where nodes absorb and process relevant information as it flows within and across networks. As we shall see in chapter 2, the networked state is no longer simply the sovereign political body within its own territory; it must now share authority and sovereignty (to a greater or lesser extent according to its size, capacities, and ongoing commitments to cooperate) with other states and with other organizations in global governance.

To sum up, then, contemporary political sociology concerns cultural politics, which is the interpretation of social meanings that support, challenge, or change the definitions, perspectives, and identities of social actors, to the advantage of some and the disadvantage of others, across state and society. In comparison, the threat of using force to impose the will of some on others is much less common. The threat of force is, moreover, itself applied according to definitions. Some groups and actions are defined as problematic, and as in need of state control. For example, illegal migrants are generally seen as a problem in wealthy liberal-democracies, rather than as an economic benefit, and as a result they are at risk of being subjected to the force of the state. In contrast, rates of conviction for sexual assault remain low, though it is clearly illegal and the numbers of incidents reported to the police have been rising in recent years.

Interpretations of social meanings involve power because shaping and achieving a degree of mutual consent to the institutionalization of definitions and perspectives closes down or marginalizes existing possibilities with which some members of society are identified. The institutionalization of some social meanings rather than others makes it easier for some actors to realize their existing projects and goals, while others have to alter and adapt as best they can to new situations. Of course, at any particular time, the greater part of social life is not politicized. For the most part, social relations that close down future possibilities for some as they open up opportunities for others continue routinely, accepted by all concerned as the proper way to go on with life in common. In part, this is because, in shaping identities and perspectives, cultural politics changes preferences. Understanding "how to proceed" in everyday life shapes individual aims and goals as well as permitting us to get along together. It is only relatively rarely that cultural politics becomes a significant force for change. Nevertheless, in complex, hierarchically ordered, and unequal societies, there is always the potential for re-assessment of the justice, feasibility, or attractiveness of existing arrangements. The main way in which settled social structures become politicized is through the formation of collective will in social movements, which makes issues and injustices visible, challenges assumptions structuring the *status quo*, and represents alternatives. Although change is a permanent *possibility* of social life, and ongoing, insofar as the reproduction of social relations requires the continual re-iteration of symbolic meanings in slightly new contexts, it is relatively rare that challenges to routine understandings of "how things are done" coalesce into large-scale or fundamental social change.

Contemporary political sociology

Arguably societies are currently going through fundamental changes linked to the development of information technology. In chapter 2, we discuss globalization, probably the most dramatic and widely acknowledged challenge to sociological models of state-centric politics. Globalization makes it difficult for state actors to control the traffic of goods, services, technology, media products, and information across borders. State capacities to act independently in the articulation and pursuit of domestic and international policy objectives have become highly politicized as a result. The political authority of the state to determine the rules, regulations, and policies within a given territory has to some extent been "scaled up" in order to try to take control of processes and flows of globalization. The "internationalizing state" raises difficult questions for contemporary political sociology concerning fundamental assumptions about society that were established by the isomorphism of state, the nation, and national territorial boundaries.

The empirical changes brought about by globalization problematize the most basic concept of sociology, "society," by disaggregating the economic, social, and political processes previously seen as bound together within the borders of distinct national societies. What Ulrich Beck calls "methodological nationalism," the construction of societies as internal to state borders, is no longer viable (Beck, 2000). Indeed, as a way of understanding empires, and the subsequent inter-connections of metropolitan centers and post-colonial states, it was always limited (see Bhambra, 2007). Social life must be rethought in terms of multiple and multiscalar networks and identities, and power and politics as an aspect of social life rather than as separate institutions within a society governed by a single determining base, as in the case of Marxism, a single inexorable logic, as in Weber's rationalization thesis, or functionalist social solidarity, as for Durkheim. Globalization opens up issues that require a wider view of power and politics than that provided by the framework of classical political sociology.

In chapter 3, we look at social movements, which displace the focus of classical political sociology on social systems and questions of causality, shifting attention to the way in which social actors make society through cultural politics. Social movements transform social relations by challenging and redefining meanings and creating new collective identities across the social field. The study of social movements also shifts the focus on relations between state and society. Social movements are at least as concerned with personal decisions and with changing the rules and routines of everyday life as they are with policies and the law. The state is often seen as biased and bureaucratic, too blunt an instrument to bring about the detailed transformation in social relations at which they aim. Nevertheless, contrary to the claims of some theorists of social movements, the activities of social movements are not confined exclusively to changing ways of life through micro-politics. Indeed, even the global social movements that have become prominent over the last decade are often engaged in redefining state policies and practices, both from below, within national territories, and from above, through the international organizations of global governance.

In chapter 4, we examine how the cultural politics in which social movements engage are transforming citizenship. Citizenship rights are as much a matter of definition as the contestation of identity, lifestyle, media representations, and ethical consumerism with which social movements are more typically linked. Citizenship involves questions of identity and membership that have been central to social movements concerned with "difference." Feminism, the gay and lesbian movement, and anti-racist movements are sometimes thought of in derogatory terms as involving "identity politics." Challenging the way particular groups have been identified as inferior, trying to change what is generally seen as a source of shame into pride, they have been criticized for giving too much attention to the politics of recognition, with demanding respect for differences between groups, at the expense of dealing with important questions of the redistribution of wealth and social democracy that were previously more typical on the Left. In addition, social movements concerned with identity have been criticized as authoritarian and essentialist, as closing down possibilities for self-creation by putting too much emphasis on particular aspects of individuals' lives. It is certainly important to understand struggles over definitions of citizenship in the context of neo-liberalizing globalization in which many of the social rights achieved in the welfare states of the twentieth century have been lost or are in question, and inequalities of wealth and poverty are growing. But, as we will see in this chapter, social movements contesting citizenship have been just as concerned with "equality" and "freedom" as with "difference," and debates over the relative weight to be given to all these issues – to recognition, to redistribution, and to the relationship between personal and social identity – have been vital to redefining social relationships as the influence of social movements has spread. Debates over citizenship in contemporary societies concern a range of problems, including how to accommodate different ways of identifying as a member of society; what diversity means for equality of citizenship rights in terms of recognition, redistribution, and political representation; and how freedom to redefine identities in the future is to be balanced with concerns for equality.

The intensity of debates over what citizenship really means, and should mean, in terms of equality, freedom and difference is matched in contemporary political sociology by questions concerning *who* should have citizenship rights and obligations, both within state territories and beyond. Globalization raises questions of post-national citizenship in relation to large-scale migration and settlement in the territories of Western states; and to the urgent necessity to respond to environmental dangers. As national identity, rights and obligations, and the sense of belonging in a territorially bounded "community of fate" come into question, citizenship itself, previously closely linked to the nation-state, is becoming de-territorialized.

Finally, in chapter 5 we look at the changing conditions of democracy in relation to globalization. Representative democracy in the West is in something of a crisis, with declining interest in political parties, and generalized mistrust of politicians (the very real hopes raised by Obama notwithstanding). Given the questions raised by globalization about the limits of the nation as establishing a legitimate democratic political community, is democratizing international political institutions a viable response to the crisis of democracy at the national level? If so, how might

it be achieved? What difference does the cultural politics of social movements make to democracy? And what is their democratic legitimacy, given
that contesting and redefining issues that are supposed to alter global
policy agendas does not involve a global public and is never subjected to
popular vote?

Notes

1   This definition of power is also adopted by Marxisant political sociologists
    (see Bottomore, 1993: 1).

2   They then go on to do just that. Although they argue for seeing politics as a
    class of actions rather than a set of institutions or organizations, in particular
    as the establishing of the rules of social organization, their primary focus is
    on government as a special set of this class, involving the setting of rules
    intended to be absolute. In practice, therefore, their main focus is again on
    the relation between state and society.

3   Although Weber's term is usually translated as "iron cage," Alan Scott has
    convincingly argued that "steel-hard housing," the casing which encloses
    machines, is actually a more accurate translation and a better metaphor for
    the constraints of modernity Weber wants to convey by it (Scott, 1997a).

4   Pluralism is categorized as Weberian here more on the basis of its intellectual
    orientation than its theoretical antecedents. It is better seen as founded by
    American political scientists, notably Robert Dahl and his school, than by
    Weber. Nevertheless, it may be taken as Weberian in relation to Marxism
    insofar as it insists on the autonomy of the political process, and sees power
    as dependent on the intentions and circumstances of social actors, rather than
    on socio-economic structures.

5   There is a growing scholarship that might usefully be analyzed here in terms
    of its neo-Durkheimian contribution to political sociology, if there were
    enough space (e.g., Alexander, Giesen, and Mast, 2006; Boltanski and
    Thevenot, 2006; Lamont and Thevenot, 2000; Smith, 2005).

Chapter 2
Politics in a Small World

Globalization may be defined very simply as increasing global interconnectedness. It involves flows of goods, capital, people, information, ideas, images, and risks across national borders, combined with the emergence of transnational and international networks. This does not mean that consciousness of the world as a whole is intensifying (*cf* Robertson, 1992: 8); nor that there is the creation of a new global, or "supraterritorial" space beyond that of nation-states (*cf* Scholte, 1996). On the contrary, the impact that increasing global interconnectedness has on the imagination of humanity, on formal political structures, and on the spaces within which social life is routinized is a matter of empirical study for contemporary political sociologists, not to be decided *a priori*, by definition (see Albrow, 1996: 88).

Economic globalization combined with digital communication networks is the main driving force of processes of globalization, especially in terms of developing new products, services, and markets. Migration, however, is also important, and invariably involves the contestation of identities, loyalties, and assumptions about who "we" are when people live in places different from those in which they or their parents were born and brought up. The spread of global media similarly enables settled ways of life to be called into question, as digital technologies and satellite communications bring the world closer together in some ways, whilst at the same time they allow people to opt out of shared systems of communication that contributed to local and national solidarities. Increased perceptions of risks across borders add to uncertainties. Terrorist networks also make use of new technologies, forms of communication and travel, and they seem more difficult to contain now than ever before as a result. Even more alarming, risks of environmental catastrophe for human, animal and plant life on the planet have become increasingly apparent as unforeseen consequences of the development of science and innovative technology that make globalization itself possible.

As people's daily lives and biographies are ever more entwined with processes of globalization, it is increasingly obvious that the founding sociological image of society as a bounded and coherent set of structures and practices governed by the sovereign nation-state is redundant. Social relations are now a good deal more complex, especially as states themselves are implicated in globalization, in trying to manage it through international institutions, but also, in the case of economic globalization, in promoting cross-border flows of all kinds.

Economic globalization – sometimes called "footloose capitalism," or even more emphatically "turbo-capitalism" – is a project of neo-liberalization in which states have been engaged, to a greater or lesser extent in different cases, since the 1980s. Following World War II, Keynesian welfare state capitalism predominated in the West. International trade was primarily of foodstuffs and raw materials, while production was organized within national economies. International economic institutions, the International Monetary Fund (IMF) and World Bank, oversaw the stability of the system through a mixture of protection of domestic markets and the encouragement of international trade. In many cases, parts of the economy considered to be strategic were owned by states themselves – airlines, railways, and steel companies, as well as hospitals and schools. Markets were embedded in governments. Since the early 1980s, the acceptance of neo-liberal ideas opposed to state planning has led governments, beginning in the US and UK, to pursue projects to free markets from state control: privatizing national industries, and lifting regulations on foreign investment and financial markets. States have been involved in *disembedding* markets to enable multinational corporations to operate transnationally, promoting flows of staff, money, information, and products across borders. States no longer control industrial processes and financial exchanges in the name of national economies; they are engaged, rather, in trying to attract multinational corporations by providing infrastructure, corporate tax breaks, and a well-trained and well-disciplined labor force that will accept their working conditions and pay. It is important not to over-estimate the extent to which the global economy is integrated. It is certainly geographically uneven: as Hirst and Thompson have pointed out, multinational corporations still tend to operate within European, Asian-Pacific, and NAFTA-Latin

American regions; the poorest countries, in sub-Saharan Africa in particular, now receive less foreign investment than in the early twentieth century. Indeed, they argue that it is important to understand how much control states still have over economic processes within national territories (Hirst and Thompson, 1996). Nevertheless, the neo-liberal project of lifting restrictions on investment, promoting the flexibility of labor markets, and creating markets for state services and the management of public goods wherever possible is now built into international economic governance in the policies of the IMF and World Bank. In this respect, economic globalization is global (Keane, 2003: 65–74; Harvey, 2005; Tonkiss, 2005).

All processes of globalization are linked to the development of new information technologies. In the case of economic globalization, they are closely linked to advances in data-processing and information technology that allow instantaneous communication across vast distances, enabling the formation of a transnational financial system and facilitating the operations of multinational corporations. The same is true of the coordination of the actions of state officials across territorial borders in international organizations and networks. The rapid communications that new information technologies make possible provide the conditions for a certain kind of dispersion of state activities in globalization, as bureaucrats, politicians, and members of the judiciary exchange knowledge and experiences with their counterparts from other states on a regular basis, as well as engaging in policy and law-making in Inter-Governmental Organizations. In terms of the diffusion of ideas and images, new information technologies create apparently endless new possibilities for mediated interaction (through social networking sites, blogging, Twittering, exchanging photos and films, and so on), as well as the rapid spread of media products like TV news, films, and music across borders, illegally as well as through officially sanctioned channels. New information technology is crucial to global social movements, too, as it enables the coordination of collective action across borders, as well as interventions online (in e-petitions, for example, or just sharing images and ideas or discussing political disagreements) and organizing off-line (where mobile phones are as important as use of the Internet). The capacity of such mediated interactions to evade state censorship is especially significant. It is not that information technology is *determining* social change: the change that information technology makes possible takes place within the limits that are imagined by its use. But, providing the infrastructure for very rapid communication of large amounts of information across huge distances, new information technology enables the shrinking of time and space that is the key feature of globalization.

In this chapter, we will first consider macro-theorizations of globalization in section 2.1. At the center of both sociological and more general public interest in globalization are its economic dimensions – the re-structuring of the world economy, and the focus on speed, communication, and adaptability that has significantly altered existing relations of production, distribution, and consumption. As a consequence, Marxist accounts of globalization have been important in mapping out the problems that are to be addressed in thinking sociologically about globalization. As we saw in chapter 1, such accounts tend to marginalize the importance of politics. This tendency is not shared to the same extent by theories of globalization as modernization, which see its development in multi-causal terms and which, consequently, give a greater importance to politics. In this section, we will also explore how both types of accounts foreground cultural change as crucial to the restructuring of globalizing social life, pointing beyond themselves towards the importance of cultural politics. We also examine the account of "world polity" theorists, which focuses explicitly on culture and politics, trying to explain how and why states around the world increasingly resemble each other. Although dealing directly with culture and politics, however, this account oddly lacks a sense of the importance of social meanings and how they are embedded in hierarchical structures. Tending to treat "diffusion" as rather a mechanical process, it actually lacks any real understanding of cultural politics.

The state is not disappearing in globalization (as some early theorists of globalization supposed [Ohmae, 1995; *cf* Hirst and Thompson, 1996; see Tonkiss, 2005]). On the contrary, the development of global markets, including the privatization of what was previously public, would not be possible without detailed and extensive state regulation. The state is, however, being transformed in global governance. In section 2.2, we investigate how state autonomy and sovereignty are being altered with the disembedding of markets and state integration into Inter-Governmental Organizations (IGOs) that attempt to "scale up" control over those markets and over other processes of globalization. The state is internationalizing in these processes. We also consider debates over whether global governance is inherently imperialist, or whether it might be steered in a more cosmopolitan direction through the development of the legal and moral framework of universal human rights. These debates involve the very controversial issue of military intervention for humanitarian reasons. Finally, in section 2.3, we consider the possibility of global political community in relation to global governance and global media. "Political community" was synonymous with "nation" in the Westphalian order of discrete, sovereign states. It seems that globalization may now offer concrete possibilities of re-imagining political community beyond the nation for the first time in history. The sociological study of what *prevents* the realization of global political community also, therefore, becomes significant for the first time now too.

2.1 Explaining Globalization

Accounts of globalization are closely linked to questions of the novelty of contemporary society. The "facts" of globalization are less disputed by political sociologists – though different accounts give different weight to those "facts" – than the question of whether we are now entering a qualitatively different era from what we might think of as "the past of modernity." If there are sufficient continuities with this past, then in principle the classical sociological theories developed in the nineteenth and early twentieth centuries can be quite easily adapted to understand forms of political action today. If not, then completely new tools for sociological analysis are needed.

Globalization as a consequence of capitalism

The most traditional sociological approach to globalization is that of the Marxists. Although, as we have seen, neo-Marxists have been very much concerned with the form and functions of the nation-state, the Marxist view of the essence of capitalism as a mode of commodity production based on the exploitative relationship between capital and labor does not require that it should be thought of as synonymous with a society organized as a territorially bounded nation. On the contrary, as a system which requires the maximum appropriation of surplus value, and which is characterized by class struggle, it is inherent in the logic of capitalism that it will seek out new sites of exploitation. Capitalism depends on the relentless search for low wages, cheap resources, and the creation of new markets for the goods it produces. The original premises of Marxist theory apparently need little alteration, then, to enable it to deal with the phenomena of globalization since, on this understanding, capitalism has inherent tendencies toward expansion beyond the societies in which it was initially developed.

The most highly developed application of Marxist theory in these terms is the world systems theory of Immanuel Wallerstein. According to

Wallerstein, there is nothing new in the global scope and orientation of capitalism. It has, of course, expanded greatly in 400 years, to the point where it now forms a world economic system, but the logic of its expansion was there from its beginning in sixteenth-century Europe. Wallerstein sees capitalism as an integrating world system which has an internal dynamic of development; capitalism needs to expand its geographical boundaries in order to combat the regular slumps to which it is prone (Wallerstein, 1990). Although the world system is, therefore, driven by economic imperatives, Wallerstein's account is neo-Marxist in that he sees states as essential to the stability of global capitalism. The capitalist world system is historically unique in that it involves a global economy combined with a political system of sovereign nation-states; it is, therefore, quite unlike previous world economies which were regional rather than global, and centered on imperial states. The capitalist world system integrates what Wallerstein calls "political states" in a common international division of labor. The core developed states, such as those of the EU, Japan, and the US, dominate on the basis of higher-level skills and greater capitalization, while peripheral areas with weak states, including the newly industrializing countries of the South, provide the conditions for capitalist expansion through their economic dependence on the core. In addition, there are semi-peripheral areas, including the "tiger economies" of South-East Asia, the oil-producing countries, and the former socialist countries of Eastern Europe, with moderately strong governmental structures and single-commodity or low-technology economies, which provide a buffer zone preventing polarization and outright conflict between core and periphery (Wallerstein, 1979; Waters, 1995: 226).

Wallerstein's world systems theory has been widely criticized for its practically exclusive emphasis on the economic aspects of globalization. Although politics actually features more centrally than class in his account, global integration seems to take place solely at the economic level; the relationships of trade and exploitation he sees as characterizing the world economy take place between relatively sovereign nation-states, each with its own relatively independent culture (Waters, 1995: 25). World systems theory therefore fails to address the changing form and role of the state in the context of the multiple and shifting sites of sovereignty which now characterize global governance (Held, 1995a: 26). Furthermore, as Roland Robertson points out, although Wallerstein has given up his original view that culture is epiphenomenal to economic processes, he tends to consider it only under the guise of "an ideological impediment" to the realization of socialism as a world system or, alternatively, as a resource for the "anti-systemic movements" he sees as opposed to the cultural premises of the core societies (Robertson, 1992: 658). These movements are, according to Wallerstein (1991), principally directed toward what he thinks of as political ends, at overthrowing or resisting state authorities. Culture, for Wallerstein, is either national, organized around and defined as such by the nation-state, or, alternatively, world culture, which would contribute to world socialism (Wallerstein, 1991). He is unable to take into account the multiple struggles over meanings which do not conform to this binary opposition. He is also unable to give any consideration to the exponential increase in cultural products which other Marxisant theorists take to be the defining feature of contemporary globalization and which may indicate the development of a form of global capitalism quite different from that of any which has preceded it.

One of the most widely respected of these theorists is David Harvey. In *The Condition of Postmodernity* (1989), he links globalization with postmodernity and postmodernism, arguing that the new form of capitalism he calls "flexible postmodernity" can nevertheless be understood in classical Marxist terms: "Let us go back ... to Marx's 'invariant elements and relations' of a capitalist mode of production and see to what degree they are omni-present beneath all the surface froth and evanescence, the fragmentations and disruptions, so characteristic of present political economy" (Harvey, 1989: 179). Globalization is not new to capitalism, according to Harvey, but flexible postmodernity involves the intensification of the time-space compression which characterizes it. Social life is speeded up to the point where space is reduced or collapses entirely, as in the case of the instantaneous transmission and reception of images around the world using satellite communications (Harvey, 1989: 241). According to Harvey, since 1970, there has been an intensification of time-space compression as a response to a crisis in the Fordist regime of capitalist accumulation; new forms of information technology and communications are now used to bring about a more flexible form of capitalism. By 1970, market saturation and falling profits exposed the disadvantages of a system based on Fordist techniques of mass production and Keynesian corporatism involving agreement between the state, capitalists, and trade unionists to guarantee high levels of employment, investment, and consumption. Capitalists successfully dismantled Fordism by introducing new manufacturing and information technology, enabling small-batch, "just-in-time" production aimed at specialized "market niches," by gaining greater control over workers with the division of the labor market into skilled, adaptable, and therefore well-paid and secure core employees, and peripheral workers who are less skilled and frequently insecurely employed; and by deregulating the global financial market so that capital flow is now to a large extent outside the control of nation-states (though they are called upon to intervene in new ways, in unstable financial markets, where currency is in danger, for example).

We are currently in a period of transition, then, to a flexible postmodernity characterized by post-Fordist techniques and relations of production. Most importantly, for Harvey, finance capital has been empowered at the expense of the state and organized labor. The nation-state has lost a good deal of the control over economic policy and labor relations it enjoyed in Keynesian corporatism. It has been forced to become "entrepreneurial," disciplining workers and curbing the power of trade unions in order to attract capital investment (Harvey, 1989: 168). Flexible postmodernity is a new, more virulent form of capitalism in which the state and organized labor are at the mercy of finance capital. The state remains a powerful actor for Harvey, however, working virtually exclusively for capitalism. In a more recent book, *The New Imperialism*, Harvey argues that we are now seeing states engaging in a new form of "capitalist-imperialism," using military, diplomatic, and political strategies to extend its interests and achieve its goals outside its own territory. We will consider this argument in the next section (Harvey, 2003).

According to Harvey, flexible postmodernity produces a postmodern culture. Following Jameson's (1984) influential argument that postmodernism is the "cultural logic of late capitalism," he sees cultural production as increasingly integrated into commodity production, resulting in a new aesthetic sensibility. The relentless search for new markets, the rapid turnover of goods, and the constant manipulation of taste and opinion in advertising produces the postmodern celebration of ephemerality, of surface images rather than depth of meaning, of montage and juxtaposition of styles rather than authenticity, and of heterogeneity, pluralism, discontinuity and chaos rather than meta-narratives of reason and progress (Harvey, 1989: chapter 3). For Harvey, postmodernism is epiphenomenal, a by-product of a new stage of the capitalist mode of production dependent on the accelerated consumption of signs and services, rather than on manufactured goods. Nothing more than "froth and evanescence," it does not require the development of new theoretical tools since it can be understood entirely from within the terms of Marxist political economy.

In fact, as Krishan Kumar (1995) points out, it is possible to read Harvey's work against his own conclusions. Rather than seeing postmodernism as simply a change of style, a surface gloss on capitalism as the driving force of contemporary social life, we might conclude that if postmodernity is capitalism with a new face, then the novelty of the situation warrants more than simply a return to business as usual. Without denying the importance of the economic dimension of postmodernity, it is important not to reduce the cultural and political dimensions to an economistic determinism of capital accumulation and ceaselessly extending commodification (Kumar, 1995: 1925). Despite his sensitivity to cultural forms, from the position Harvey takes within a political economy developed to deal with a very different kind of social life, one in which signs were less obviously effective in identity formation and contestation and in the structuring of social practices. In reducing cultural forms to economic determinism, Harvey cannot engage with the potentially transformational dimensions of cultural politics.

For Harvey, real politics is essentially class politics. Though on occasion he commends social movements for "changing the structure of feeling" and articulating the rights of the marginalized to speak in their own voices ("women, gays, blacks, ecologists, regional autonomists," Harvey, 1989: 48), at the same time, he suggests that such movements tend toward "place-bound" resistance which only serves the fragmentation upon which flexible accumulation feeds (1989: 3035). As Meaghan Morris (1992) notes, he gestures toward acknowledging the equal importance of "differences" and "otherness" and the necessity of incorporating them into a more inclusive historical materialism, but he continually rewrites "differences" as "the same,"; ultimately, all these groups are simply further victims of capitalist exploitation. For Harvey, it is only class politics that can be genuinely emancipatory (Harvey, 1989: 355, 1993; Morris, 1992).

In *Economies of Signs and Space* (1994), Scott Lash and John Urry expound a similar argument to Harvey, using a Marxist framework to explain globalization. Like Harvey, they also see the terms "postmodernity" and "postmodernism" as usefully summing up new features of contemporary life, while grounding them in the continuity of dynamic capitalism as the driving force of history. However, Lash and Urry do integrate these new features into their account of what they call alternatively "disorganized capitalism" and "postmodernity" to a greater extent than Harvey. In fact, in this respect, their account breaks through the modern Marxist paradigm to which they are anxious to remain committed.

Lash and Urry give more emphasis than those who think in terms of post-Fordism and flexible specialization to *consumption* as a leading practice in contemporary capitalism. For them, it is consumption and service industries rather than finance capital and post-Fordist production that demonstrate the progressive features of disorganized capitalism and which are therefore at its core (Lash and Urry, 1994: 17, 60). This is an important difference in emphasis because it leads them to place culture and symbolic value at the center of their analysis. In their view, the economy is now based primarily on the circulation of signs: the cognitive signs that are informational goods and the aestheticized signs of what they call postmodern goods such as media products, leisure services, and designer products (1994: 4). Alongside the changing *objects* of capitalism, disorganized capitalism also involves the emergence of a new, more highly reflexive *subjectivity*. This is, in turn, both cognitive and aesthetic. In cognitive terms, it involves the monitoring and formation of the self in the reflection on information given by experts. In aesthetic terms, it involves the interpretation and formation of the self through the consumption of goods, ideas, and images. Lash and Urry see reflexivity of both kinds as central to the reproduction and modification of the socio-economic processes of postmodernity; it is both the result and the condition of a continual "de-traditionalization" which constantly revolutionizes patterns of production and consumption.

For Lash and Urry, postmodernity is intrinsically global. Organized capitalism was centered on the nation-state; like Harvey, they see the previous capitalist system as one in which class interests were incorporated into a Keynesian national agenda set through negotiated compromises and state regulation (Lash and Urry, 1987). Disorganized capitalism cannot, however, be analyzed as a society, a set of structures bounded by the nation-state (Lash and Urry, 1994: 320–2). Flows of capital, technologies, information, images, and people do not recognize territorial boundaries and collapse the globe as they circulate across greater distances at greater velocity. Expanded and speeded-up flows across borders are increasingly outside the control of national governments, or, indeed, of any individual organization or group. Nothing is given or fixed in disorganized capitalism, according to Lash and Urry, and the reflexivity resulting from ever-increasing knowledge and information serves only to disorganize it still further (1994: 1011).

Lash and Urry begin and end *Economies of Signs and Space* by invoking the name of Marx, to resurrect the "dinosaur," as they put it. However, it is arguable that the theory they present breaks significantly with the economism of orthodox Marxism in seeing the circulation of goods, capital, and labor in symbolic terms and therefore as at least as much a matter of culture as of economics. On one hand, they seem to argue for a weak version of economic determinism, seeing postmodern culture, reflexivity, and other features of postmodernity as caused by global economic flows, as "effects of [the] highly informationalized socio-economic core" (1994: 13). However, as Kumar notes, at the same time, they also see the postmodernized economy as inseparably intertwined with culture, rather than as occupying a separate sphere from which it could be said to be causing cultural effects (Kumar, 1995: 118). They argue that what it is important to grasp in order to understand contemporary capitalism is precisely "the extent to which culture has penetrated the economy itself, that is, the extent to which symbolic processes, including an important aesthetic component, have permeated both consumption and production" (Lash and Urry, 1994: 601). This second thesis is also a good deal more consistent with the idea of reflexivity as productive of the flows in which it is embedded; flows of goods, information, and people are modifiable just to the extent that they are, as Lash and Urry argue, meaningful for those engaged in them because they are imbued with symbolic value. The reflexivity of the economy is both cause and effect of the way in which it is, in Lash and Urry's terms, informationalized and aestheticized. In fact, Lash and Urry's theory of capitalism is barely recognizable in terms of Marxism's privileging of the economic sphere as determinant of social relations and cultural forms.

Lash and Urry give little consideration to politics in either the narrow or the wider sense. They see the nation-state as increasingly internationalized in that many attempts to govern globalized capitalism can only be made at the level of the international political order. However, they do not discuss politics at this level in any detail. Nor do they explicitly address the issues of cultural politics with which we are concerned in this book. Nevertheless, their analysis of reflexive capitalism points towards the need for an understanding of cultural politics as it is concerned with the formation and contestation of identities and social practices. Lash and Urry's analysis of disorganized capitalism might be seen as entirely pessimistic, as the demise of organized labor and diminishing of the power of the nation-state reduces capacities to regulate capitalism in the interests of citizens. However, it also points towards a different understanding of politics, as the way in which the social is actively constituted through the manipulation of meaning suggests the possibility of globalization which would not necessarily be dominated by the imperatives of capitalist expansion. According to Lash and Urry's account, cultural politics is increasingly important in disorganized capitalism. Not only, they argue, is the individual forced to make choices to an unprecedented degree, especially concerning his or her self-identity and consumption of goods and services, but it is consumerism that is now leading capitalist economies. It follows, then, that forms of politics centered on information and aesthetics are increasingly crucial to structuring social relations between individuals and collective forms of life.

On Lash and Urry's account, the form of politics most pertinent to the restructuring of disorganized capitalism would seem to be consumer politics. Consumer politics, though it has a long history, has, indeed, become a good deal more prominent in the last few decades (Micheletti et al., 2004; Sassatelli, 2007). New terms that have entered our vocabulary, "ethical consumption," "citizen-consumer," are indicative of new practices and identities (Micheletti et al., 2004: xiv). In large part, this is due to the revolution in advertising from the mid-1980s when, as Naomi Klein puts it, management theories realized "that successful corporations must primarily produce brands, as opposed to products" (Klein, 2000: 3). Brands are designed to symbolize value to consumers: to assure us of the quality of a range of products, but also to help us (safely) experiment with, or to re-confirm, our identity by buying and using them. Advertising, sponsorship, and logos are vehicles that are intended to convey the meaning of a corporation for our lives, and, at the same time, the meaning of our actions and who we are in consuming the corporation's products. Brands make corporations hugely successful; as Klein argues, in some cases the products hardly seem to matter at all any more. But they also make huge, sprawling transnational corporations extremely vulnerable at the same time. If consumers can be successfully mobilized to boycott a brand, or even if leaders of corporations fear that there might be a sharp fall in purchases of branded products, they can be brought to change their practices. Through activities such as boycotts, demonstrations, court cases (e.g., McLibel), culture-jamming (subverting advertisements with graffiti), and even Internet rumor (see Lury, 2004: 144–5; Perretti and Micheletti, 2004), corporations such as Nike, Gap, Calvin Klein, and McDonalds have been brought to change certain of their practices, from employing child labor to production processes that damage the environment.

There are certainly limits to this kind of politics. Changing buying habits relies on relatively high levels of disposable income and/or careful budgeting, and it may therefore be marginalizing and disempowering for some (Micheletti et al., 2004: xv). It is controversial where it affects labor practices in the developing world; those involved in boycotts may not be aware of the difficulties faced by people involved in producing branded products if they lose their jobs (Spivak, 1999: 415-21). Finally, unless consumer politics is quite organized and systematic, it may be rather capricious in its effects, ultimately removing any incentive for corporations to change how they act. On the other hand, ethical consumption may itself be simplified and rationalized by branding as, for example, in the case of the Fairtrade mark in the UK, which denotes production and marketing that gives a reasonable return to producers (Lury, 2004: 138). The cultural politics of branding is developing, but it undoubtedly needs organization as part of social movement politics if it is to realize its potential to reform global capitalism (Bennett, 2004).

Globalization as modernization

An understanding of cultural politics as intrinsic to social life is much more highly developed in the sociology of reflexivity, the main alternative to Marxism as a way of theorizing globalization from a starting point within the terms of traditional sociology. Anthony Giddens and Ulrich Beck advocate a multi-causal explanation of globalization in which it is seen as a consequence of modernity, rather than the mono-causal account of Marxists in which capitalism is presented as its driving force (McGrew, 1992: 69).

Giddens (1990) sees globalization as the outcome of the dynamism of modernity, which involves what he calls the disembedding of social relations in time-space distanciation and the reflexive appropriation of knowledge. He contrasts modernity with previous epochs in which time and space were always linked to place, to the immediate location of co-present social actors. In modernity, time and space are "emptied," abstracted from particular social rhythms of life; they are represented by clocks and maps which allow them to be used independently of any particular social location. Time-space distanciation makes possible the development of disembedding mechanisms which "lift out" social activity from localized contexts, and reorganize it across time and space. There are two types of disembedding mechanisms, according to Giddens: symbolic tokens, of which the only one he discusses is money, used as a universal token of exchange; and expert systems in which technical knowledge is used to organize material and social environments: that of engineers, architects, doctors, psychologists, and so on. Expert systems contribute to the reflexivity of modernity, to the continual monitoring of what is known, and to the decisions that have to be made concerning how to proceed in everyday life. In modernity, there can be no reliance on tradition, since every aspect of life is potentially subject to reason and can only be justified in the light of this consideration. The reflexive monitoring intrinsic to human activity is thus radicalized in modernity; social practices are continually constitutively altered by the understanding social actors bring to bear on them in their daily routines (Giddens, 1990).

According to Giddens, the dynamism of modernity leads inexorably (if unpredictably, since there are always unintended consequences in social life) toward the globalization of its institutions: capitalism, industrialism, and the administrative surveillance and control of the means of violence which are concentrated in the nation-state. In Giddens's view, it is the importance of the rise of the nation-state, and now of the nation-state system of global governance, which is neglected in Marxist accounts. He agrees with Wallerstein that capitalism is inherently expansionist, but he argues that the concentration of power in the nation-state enabled the mobilization of social, economic, and military resources far beyond those available to pre-modern systems and that this, combined with capitalism and industrial production, is what has made the expansion of the West irresistible (Giddens, 1990: 62–3). Giddens sees the nation-state as retaining its importance in globalized modernity insofar as there is no area of the Earth's surface which is not under the legitimate control of a state and insofar as states continue to have a successful monopoly over the means of violence within their territories. However, the modern state has always been involved in a dialectic in which it trades control over practices within its territories for more global influence by joining with other states. Working through international agencies, a state may gain control over military operations, for example, which do not depend solely on the control it exercises within its borders; at the same time, it loses a degree of independence of action through that cooperation. In late modernity, given increased time-space distanciation in all areas of activity and the resulting flows across territorial borders, there is a tendency toward a greater degree of cooperation and a consequent diminishing of autonomy for the nation-state.

As Giddens sees it, then, we are still within modernity, albeit a radicalized modernity which has many of the features others attribute to postmodernity. He sees radicalized modernity as characterized by disenchantment with teleological models of history involving the progress of some intrinsic human capacity or activity, such as reason or labor, and also by the dissolution of foundationalism in which the absolute and fundamental grounds for truth or morality are sought in reasoned reflection (Giddens, 1990).

Giddens has developed one of the most pertinent accounts of cultural politics in relation to globalization. He compares the "emancipatory politics" of modernity, including Marxism, liberalism, and conservatism, with the "life politics" of the contemporary period of late modernity in which both the political end, and the means, are the transformation of the self. He gives rather a sketchy account of emancipatory politics as concerned with liberation from exploitation, inequality, and oppression, and as seeking justice and participation through democratic participation (conservatism is seen as a reaction to these ideals in radicalism and liberalism). It works with the conventional, modern notion of power as the capability of an individual or group to exert its will over others that we have encountered as the dominant definition in political sociology (Giddens, 1991: 210–14). By contrast, "life politics" is a politics of individual lifestyle. It involves the individual in continually making choices in a reflexively ordered environment where tradition no longer provides the parameters of everyday life. It is closely connected to globalization, according to Giddens, "where globalizing influences intrude deeply into the reflexive project of the self, and, conversely, where processes of self-realization influence global strategies" (1991: 214). The consumer choices we examined at the end of the previous section would also be a good example of Giddens's ideas about "life politics"; as a result of the efforts of environmentalists, there is now extensive public awareness of the impact of lifestyle decisions that people make in the over-developed West on the environment here and elsewhere. There is also awareness of the differences that could be made to global environmental risks if people made lifestyle changes.

Giddens does not see the nation-state as irrelevant in life politics. The state remains crucial to democratization, emancipatory rights are still important, and issues of life politics are likely to become increasingly significant in the public and juridical arenas of states. However, life politics are currently more prominent outside the state, often carried by social movements. The feminist slogan, "The personal is political," exemplifies this kind of politics, as does the environmental slogan, "Think global, act local." Such forms of politics may, therefore, Giddens argues, lead to new forms of political organization, both within states and at the global level, that are more appropriate to their concerns (Giddens, 1991: 226–8).

Discussion of these new forms of political organization is further advanced in Ulrich Beck's work on "risk society." Beck's theory of cultural politics is similar to that of Giddens in many respects, despite their different starting points (Beck, 1992: 78). Beck's understanding of "risk society" draws sociologists' attention to the way in which contemporary social life is characterized by an unprecedented degree and number of fabricated risks, many of which are global in scope, such as environmental pollution or nuclear war, and which are likely to become more so as the overproduction, which is currently a feature of advanced industrial societies, intensifies across the world. Risk society is necessarily global, in Beck's view, because the dangers we must now deal with are not clearly limited in space and time. Furthermore, responses to risk may also be global: modernization is the driving force of globalization, but risk accelerates it insofar as modernity is reflexive. Beck argues, from rather an optimistic point of view, that we are now on the threshold of a radicalized modernity in which "global dangers set up global mutualities" such that self-conscious, collective reflection on risk displaces the modern privileging of progress and wealth production in order to avoid global destruction (Beck, 1992, 1996: 29).

In Beck's view, the realization of the potential for reflexive modernity depends on what he calls "sub-politics." For Beck, it is very clear that new forms of politics are developing which do not directly address the nation-state but, nevertheless, alter it from below. Modernity has resulted in a gap between the state as the supposed political center which actually has no influence over the most important decisions concerning risk, and the decisions taken outside this arena, in different institutional contexts where contingent decisions must be made in the light of the knowledge of different possibilities with different implications for different groups (Beck, 1992: 222). Beck's chief example is the "citizens-initiatives" groups in Germany in the 1980s and '90s, but he argues more generally that citizens now have a public voice in media debates, in political campaigns, in decisions concerning ethical consumption, in petitioning the courts on matters of public concern, in private lifestyle choices, and in addressing professional organizations. Scientists and technicians have an especially important role to play in "sub-politics" because of their expertise in risk assessment. All these "citizens-initiatives" must be taken seriously by governments, multinational corporations, and other citizens. As Beck sees it, in reflexive modernity, there is a re-moralization of economic and social life in which the supposed objectivity and necessity of technical requirements and the outcomes of government policies are continually called into question and opened up to new opportunities for democracy. Beck's principal example here is the politics of the environmental movement which has been largely effective outside political parties and the bureaucratic procedures of the state, using a range of means to get its message across where everyone is uncertain about the extent and depth of the real risks involved in the everyday use of science and technology.

Beck's analysis of "sub-politics" goes beyond Giddens's theory of reflexive modernity in offering the theoretical possibility of a complete transformation of social forms. For Beck, decisions made in sub-politics may now alter the institutional contexts in which they are made; such decisions precisely concern the realization of one course of action, and thus the constitution of one possible institutional form among various possibilities. Most strikingly, Beck argues that the state is currently being remade completely, behind the façade of what is still understood as the modern nation-state. He calls "the nation-state" a "zombie" category: a fiction, only apparently a reality. Sociologists have remained focused on the nation-state, Beck argues, where they have failed to overcome "methodological nationalism," the perspective from which most sociological concepts have been developed and which took what happened within a territorial state for granted as the basis of analysis: society was equated with national society. Such an approach is of no use for understanding what is happening in the world today. What is needed, rather, is "methodological cosmopolitanism" to grasp how dualities of global and local, national and international are being dissolved (Beck and Sznaider, 2006). Whilst, historically, nation-states were formed and sustained by and for war, the situation is very different where populations are faced, instead, with global risks. The state itself must now adapt to the new situation of the risk society and to the sub-politics of social movements, citizens' initiatives, and professional associations (Beck, 1998).

Globalization as world culture

"World polity" theorists, a school of sociologists led by John Meyer, put the nation-state at the center of their analysis of globalization (Meyer, 1999; Meyer et al., 1997; Boli and Thomas, 1997; Meyer and Jepperson, 2000; Lechner and Boli, 2005: 43–7). Globalization is not the result of capitalism; the changes that are taking place across a variety of different areas of social life cannot be seen as economically determined. Nor is it a product of the inexorable logic of modernization. The establishment of the world polity is due rather to the effective influence of individuals and organizations since the nineteenth century who have successfully spread universal ideals around the world. Since World War II, "world culture" has become all-pervasive. There is a "world society" of national and international actors, and the diffusion of norms concerning how political life should be organized have become part of the practices of every nation-state in the world. It is the contingent success of this diffusion of cultural norms that warrants the term "world polity" as a description of global political integration.

Meyer and his associates are very clear about the causes of the world polity. In terms of actors, world society is made up of what Meyer calls "Rationalized Others," individuals and organizations that advise nation-states and others about their responsibilities and true purposes (Meyer, 1999: 128–30). There are four main elements of world society that contribute to and implement the tenets of world culture: International Governmental Organizations (IGOs), especially those in the United Nations system; nation-states, which copy each other's ways in ways that lead to the diffusion of cultural norms of political and social organization world-wide; voluntary associations in different fields, especially those that are attached to social movements; and scientists and professionals, experts who give advice to other actors of world society (Meyer et al., 1997: 162–6). Perhaps the single most important elements of world society are International Non-Governmental Organizations (INGOs), which represent, carry out, and elaborate global principles. They are "built on world-cultural principles of universalism, individualism, rational voluntaristic authority, progress, and world citizenship" and they promote those same principles (Boli and Thomas, 1997: 180).

World polity theorists understand the nation-state as culturally constructed and embedded in world culture (Meyer, 1999: 123). Their theory of world culture is an attempt to understand the "isomorphism," or structural similarity, between states across the world. The question world polity theorists set out to explain is the following: Why do nation-states adopt similar constitutional forms, public educational systems, welfare systems, policies on women's rights, and so on, regardless of their appropriateness to local conditions (Meyer et al., 1997: 152–3)? They argue that world society actors fashion nation-states in such similar terms through three processes. First, they produce models to which nation-states should be seen to conform. For example, joining the United Nations involves demonstrating appropriate understandings of sovereignty, control of populations, territory, and so on. Second, world society systematically works to maintain the identities of state actors as committed to those models. If, for example, state actors resist putting into practice the goals to which states have formally committed themselves – by violating human rights agreements, or failing to meet goals of socio-economic development, for example, – they will come under the scrutiny and the criticism of external actors, especially IGOs and INGOs. Third, world society legitimates citizenship, individual rights, and democracy. In this respect, it creates links between local actors and world culture, so ensuring that individuals and social movement organizations are also active in holding states to the promises they have made to uphold universal principles of world culture.

Meyer and his associates argue convincingly that sociologists should overcome their historic reluctance to consider the importance of culture in explaining political change. Their own model, however, is problematic in this respect. They explicitly counter-pose cultural explanations of global development to those theories that consider "patterns of influence and conformity" as solely matters of power relations (Meyer et al., 1997: 145). It is important, however, not to oppose "culture" and "power" in this way.

A useful way to understand how culture and power are inseparable in the international arena is Joseph Nye's categorization of "soft power" as on a continuum with "hard power." Soft power involves charismatic leadership, communication, persuasion, and exemplary behavior, compared to hard power, which involves military or economic coercion or payment (Nye, 2005). Clearly, there is not always a strict separation between the two types of power. As Meyer et al. themselves note in the example they give of nation-states that apply to join the United Nations, in order to be able to benefit from belonging to it – and there are very real dangers in terms of "hard" power of not belonging – they must clearly demonstrate that they "fit." This is far from a neutral, technical exercise of demonstrating competence. Indeed, Nye developed the idea of "soft" power precisely in order to convince US authorities that persuasion is a much more effective way of leading the world than coercion, even during times when the US may be threatened by the rise of other states, especially China. It is an argument for maintaining US dominance in the multipolar world of IGOs and NGOs through the power of ideas. Dominance through persuasion is possible, not only because the US still has far more military and economic strength than any other state, but also because the universal ideals on which legitimate states must model themselves are derived from, and fit much more easily, some societies than others, enabling them to maintain their advantages in the international arena.

World polity theorists consider their theory rigorously neutral and scientifically verified. Indeed, they have produced a massive amount of statistical detail concerning the diffusion of norms of world culture (e.g., constitutional models [Boli, 1987], educational systems [Meyer et al., 1992], and organizational forms of world society [Boli and Thomas, 1999]). One failing of this methodology, however, is that, although world polity theorists are concerned with culture, they have practically no interest in the interpretation of *meanings*. They note that there are very often important differences between the ideals that states set themselves and their practices; states frequently fall short of constitutional commitments, for example, and they invariably fail to live up to policy promises in terms of welfare, health, and education (Meyer et al., 1997: 157). There is also room in their account, at least theoretically, for conflict over the universalist principles that underpin these ideals. But they have little or no interest in differences, either in the diversity of interpretations of those principles, or in alternatives that are not adopted, which are marginalized or ignored. This methodological failure is actually consistent with their theory of culture. For Meyer et al., cultural meaning is "more cognitive and instrumental than expressive" (Meyer et al., 1997: 149); it concerns the communication of knowledge and technical reasoning rather than what is more commonly understood by "culture": active interpretations of events and processes, strongly held or deep-rooted beliefs and values, and passionately embodied identifications. Indeed, Meyer et al. explicitly see the diffusion of cultural norms in terms of a set of scripts that can be, and are, adopted without much difficulty anywhere.

More interpretative methodologies lead to a set of questions that are not easily addressed from within the terms of the theory of "world polity." If the globally diffused "scripts" of human rights, development, universal education, and so on regularly fail in practice, although they are apparently legitimated by world society actors, surely this points to differences in the meaning of these scripts in different settings. Who defines what form states should take in practice, and how? To give an example in terms of human rights principles, there is no doubt that agreements on civil and political rights are far more important to IGOs than those that require international cooperation to further the social and economic rights of the most impoverished people in the world (An'Naim, 2002). This is despite the fact that the vast majority of states in the world have signed and ratified the Universal Declaration of Human Rights (UDHR) which (especially as it is supported by the International Convention on Economic, Social and Cultural Rights [ICESCR]) in principle commits them to do all they can to ensure that everyone in the world has certain basic minimum requirements in terms of food, shelter, education, and healthcare. International law has been established concerning human rights to alleviate poverty, and there has been continual emphasis on the importance of such rights by the leaders of developing countries and by INGOs, but its very existence is practically unknown outside certain circles (see Nash, 2009a: chapter 5). Insofar as world culture is unified, it is because it is very difficult for those without authority to challenge the assumptions of the leaders of Western states about who and what is important. Theorists of "world polity" do not ask questions about power and interpretation that would enable us to understand how establishing the unity of the world polity, if it is indeed possible, is inevitably caught up in challenging and re-creating hegemony.

The theory of "world polity" is an important and influential contribution to understanding the development of globalization in terms of political institutions. Although the positivist methodology adopted by Meyer and his colleagues creates problems in terms of understanding differences of perspective and power in the creation of global norms and practices, world polity theorists have carried out an impressive mapping of the principal cultural norms, and the actors and organizations, that need to be taken into account in understanding global politics. What also remains oddly under-theorized in this account, however, is the development of relations *between* the actors involved in global politics. Meyer et al stress how crucial the nation-state is as a "carrier" of global cultural norms, but they do not consider how globalization might alter the very form of the state itself. It is to this question that we now turn.

2.2 State Transformation and Imperialism

"Methodological nationalism" allowed sociologists to treat societies as if they were coherent and bounded entities, distinct from one another, and contained within the territories of nation-states. Understanding globalization means an end to this fiction, and the necessity of taking seriously what was previously the domain of historical sociologists and of the discipline of International Relations, the way in which states are formed in relation to each other. Globalization involves a growing density of international organizations that deal with border-crossing flows. Far more than a matter of relations between states, global governance is significant for all aspects of social life, including the formation of states themselves.

It is misleading to think of "the state" as if it were a singular, integrated, and fully formed agent that is now taking on a new role on the world stage. A state is better seen as a fluid grouping of institutions with unstable boundaries which create official positions from which social actors negotiate their tasks and capacities, both *internally*, with others who act "in the name of the state," and *externally*, with officials of other states and with representatives of other social and economic organizations. In other words, "the state" is always an unstable and temporary outcome – however long a particular formation may last – of ongoing cultural politics. It is as important to pay attention to the contestation and reformation of its internal structural form in processes of globalization as to its external interface with other states and other actors.

"Global governance" describes a world in which states must accommodate themselves to the development of international and transnational organizations, not just to prevent or deal with conflicts between states themselves but increasingly to address every possible issue of national or international concern. Most importantly, global governance itself is not exclusively concerned with relations between states, but also with activities within states in ways that impinge on modern notions of state sovereignty. As James Rosenau describes it, global governance consists of "governance without government – of regulatory mechanisms in a sphere of activity which function effectively even though they are not endowed with formal authority" (quoted in McGrew, 1997: 15).

Widespread networks of Inter-Governmental Organizations that deal with a vast array of transnational issues are at the core of global governance. Some are global, most notably the United Nations system (UN), including the World Bank and the International Monetary Fund (IMF). Others are regional, including the European Union (EU) and the North American Free Trade Agreement (NAFTA). Some are selective along lines of wealth and military capacity, for example, the G8 (which includes Canada, France, Germany, Italy, Japan, the UK, the US, and Russia), and the North American Treaty Organization (NATO, an alliance of 28 countries in North America and Europe). Some are selective on other bases; the Commonwealth, for example, includes 53 states from all parts of the world that were originally part of the British Empire.

At the same time, alongside IGOs, in almost every sphere of activity, there are a growing number of Non-Governmental Organizations which are actively engaged in trying to influence states from below and above. NGOs and INGOs are legal entities, formally independent of states, and non-profit-making. The increase in the numbers of INGOs alone is astounding. Around one-quarter of the 13,000 now in existence were founded after 1990 (Anheier, Glasius, and Kaldor, 2004: 4). In addition, there are tens of thousands of NGOs that, besides working within national territories, are also oriented towards IGOs and to addressing states other than those in which they are set up. INGOs include social movement organizations like Greenpeace, but also large, charitable operations like Oxfam and scientific and professional bodies like the International Association of Nutritional Sciences and the International Sociological Association (McGrew, 1995: 35). All these organizations, of necessity, tend to engage in forms of "soft" power, depending on publicity, knowledge, and communication.

In contemporary society, what we will continue to call "the state" for the sake of convenience is currently undergoing transformation in global governance. It is not that states are *undermined* by globalization, as if it came from outside. On the contrary, the way in which states are themselves involved in global projects is one of the most important and dynamic aspects of globalization itself. By comparison with the sovereign nation-state, the internationalizing state is becoming disaggregated as it is restructured within and across territorial borders. It is better, then, to think of the state, as Saskia Sassen suggests, as an *assemblage* of territory, authority, and rights, a bundle of institutions that form over a long period, but which can be disassembled and re-bundled in different ways when specific historic conditions make it possible and attractive to key social actors (Sassen, 2006: 6). Whilst the national state bundled limited territory, the authority of state officials, and citizens' rights together, the internationalizing state is beginning to remake each of these elements across national borders.

First, the internationalization of the state is marked by the integration of policy and even law-making across borders. Each branch of the domestic state now takes on an international dimension, resulting in trans-governmental networks that share information, harmonize regulation, and develop new ways of enforcing international law. Anne-Marie Slaughter distinguishes between vertical and horizontal networks. In horizontal networks, state officials come together with their counterparts from other states: as regulators, bureaucrats, judges, or elected politicians. They share information and they may set standards for regulating activities within and across territories, as well as developing agreements and enforcement mechanisms. The networks involved in IGOs are mostly of this kind, but there is, in addition, now a vast array of meetings between governmental officials as well as continual information gathering and exchange amongst those who share globalizing sympathies. In vertical networks, on the other hand, state officials delegate some of their authority to a "higher" or "supranational" organization which is authorized to make binding decisions for its members. The institutions of the European Union are the most highly developed supranational organizations. Also supranational in this sense are the growing variety of international courts (for example, the International Criminal Court, the International Criminal Tribunal for the Former Yugoslavia, and so on) which have been authorized by some, not all, state officials to make judgments that are, at least in principle, binding on states themselves (Slaughter, 2004).

Second, there is a trend towards the "de-statization" of the political system as a product of neo-liberal globalization (Jessop, 1997). De-statization involves the state, which often nominally remains the major sponsor and director of economic and social projects, cooperating to an increasing extent with NGOs and para-governmental organizations to realize its objectives. In such cases, the state does not give up authority within its own territory. It rather hires it out to other agencies. This shift is very evident in Britain as a product of neo-liberalist reorganization of relations between the state and the market. There has, for example, been some privatization of branches of the British state, with semi-autonomous agencies taking over many of the functions of civil service departments. Tasks such as prison security and assessing social security benefit claims are now carried out by contracted firms. While governments have always relied on other agencies and organizations to realize state objectives, and while they continue to set the framework within which services and goods are provided in the name of the state, they are now more likely to do so in negotiation with influential partners on whom they rely to a greater extent than was previously the case (Jessop, 1997: 575).

The internationalization of the state involves processes that are disassembling its previous form, contained within national borders, and reassembling it in new forms across borders. Saskia Sassen argues that this reassembling is in part strategic, to effect a changing balance between different branches of the state in order to increase the power of the executive relative to the legislative. The US is exemplary of such tendencies towards presidentialization, but it is a more general phenomenon (Sassen, 2006; see also Poguntke and Webb, 2005). In the US, it means that Congress is now much less able, and also much less likely, to question policies that the executive puts in place in terms of privatization, deregulation, and the marketization of public functions. There is an increase of specialized regulatory agencies within the executive, which often work in secret, that have taken over some of the oversight functions of the legislature. This shift in the balance of power from the legislative to the executive has been exacerbated by the declaration of the "war on terror" following 9/11, raised security alerts, and increased powers of surveillance, detention, and information gathering that the legislative find difficult to challenge, politically and legally.

It is in this context that we should understand the popularity of the work of Georgio Agamben on state sovereignty in recent years. Agamben explains state powers to suspend the rule of law in order to treat terrorist suspects quite differently to others suspected of criminal activities as a function of state sovereignty, arguing that it has always involved a distinction between those who are included within the state and those outside, who may be "killed without sacrifice" (Agamben, 2005: 4). Agamben understands state sovereignty as intrinsic to the formation of states: the origins of law lie in the distinction between *zoe* (bare life), which can always potentially be killed without sacrifice; and *bios* (political life), the life of citizens, which is preserved by the state (Agamben, 1995). The sovereign declaration of a state of exception is always, then, a possibility that exists within the rule of law, enabling the law to "withdraw from its usual jurisdiction" (Butler, 2004: 60). Agamben's theory has gained in importance in the US and Europe, where there have been declarations of states of emergency which have enabled the suspension of the rule of law to detain terrorist suspects in Guantanamo Bay, Belmarsh Prison, and elsewhere without trial, without access to the evidence against them, and, for many years, without even the right to legal counsel. Once prisoners are kept in such conditions, forms of cruel and degrading punishment and interrogation techniques involving torture are all too common and, as we now know, they were certainly a feature of detention in Guantanamo Bay (Johns, 2005; Nash, 2009a). Here we appear to see a form of state sovereignty that remains unchanged since ancient times, all discussions of state transformation in globalization notwithstanding.

It would be a mistake, however, to understand state sovereignty as timeless in this way. The ongoing internationalization of the state makes for a very particular context for these executive enactments of state sovereignty. The rhetoric of the "war on terror" certainly did enable the executive in the US and UK to seize extraordinary powers to disregard the human rights of terrorist suspects, and to enact legislation, like the Patriot Act in the US, that encroached on the established civil rights of citizens by legalizing intrusive forms of surveillance. It is in the context of measures that increase surveillance, technologies of control like biometrics, and security measures of all kinds, that we have seen the rise of what some have called "the security state." At the same time, however, Sassen argues that the power of the judiciary relative to the executive is increased in current state transformation. She is especially concerned with judicial review of the executive's regulatory activities where the legislative mechanisms for oversight are now disregarded. It is notable, however, that, while the legislative did little to challenge the emergency powers of the executive in the "war on terror," the Supreme Court did confront the Bush Administration's definition of its own powers to override fundamental prisoners' rights (Sassen, 2006: 178). In the UK, the relative power of the judiciary to challenge the executive was even more striking, especially as it derived from the European Convention of Human Rights incorporated into national law. The highest court in the UK, the Law Lords, required parliament to release detained terrorist suspects where it judged the government was in breach of European human rights (Nash, 2009a). This is not to say that there is now an appropriate balance between security and rights, but rather to note that sovereignty is being restructured in complex ways *internally* to internationalizing states, with the legislature losing ground to the executive and the judiciary.

Even more dramatic is the restructuring of state sovereignty *externally* in global governance. Interpretations of global governance, in political sociology and also amongst those who challenge, or who are trying to influence how it is developing in practice, broadly turn on questions of "sovereignty" and "imperialism." Contemporary political sociologists are divided over whether global governance is inherently imperialist, or whether it can be steered in a more cosmopolitan direction. Political cosmopolitans are not pro-Empire, but, from the point of view of "anti-imperialists," they are insufficiently attentive to the historical conditions and dangers of imperialism and how that might affect and influence imperialist tendencies in global governance today.

There is no doubt that global governance differs *formally* from imperialism in that it ostensibly involves relations between sovereign states. It is different, then, from Empires that owned and ruled sections of the world directly (Ferguson, 2008) On the other hand, an unconditional commitment to state sovereignty, regardless of a state's democratic structure and the respect of its officials for the rule of law, is a problem for political cosmopolitans, who see limitations on state sovereignty as entirely legitimate where states are involved in torture and murder, or where they systematically fail to enforce laws against routine violence that takes place within their own societies. Particularly at risk here are women, when violence in the "private sphere" of family life is treated as normal and goes unpunished; and ethnic minorities, where fear and hatred erupts, especially on the part of those who are able to access and use states' means of force. Political cosmopolitans consider that sovereignty should be reassessed and reformed: it should be *shared* in a democratically reformed UN in which state representatives agree on the legitimate limits of state activity. Breach of those limits could involve interference in states' domestic affairs. Political cosmopolitans see shared sovereignty as already developing as a legal possibility, and argue that intervention may be justified in certain cases, legally and morally (Held, 1995a, 1995b, 2002; Habermas, 2006). In contrast, those who interpret global governance as inherently imperialist see such interventions as linked to continuing attempts to dominate and exploit people who live in post-colonial states that have achieved only a precarious and formal recognition of sovereignty: global governance in general, and especially the use of military force on other states, is a way of extending imperialism (Chomsky, 2000; Hardt and Negri, 2000; Harvey, 2003, 2005; Amir, 2007; Douzinas, 2007). What "human rights" mean, and to whom; how societies are to be structured for the good of all; and who is to decide: these are the objects of the cultural politics of global governance for sociologists as well as for those directly involved in the organizations of global governance.

The distinction David Held has made between state autonomy and state sovereignty is useful to separate out issues that are often conflated under the heading "sovereignty" in these debates. It can be hard to separate them in practice, but analytically, it is useful to distinguish between "autonomy," which refers to the independence of state actors in taking action; and "sovereignty," which concerns their political authority and legal jurisdiction. Political cosmopolitans tend to be concerned less with autonomy than with sovereignty, while anti-imperialists understand global governance as enhancing both the autonomy and sovereignty of over-developed states at the expense of post-colonial states.

Autonomy concerns the capacities a state possesses to act independently of other states and of other economic and social organizations to articulate and pursue domestic and international policies (Held, 1995a: 100). Manifestly, no state has ever been fully autonomous; as we saw in chapter 1, the extent to which the modern state has been subject to the imperatives of capitalist accumulation has been one of the most debated issues in Marxist political sociology. However, the debate has taken on new life insofar as theorists of globalization argue that global economic processes now systematically undermine state autonomy to the point where governments are reduced to managing processes over which they have no control, even in principle, since they are not contained within national borders. Similar arguments can be made with regard to other border-crossing activities. Satellite broadcasting systems and digital technologies make censorship difficult, threaten national broadcasting systems, and facilitate transnational terrorist activities and civil disobedience that create insecurity. Environmental risks are created in particular places but they cause problems elsewhere, potentially for everyone on the planet. As none of these activities respect national boundaries, they cannot be controlled by individual national governments.

In effect, globalization means that states must cooperate in order to gain some degree of autonomy over cross-border flows that they cannot control alone. However, states never begin cooperation from the same starting point; inter-state relations are already embedded in long-standing structures of economic exploitation and dependence. The fate of post-colonial states has long been connected to that of metropolitan centers, and global governance exacerbates rather than ameliorates imperialist tendencies. In the first place, then, global governance should be seen as allowing economic practices in which over-developed states put pressure on those that aim to become better integrated into the global economy, to open up new markets, to privatize common and public goods (including nature), and to exploit and export cheap raw materials and manufactured goods (Tonkiss, 2005: 16–28). This is happening in a context in which world trade outside the highly integrated states of the global economy in Europe, North America, and East Asia is actually falling, leading to greater impoverishment for people elsewhere (Amir, 2007). It is in this neo-imperialist context that global governance enhances the autonomy of over-developed states at the expense of that of post-colonial states.

The most important factor in this respect is the "Washington Consensus," shaped by the US Treasury, the World Bank, and the IMF, that dominated global governance until the late 1990s. It involved neo-liberal commitment to the creation and extension of markets, and to decreases in tax and public spending. The "Washington Consensus" has been modified somewhat in recent years, following the global financial crisis of the 1990s, and talk in the IMF and World Bank is now of "good governance" rather than "free markets." What is sometimes called the "post-Washington Consensus," though there is some doubt about how wide this consensus might be, is, however, close to its predecessor in the restrictions it imposes on state autonomy: by creating conditions for financial investment to be easily transferred across borders, and making it necessary for states to take measures (discouraging trade unionism, creating tax incentives and infrastructure for multinationals) to encourage business that may go against citizens' best short- or long-term interests. International economic policy is the framework within which states must set their own national economic policies, regardless of whether most people within that state agree with it (Fine, Lapavitsas, and Pincus, 2001; Tonkiss, 2005: 66–70).

Where economic policy is negotiated in conditions of gross inequality in global governance, it is unsurprising that the results impact on the autonomy of states in radically different ways. First, the leaders of over-developed economies do not subject themselves to the rules of market liberalization they attempt to impose on others. Most remarked on recently are the subsidies North American and European states give to agriculture in their territories, and the way in which they then dump agricultural surpluses in developing countries. Both these practices work to prevent the development of local agricultural markets and global competition. This is especially problematic in areas where monoculture was established for imperial trade. Second, the effects of free markets, where they exist, are different for different economies. Developing economies may need a level of protectionism and support from state subsidies similar to that enjoyed by "infant industries" in the West which were often them-selves developed through imperial exploitation and the closing down of production in the colonies (the British closing down the cotton industry in India to develop it in Lancashire is the classic example). Third, a large number of developing countries are still bound to pay back escalating debts that were loaned by the IMF in the 1960s to develop modernization projects (dams, roads, airports), often to corrupt and unscrupulous politicians, and with little regard for their feasibility and long-term benefits. States are bound to make serious reductions in public spending if they are to pay back what is known as "odious" debt, irresponsibly offered and promoted by the IMF. Fourth, global economic governance may even on occasion involve direct intervention in the internal affairs of states. For example, the IMF may grant financial assistance to governments who ask for it under conditions which the government in question may have no part in negotiating. Although the IMF officially prefers to negotiate Structural Adjustment Programs with governments, the extent to which it actually does so is largely governed by that state's size, reputation, and importance to the global economy. As David Harvey points out, the enormous foreign debt of the US (to other states, especially China and Japan) would make it a macro-economic basket-case under IMF rules, and subject to intense pressure to restructure its economy (Harvey, 2005: 72; see also Sen, 1999; Chomsky, 2000: 101–7; Tonkiss, 2005).

"Sovereignty" concerns political authority, the "right to exercise the powers of the state and to determine the rules, regulations and policies within a given territory" (Held, 1995a: 99–100). The word "sovereignty" sums up ultimate state authority, what authorizes the state to have the "last word" within its own territory (Montgomery, 2002: 5). As the formal right to exercise authority, sovereignty differs, then, from state autonomy, which concerns the actual capacities of states for independence from others. A relatively simple idea, the practice of sovereignty is highly complex because of the way in which external sovereignty, ensured by international law that prohibits other states intervening in domestic affairs, is intrinsic to, but not the same as, internal sovereignty, the jurisdiction of states over their own territories and populations. Furthermore, the history of sovereignty is highly contested, and how it is understood makes a significant difference to how sovereignty is seen today.

Political cosmopolitans see state sovereignty as integral to the modern international state system, known as the Westphalian order, after the Treaty of Westphalia that inaugurated it in 1648. According to Held, this system supported the exclusive right of each nation-state to rule over its citizens and to conduct its own internal and external affairs without intervention (Held, 1995a: 38–9; 2002). A difficulty with this view of history is that formal Empires – of the kind conducted by the British in India, which involved directly governing inside state territory – have then to be seen as a breach of international law. If, however, an international agreement is more honored in the breach than the observance, it is difficult to see it as *law*. It was only after conflicts between the Great Powers about how the world should be divided led to the First World War that questions of Empire began to be seriously raised in international affairs, at a time when the high-point of European Imperialism was already passed. Until then, David Chandler argues, the international states system *supported* formal imperialism because it was based solely on the recognition of sovereignty as effective power. Chandler argues that the Westphalian system enabled the development of Empires because states that did not "count" as such could be appropriated, subject only to the resistance of those who lived there and to accommodation with other imperial states (Chandler, 2006: 122–7).

These differences of historical interpretation are crucial to contemporary understandings of global governance as inherently imperialist or as having progressive potential. Political cosmopolitans and "anti-imperialists" fundamentally disagree on what international law now means. David Chandler sees the ending of World War II as the beginning of a genuinely world-wide system of equal sovereign states, formally recognized by the UN, which undertook to maintain the peace by preventing states from interfering in each other's affairs. The UN Charter restricted the political sovereignty of the Great Powers, and inaugurated a law-bound international society of states for the first time, basing the authority of all states on the "equal rights and self-determination of peoples" (Article 1) (Chandler, 2006: 126–7). Held, however, interprets the UN system quite differently, seeing fundamental changes in international law following World War II as going beyond the Westphalian system and supporting the rights of individual *persons* rather than states (Held, 1995a: 74–89; 2002). In fact, these contradictory accounts of the development of global governance after World War II are different interpretations of aspects of the same legal system, described by Costas Douzinas as schizophrenic (Douzinas, 2007: 244). The UN system both inaugurated formal respect for the integrity of self-determining sovereign states, whilst the long process of developing human rights law to protect individuals within those states began at the same time.

Held argues that cosmopolitan law is still in development, following principles that were first outlined in the Nuremberg trials. First, individuals became criminally accountable for violations of the laws of war ("just obeying orders" was no longer a legitimate legal defense, however lowly a position the accused held in the military or state hierarchy). Second, principles of human rights began to be developed that prescribed limits to a government's conduct towards its own citizens to apply in times of peace and war (Held, 1995b: 101–2; see also Ratner and Abrams, 2001: 4). This second principle was carried forward and extended with the Universal Declaration of Human Rights, beginning international human rights law in the UN human rights system. In contrast to Westphalian international law, cosmopolitan law reaches inside states, piercing nominal state sovereignty and enforcing claims against human rights violators. Where international law governs relations between states, cosmopolitan law (or what Habermas also calls the constitutionalization of international law) is a law of *individuals*, not of *states* (Habermas, 2006: 124; Hirsh, 2003). For political cosmopolitans, the development of the European Union, though lacking in some respects, is indicative of the concrete possibilities of these cosmopolitan ideals in practice (Beck and Grande, 2007; Habermas and Derrida, 2005; Rumford, 2007). The European Union has achieved the peaceful incorporation of states that were long-term enemies by external expansion: integrating states into a supranational organization has been much more effective than a balance of powers based on mutual fear of the use of force. Although there are continual political struggles within Europe over sovereignty and national independence, European human rights law is relatively effective in bringing pressure to bear on member states, and it also influences prospective member states which must show they comply with it before they are allowed to join the European Union. In this way, the European Union spreads human rights principles peacefully beyond its own borders. The international courts that try individuals for crimes against humanity are also examples of cosmopolitan law: as long as the court's protocols are observed and there appears to be sufficient evidence against the accused, the individual's status within a state – citizen or non-citizen, elected or appointed leader – is irrelevant. According to "Nuremberg principles" of cosmopolitan law, there are no reasons, not even reasons of state, that can possibly justify certain actions, whether in peacetime or when a state is at war.

Initially a side-show to the main event of setting up the equal sovereignty of states in the UN system, the development of human rights agreements into cosmopolitan law now strikingly contradicts its premises, at least in some respects. It should be stressed here that, for the most part, human rights policies are agreements that state actors themselves define and institutionalize within their own territories. The UN system is designed to allow maximum autonomy to states in this respect, as we will see in chapter 5. Nevertheless, cosmopolitan law is at odds with state sovereignty because it is *only* where state actors are involved that violence against individuals or groups is considered as violating human rights. State actors define human rights, and agree on what they mean and how they should be institutionalized. In all these ways, they are the guarantors of the human rights of individuals within their jurisdiction. But in international human rights law it is also state actors who violate human rights. What is to be done when state actors do not respect the human rights norms to which their state has committed itself by signing and ratifying international human rights agreements?

The most controversial answer to this problem in recent years has been calls for military interventions led by the US and its allies. Such occasions raise very difficult dilemmas for political cosmopolitans. If individuals are being tortured, raped, and murdered, often with the cooperation of militarized sections of their own state, who is responsible for ensuring that rights they have as members of the "universal community" of humanity are guaranteed? In fact, "actually existing" cosmopolitan law offers little help with this dilemma. As it currently stands, legal support for military action that is not taken in self-defense is very weak. Although the cosmopolitan law of human rights has been fostered by the UN system, it is distinctly at odds with the UN's statist Charter, developed to preserve the sovereign integrity of states to ensure world peace. The duty to intervene in a state's affairs on humanitarian grounds may be extrapolated morally from "the Nuremberg Principles," and from human rights agreements ratified by states and developed since the UN was founded in 1948. They are the basis of the "responsibility to protect" enjoined on states, and on the international community where states fail to protect people inside their borders, that was endorsed by the UN Security Council in 2006. Nevertheless, the Security Council, the only international body with the authority to allow war to be declared legitimately, has not so far given agreement for military interventions on humanitarian grounds. On the other hand, states involved in military actions taken on the grounds of humanitarian intervention have consistently sought permission from the Security Council, and if UN approval for military action were given, it would consolidate cosmopolitan law in this area (see Douzinas, 2007: chapter 9).

The work of Jurgen Habermas on developing cosmopolitan law is interesting in this respect. Habermas saw the humanitarian intervention in Kosovo in 1998 as morally, if not legally, justified. The US and its allies had no UN mandate to attack those carrying out "ethnic cleansing," but Habermas argues that they were right to act against existing international law in this case, even if the precedent it set in overriding state sovereignty was dangerous, in order to protect people against the arbitrariness of their own government (Habermas, 1999, 2006: 85–7). On the other hand, war on Iraq to topple Saddam Hussein and achieve "regime change" was neither morally nor legally justified (Habermas and Derrida, 2005). What makes the difference is that, in Kosovo, human rights violations were actually ongoing, so that there was a chance of stopping them, and the liberal-democratic states involved in the bombing and invasion of the former Yugoslavia had acceptable human rights records. In the case of war in Iraq in 2003, on the other hand, the US acted much more unilaterally, opposed by a number of previously close allies, justifying the decision to invade on very dubious grounds, and putting together a "coalition of the willing" that included states which themselves had poor human rights records (Habermas, 2006: 85–7). What is necessary, then, according to Habermas, is the development of cosmopolitan law out of international law involving deliberation on the facts and principles justifying humanitarian intervention on a case-by-case basis. In this way, there is the possibility of building a world organization in which states bind themselves to respect limitations in terms of respecting individual's rights, or face the legitimate enforcement of cosmopolitan law by military or (where criminal prosecution of a particular leader is the object) police force (Habermas, 2006).

On the other hand, for those who see global governance, and especially the justification of any kind of humanitarian intervention, as inherently imperialist, however subtle the arguments for cosmopolitanism may be, they are at best deluded and naïve, and at worst cynically motivated legitimations of force for personal gain. The traditional version of this argument in political sociology is Marxist, and it is put forward clearly and forcibly by David Harvey (2003). Harvey argues that capitalism requires imperialism, and so-called "humanitarian interventions" are actually geo-political conflicts led by the US to secure its long-term interests. In particular, the Iraq war was intended to bring about regime change to give the US a foothold in the Middle East which would enable it to control the flow of oil on which the global economy depends. According to Harvey, capitalist imperialism is always faltering and inconsistent because it involves two, often contradictory, logics: that of the state, which concerns regulation backed up with the threat of coercion and which is therefore necessarily concerned with territory and the limits of military and legal reach; and that of capitalist accumulation which involves exploiting uneven global development in order to maximize returns on investments by keeping the costs of raw materials and labor low. In Harvey's view, changes in international law that cosmopolitans see as progressive are no more than a cover for US imperialism, which combines the use of hegemonic ideals of human rights with superior military force to make resistance extremely difficult. On this account, the events of 9/11 provided a perfect pretext for imperialist expansion masked as military humanitarianism.

A fundamental problem with this kind of account is that, as an explanation, it relies on an unexamined functionalism. Harvey's account explains the facts of what happened in the invasion of Iraq in 2003 in terms of a circular logic: because capitalist accumulation *requires* imperialism, humanitarian interventions have now become something of a norm in global governance, if not in international law. His account explains historical events by recourse to the *necessity* of the capitalist system: what the system needed to happen, did happen. Functionalism is a recurrent problem for Marxist explanations. As Giddens puts it, because Marxism is a theory of social reproduction, it is rather prone to the formulation, "Capitalism has its own 'needs,' which the system functions to fulfil" (Giddens, 1979: 112).

By what mechanisms does capitalist imperialism achieve what it needs? In fact, it can only do so through the situated and contingent judgments and actions of actors who must decide how to proceed based on their necessarily limited perceptions and assumptions. Thus, at odds with the fundamental functionalism of his theory of capitalism's need for imperialism, Harvey has to admit that, although US elites may be motivated by calculations concerning their long-term geo-political interests, they do not know how to achieve them. In fact, US activities in the Middle East do not appear rational at all if the aim is to achieve control over oil reserves. The principal difficulty here is US support for Israel. It has long been underpinned by assumptions concerning Israel's strategic importance, as well as its moral superiority, in the Middle East, but rationally it would make much more sense for the US to put pressure on Israel to come to terms with at least some Palestinian demands for territory and security in order to extend hegemonic influence in the region (Lieven, 2004). Indeed, Harvey himself notes that it is very far from obvious that the Iraq war will be successful in giving US elites control of Middle East oil reserves; such an outcome depends not only on Iraq becoming a prosperous, democratic, and capitalist state under US influence, but also on an Israel-Palestine settlement that would be acceptable to surrounding Arab states, and a dampening of nationalist sentiments in the region that might otherwise put constraints on the circulation and accumulation of capital (Harvey, 2003: 199–207). In this respect, Harvey agrees with Michael Mann that the US is an incoherent empire, lacking the organized political will and military strength to carry through any systematic project to make capitalist investments secure and profitable across the world (Mann, 2003).

A more contingent, less functionalist and rationalist account of imperialism, linked closely to the changes in international law that cosmopolitans see as potentially progressive, is that of Michael Ignatieff. It is all the more striking because Ignatieff is himself a liberal champion of human rights. He argues, however, that human rights politics should be treated pragmatically, and that "human rights culture" is imperialist, not because of elite interests in capitalist accumulation, but because human rights have taken on an absolute value such that their extension appears now as a kind of "anti-politics." He argues that we must understand that claims for human rights no more transcend neutrality and partiality than any other political claims. It is not the morality of developing cosmopolitan law that should be at issue, or even its legality, according to Ignatieff, but the *politics* of the human rights movement. What kind of vision does it promote? Whose interests are at stake in any particular case? What compromises does it make possible, and how are its representatives to be made accountable? In practice, Ignatieff argues, the criteria that have emerged as crucial in decisions to intervene in order to prevent human rights abuses have been strategic as well as moral: not only must military intervention stand a chance of stopping gross violations of human rights, but those violations have to be a threat to international peace and security in the immediate surrounding region. Most crucially, the region in question must be of vital interest to a powerful state in the world, and the exercise of force must be unopposed by another powerful nation (Ignatieff, 2001).

According to Ignatieff, the US is leading human rights imperialism, supported by European money. Although the US is often reluctant to compromise its democratic sovereignty by binding itself to international agreements, its role as leader of the world in establishing international human rights is far from new. Since Eleanor Roosevelt led the committee that drew up the Universal Declaration of Human Rights, the US has been at the forefront of promoting human rights norms across the world. Now the US is the only state with the military capacity for humanitarian intervention, and since 9/11, it has been willing to exercise its military strength in the name of national security. At the same time, however, it is in part the fact that Americans continue to see their state as *anti*-imperialist, as having freed itself from British imperialism and as supporting self-determination and democracy, that makes the new "humanitarian" imperialism problematic. Ignatieff argues that Bosnia, Kosovo, Afghanistan, and now Iraq, despite nominal sovereignty and democracy, are actually ruled from imperial capitals, especially Washington and London. These states are independent in name only; in fact, they are protectorates of large, wealthy, and internationally prominent states that have as their aim "the maintenance of order over barbarian threat" (Ignatieff, 2003: 22). Following military action in these countries, the US and its allies have planned to re-build nations quickly, from the top-down, with minimal engagement from local political figures and citizens. This approach to building stable and satisfactory democratic states cannot succeed, but neither will long-term occupation. States may be internationalizing, making "sovereignty" a highly contested issue, but in the twenty-first century, imperialism will always meet strong opposition because national self-determination remains the only legitimate form of political rule for virtually everyone around the world, especially where it is threatened by the military force of other states, or where national independence has long been an as yet unrealized dream.

2.3   We Are the World?

So far in this chapter, we have looked at the politics of globalization in terms of restructuring the economy, the state, and relations between states. We have also touched on the continuing significance of "the nation" as meaningful to many across the world. In this section, we look directly at what politics in a small world might mean for political community. "Political community" has been synonymous with "nation" in democratic politics since the American and French revolutions of the eighteenth century, denoting a horizontal sense of "we" who belong together, and a vertical relationship to the state through which the rules by which we live together, sharing a common fate, are made and, ultimately, enforced. Nation-states carefully, and very successfully, fostered political communities as "national" in relation to rule-setting state regulation through education and propaganda, the control of media and the celebration of historical memory in national festivals, museums and so on (Gellner, 1983).

The very use of the phrase "political community" rather than the word "nation," then, opens up questions regarding "who": who shares a fate, and who decides "our" collective life? Indeed, with the transformation of the state, especially as it is accompanied by the growth of global media, we might expect new possibilities of political community beyond the nation. In this section, we are concerned with the "horizontal" relations of political community, rather than with structures of governance, though of course they are related. Does the idea that "we are the world" remain no more than a slogan? There does seem to be increased awareness of humanity as living together, sharing the fate of planet Earth. And, certainly, the *ideal* of what we might call cultural cosmopolitanism (as distinct from political cosmopolitanism) as detachment from the nation seems to be growing in some circles, amongst global elites, intellectuals, and supporters of human rights (see Cheah and Robbins, 1998; Vertovec and Cohen, 2002). But is this just, in Craig Calhoun's resonant phrase, the "class consciousness of frequent flyers" (Calhoun, 2002)? Or are new, concrete possibilities emerging, in which imagining who "we" are begins to take everyone – not just the elites of global governance, intellectuals, and those engaged in radical politics – beyond the limitations of national politics?

Following the enormously influential work of Benedict Anderson (1983), it has become commonplace to see nations as "imagined communities": "imagined" because members of nations never meet most other members; "communities" because the nation is always conceived in terms of deeply felt comradeship. According to Anderson, the media played a key role in how the nation was imagined historically. Nationalism developed out of the revolution enabled by the printed word, which completely transformed the geography of the Middle Ages through practices of identification with fellow-nationals. Printing resulted in the replacement of the sacred languages of the Middle Ages – Latin, Arabic, and Chinese, each of which united a vast territory with diverse regional, vernacular languages which were then standardized and spread in novels and newspapers. Anderson argues that in eighteenth-century Latin America and North America, the development of print enabled millions of individuals to represent their fellow-readers to themselves as compatriots. This was particularly marked in the case of daily newspapers because fellow nationals imagined themselves together as they read the same news simultaneously (Anderson, 1983). The most important conclusion of Anderson's historical investigations is that belonging to a nation is an ongoing process of construction and identification rather than an objective fact or a timeless loyalty to the land and people (though it may well be imagined in such terms).

Nationalism depends at least as much on love as on hate – as Anderson points out, people see themselves as willing to die for their country, not so much to kill for it (Anderson, 1983: 21). Indeed, as Craig Calhoun has argued, sociologists tend to generalize from "bad nationalism" and to neglect positive aspects of national solidarity. Nationalism does not involve only narrow and authoritarian patriotism. It has also been the basis of affective ties and cooperation between strangers which have been creative and positive. Most importantly, nationalism has underpinned the redistribution of wealth between citizens and the setting up of systems of education, health, and social assistance in post-Second World War welfare states (Calhoun, 2007). As we shall see in chapter 4, the politics of citizenship is still largely, though not exclusively, concerned with preserving, improving, and extending rights that were established nationally.

But national political communities are not only dependent on bonds of fellowship. They are also formed in opposition to the nation's "Others," people who not only do not happen to belong to the nation, but who are seen as unworthy to be included within it. Nationalism is inherently exclusionary; everyone in the world cannot be a member of a single nation (it would cease to be a nation). The extent to which exclusion is "Othering" varies, however: those who are excluded may be ignored or respected; they are not necessarily treated with suspicion and hostility. "Civic nationalism" is the name given to that variety in which anyone can, in principle, be a member of the nation, as long as they respect the rights of other citizens and meet their civic obligations. Those who happen to be excluded from this type of nation are not seen as inherently different in kind as human beings: they just happen to be members of other nations. The nations to which they belong may, however, themselves be coded as "Other" for civic nationalists: in order to be acceptable they should also adhere to universal principles of rights and obligations and to peaceful coexistence between states. In principle, nations may then be treated as equals. In contrast, "ethnic nationalism" denotes the kind of nationalism into which one must be born: to belong to an ethnic nation is to come from original stock, with its particular inheritance of physical attributes, language, customs, and history. The ethnic nation is inherently "Othering" to a greater extent than the civic nation, because those outside are seen as different in kind from those inside (Ignatieff, 1994: 3–6; Calhoun, 2007). Although the difference between civic and ethnic nationalism is clear in theory, and nations can be identified on a continuum between civic and ethnic (with the US and France in the civic camp, for example, and nations like Germany in the other), because the nation is necessarily exclusionary, the distinction between them is invariably much less clear-cut in practice.

The nation's "Others" may be internal to the national territory, where minorities are "racialized," considered as inherently or culturally inferior in comparison to the majority, and not, therefore, really part of the nation (see Gilroy, 1992, 2004; Morrison, 1992). A prominent example currently is the Othering of Muslim citizens within European states around issues of women's appearance. In multicultural Britain, for example, women covering part of their faces in public has repeatedly provoked anxiety, as it is seen as symbolizing identification *against* British values, and therefore, with support for Islamic terrorism (Fortier, 2008: 95–6). As a result, Anne-Marie Fortier argues, young Muslims, and other racialized "insider-outsiders" too, are required to demonstrate their loyalty and belonging to the nation in ways that are not demanded of the majority of British citizens (Fortier, 2008). In France, which has long considered itself, and been considered as, exemplary of a civic nation, Muslim heads-carves have been banned in schools which tolerated pupils wearing other "religious" symbols, such as the cross. There is currently, as I write, an attempt on the part of the French government to ban Muslim women covering their faces anywhere in public. In a speech in June 2009, President Sarkozy declared, "That's not our idea of freedom" ("Degrading' Islamic veils not welcome in France," says Sarkozy in historic speech," *The Guardian*, 23 June 2009). It is clear that some are outside "our" nation here, even if as citizens they live, work, raise children, pay taxes to the state, and obey French law under which individuals have historically enjoyed the freedom from state intervention to wear religious dress in public places (though not necessarily in state institutions, coded secular) if they please. This is not to say that debating the position of women within particular communities should be forbidden – though it is certainly paradoxical that the state here apparently wants to *dictate* autonomy and equality to women (Benhabib, 2004: 190). Great care is needed, however, to ensure that issues are debated in their complexity, rather than collapsing positions into stereotypes that confirm majoritarian suspicions of minorities as inherently unworthy to be included in the political community.

The "Others" of national political communities are also external, most commonly other nations. Most modern nations were formed through relations of conflict and competition with other nations and peoples, especially since the nineteenth century, as the form of the nation-state has been generalized across the world (Balakrishnan, 1996). More or less virulent forms of nationalism are the result of these, often long-standing, conflicts. "Hot" nationalism may be somewhat out of date now amongst sophisticated people in the West, especially on the Left, at least when a nation is not actually at war, but as Michael Billig has taught us, "banal nationalism" is evident in all sorts of signs that mark out the nation as different from, and generally superior to, other nations (Billig, 1995). One not-so-banal, example is the mediated mourning of members of the nation in comparison with disregard for the lives of members of other nations. This has been very marked in recent years in the wars in Iraq and Afghanistan, as the media represents public displays of grief by family, friends, and colleagues for Western soldiers killed there, whilst most other victims of the war, many of them civilians, are nameless and faceless, represented only as statistics and as the names of places on maps. Judith Butler argues that the unevenness of these representations fore-closes our ability to conceive of some people as having *lives*. In this way, inflicting such casualties is made bearable: it is literally imaginable because the lives of "Others" are already unreal, not really human (Butler, 2004: chapter 2).

Butler is hinting here at an alternative, that the media might unify, rather than divide, a political community around our common humanity. We may not share a human condition, given that we live in such different ways around the world, but we may share the conditions in which the question "who is human?" becomes a global question. Alongside the changing structures of global governance we discussed in the previous section, the principal change in this respect is developments in global media. Global communications systems involve integrated satellite and cable systems that transmit information quickly and cheaply across huge distances, while transnational communications conglomerates are expand-ing the global trade in information and communication products (Thompson, 1996). Changes in global media potentially alter the condi-tions in which the question "who counts?" is raised beyond the nation. This is especially the case with satellite TV: news stories and pictures of distant events are sent into homes around the world, enabling "imagining beyond the nation," even the creation of a global political community. As Bruce Robbins puts it:

> If people can get emotional as Anderson says they do about relations with fellow nationals they never see face-to-face, then now that print-capitalism has become electronic- and digital-capitalisms, and now that this system is so clearly transnational, it would be strange if people did not get emotional in much the same way, if not necessarily to the same degree, about others who are not fellow nationals, people bound to them by some transnational sort of fellowship. (Robbins, 1998: 7)

Global media, along with changing structures of global governance, seem to offer the conditions in which "we" might experience ourselves as belonging together with others who have rights and obligations that really count across borders, not just in law or morality, but through solidarity and political action. Certainly, what John Urry calls "banal globalism" is increasingly evident in the media: images of planet Earth, of the diversity of humankind, of world-famous celebrities, and of campaigns concerning global risks are now quite routinely shown to denote our commonality in living in one world (Urry, 2000: 182–3). Nevertheless, the idea of a global community bound by sentiments of solidarity does sound very idealistic given that, as Butler's example shows, the imagined boundaries of the nation appear still to be strong. Perhaps the important question to ask, then, is why, given the developing conditions of globalization and especially the potential of global media, global political community is *not* materializing?

In *Distant Suffering*, Luc Boltanski has explored the fundamental ways people may respond to the images of suffering that we see in our living rooms on a routine basis. He argues that we *must* respond to this suffering, emotionally and through action, whether that action involves offering some form of help, or just turning away. Even if we commit ourselves to helping, however, our options are limited. Generally the most we can do is to *speak*, to report on what we have seen to other people, how it has affected us, and what we think should be done about it. In some cases, this "speaking" may lead to public debate and to widening commitments to action, whether this involves commitment to send money, to demonstrate for justice or to demand humanitarian intervention (Boltanski, 1999). Where representations of distant suffering lead to debates over what is to be done, they may contribute to solidarity across borders, and even to political action for global justice.

Global media facilitates such action but, at the same time, the way in which the media is structured also makes it unlikely. Images and stories of suffering are distributed around the world through global media, but their collection and distribution is not global. The main international news agencies have their roots in London, Paris, and New York, and this Western bias continues to influence how they collect and assemble news; while broadcasting systems (the BBC and CNN, for example), select and edit news to fit regional, national, and local tastes and interests (see Hafez, 2007). At the same time, moreover, the increase of multiple channels directed at specific audiences, computerized programming, and the use of video-recording makes for what is sometimes called "narrowcasting," greater personal choice over viewing and a greater fragmentation of audiences (Castells, 2009: 60). In these conditions of competition, the aim of broadcasters is to create, capture, and keep a share of the audience, and in order to do so, they must take care to give people what they think they want.

Lilie Chouliaraki has shown, through a detailed investigation of coverage of humanitarian crises in the news media, how stories are selected and coded in ways that construct responses to suffering in "the West" in quite different ways to suffering in "the Rest." Chouliaraki analyses coverage of humanitarian crises as falling into three types. Crises may be covered as an "adventure," as a series of random and isolated events, briefly described in factual terms, in ways that make no attempt to demonstrate sufferers' agency, and which restrict spectators' sense of proximity with those suffering to representations of their physical plight. Coverage of crises as "adventure," she argues, fails to make any ethical demand on spectators to respond to the suffering they report. It generally involves people in countries far away, where the events have no obvious consequences for people in the West. Localized flooding or earthquakes in places outside the West, for example, are generally covered as "adventure." Second, humanitarian crises may be covered in terms of "emergencies," which shrink the distance between spectator and sufferer, and to which the appropriate response is pity and some kind of action. Long-term and complicated situations in most parts of the world are not reported as "emergencies" unless they become relevant to the West or become sensational in some other way. Third, humanitarian crises may be represented as "ecstatic." This involves live coverage, which often interrupts other programming, and creates a close sense of identification between the spectator and those suffering. The example of such coverage Chouliaraki analyses is that of the events of 9/11. Chouliaraki argues that, rather than opening up the imaginary of a global political community, portrayal of the suffering of those far away actually only registers in the West insofar as it involves sensations the Western media already cultivates: it is only insofar as the other is in some obvious way "like us" that they are eligible to become a spectacle of suffering with which we can identify and to which we must respond with words and action (Chouliaraki, 2006: 209–11).

Demands for action "from below" to address the suffering we may see routinely on TV – until we turn over – are rare. They predominantly involve demands for charity, to respond to emergencies like famine or flooding. Very occasionally, as in the Make Poverty History campaign, there are demands for global justice, but this requires social movement organization as well as media coverage, and a mixture of entertainment, celebrities, education, and audience involvement (Nash, 2008). Moreover, even when such campaigns do gain momentum, representations of the strangers in need are very often patronizing, celebrating "our" generosity: "we" *are* the world and they are no more than the grateful recipients of our help, passively poor and needy. Such responses prevail *despite* global interconnectedness: "our" Western governments are very often implicated in creating the conditions of humanitarian emergencies in the first place. Representations of Westerners as helping, never as involved in creating humanitarian disasters, involve more an imperialist than a cosmopolitan imagining (Stevenson, 1999, 2007). Certainly, it seems that, even as processes of globalization mean that we all increasingly share a common fate across borders and that, perhaps, a common sense of humanity may slowly be growing, most people continue to identify more readily with strangers connected by bonds of nationality than with strangers outside the nation.

Chapter 3
Social Movements

Social movements play a very important role in contemporary political sociology. First, they have been directly influential in its development within the university. That social movements have such a central place in the understanding of new forms of politics in the field is largely due to the way in which they have been placed on the research agenda by those sympathetic to, or actively involved in, those politics. In particular, in the 1970s, it was those who identified with social movements who worked to make dimensions of inequality and exclusion other than class significant. Similarly, debates in the 1980s and '90s over how identity formation should be understood were closely related to the "identity politics" of social movements. In the '00s, issues of global justice brought to our attention by social movements have become prominent in contemporary political sociology. Second, the understanding that members of social movements bring to bear on social life has been important. Where society is seen in terms of struggle and conflict, sociological explanations that treat the reproduction of the social order as practically inevitable are likely to be discredited, even to be seen as complicit with the *status quo*. This has been the fate of Marxism, now seen as over-deterministic and insufficiently sensitive to the possibilities of radical change at the micro-political level. Third, as a topic of study, social movements problematize older models of sociological explanation insofar as they see politics as organized solely around the nation-state. Social movements see themselves, and they are analyzed in contemporary political sociology, as involved in struggles over the definition of meanings and the construction of new identities and lifestyles, as well as addressing formal political institutions. They, therefore, bring the consideration of cultural politics to the center of sociological concerns with social change.

Social movements became a significant area of research in sociology in the guise of "new social movements." "New" here is indicative of the way in which social movements seemed to erupt onto the social scene in the 1960s, including the civil rights movement, the student movement of that time, the women's movement, the gay liberation movement, and the environmental movement. They were seen as "new" in terms of their orientation, organization, and style by comparison with the "old" labor movement, from which they were distinguished as:

1   Non-instrumental, expressive of universalist concerns and often protesting in the name of morality rather than the direct interests of particular social groups.
2   Oriented more toward civil society than the state:
  (a)   suspicious of centralized bureaucratic structures and oriented toward changing public views rather than elite institutions;
  (b)   more concerned with aspects of culture, lifestyle, and participation in the symbolic politics of protest than in claiming socio-economic rights.
3   Organized in informal, "loose," and flexible ways, at least in some aspects, avoiding hierarchy, bureaucracy, and even qualifications for membership.
4   Highly dependent on the mass media through which appeals are made, protests staged, and images made effective in capturing public imagination and feeling. (Scott, 1990: chapter 1; Crook et al., 1992: 148)

In comparison, the labor movement was seen as directing its attention toward the corporatist state with the aim of economic redistribution and the extension of citizenship rights, as organized in bureaucratic trade unions and parties which defend members' interests, and as showing very little concern with wider issues or more inclusive political participation.

Perhaps unsurprisingly, this sharp and rather simplistic contrast between old and new is not sustainable once it is looked into more closely; there has, in fact, long been a multiplicity of different kinds of social movements. As Craig Calhoun has shown, in the early nineteenth century there were many movements, including the feminist movement, nationalist and religious movements, and even aspects of the a class movement, such as the utopian communitarianism of Robert Owen, which were less like the conventionally defined labor movement than they were like new social movements. Very much concerned with lifestyle and identity politics, they were often organized in non-hierarchical ways in order to prefigure the social order they aimed to bring about, and they used unconventional means, such as direct action, rather than working through the "normal" political institutions of the state. As Calhoun sees it, they tended to be ignored by sociologists because of the rationalist, instrumentalist bias of sociology itself. Once the labor movement was institutionalized in the late nineteenth century with the extension of the vote, it came to be seen as *the* social movement of industrialization and progressive social change. Other movements, at least as much concerned with transformations of the self, lifestyle choices, and aesthetic criteria for judging personal and social arrangements, were ignored as irrelevant to rational, material progress (Calhoun, 1995).

However, as Calhoun himself acknowledges, the institutionalization of the labor movement also *actually* marginalized other social movements from the mid-nineteenth century. As Charles Tilly has shown, the labor movement and the modern state developed together. The extension of the franchise and the relative willingness of state elites to respond to working men's concerns meant that the very form of the state itself was shaped by the labor movement. This process culminated in the corporatist welfare state, in the period following World War II, in which negotiations between capitalists, workers, and government were formalized (Tilly, 1984). For example, although it is true that the women's movement never completely disappeared, following the extension of the vote to women in the early twentieth century it was absorbed into mainstream politics. Women's groups worked either within the state, advising on liberal policy and lobbying ministers or, in the working-class movement, campaigning for better social conditions for poor wives and mothers (Pugh, 1992). The more lifestyle-oriented politics of the earlier links between feminism and socialism were marginalized to the point of extinction (see Taylor, 1983). As sociological theory was established at the same time as these developments, sociologists were also led to focus on the state as the site of modern politics and the labor movement as the dominant political force. This resulted in the narrow understanding of politics in traditional political sociology that we looked at in chapter 1. Social movements that did not resemble the labor movement, with its organized political parties and instrumental demands for improved social conditions, tended to be ignored as not political.

At the same time, it is important to note that social movements in general share some of the features attributed to the "old" labor movement. This is clearest when their organization is considered in detail. Some aspects of the organization of new social movements do distinguish them from formal political organizations, to the extent that the term "network" is often a better description than "organization." They are often locally based or centered on small groups rather than nationally oriented; organized around specific issues rather than offering general solutions; experience vacillations of high and low activity rather than enjoying a relatively stable membership; and are run by fluid hierarchies and loose authority structures (Scott, 1990: 30). However, the organizational forms of social movements are best seen as a continuum, and where organizations are formed to address movement demands to states they may be as bureaucratic and hierarchical as any political party. Indeed, the green parties associated with the environmental movement are a case in point, even if there is still ongoing discussion within these parties about how to avoid bureaucratization and hierarchies. This is also the case wherever NGOs are formed as part of a social movement network, though they do vary. Social movement organizations that rely on the subscriptions of members without involving them in decision-making or action are at one end of the continuum. Greenpeace is a well-known example of this type of environmental organization; its members are not themselves involved in the well-planned, dangerous, and often illegal direct action it undertakes. In contrast, Friends of the Earth is run more on the basis of the participation of members who are actively involved in their own localities, and employs a minimum of professional staff.

The contrast between old and new social movements in terms of their orientations toward the state or civil society is also over-drawn. It is certainly important to note that a large proportion of social movement activity is addressed to changing practices and identities in civil society. This is clear in the case of the women's movement, for example, which has been extremely influential in opening up virtually all aspects of the relations between the sexes to public debate and in creating the necessity for individuals to make lifestyle choices in terms of their personal relationships and employment practices; in recent, so-called political correctness disputes, which largely concern the contestation of language; in questions raised by the environmental movement concerning ethical consumerism and life-style; and in struggles over ethnic identity, often articulated around music, dress, and in relation to the construction of historical narratives. Legislation is too blunt an instrument to deal with most of the issues raised by social movements, and changes in the law and social policy are often less the direct objective of their activities and more a consequence of changes in civil society which they have brought about. However, it is also the case that all social movements which organize to improve their constituents' social conditions have aimed to extend citizenship rights. This is not a unique feature of the workers' movement; it was the case for the civil rights movement, for example, and it has long been a feature of at least some aspects of feminist activities. Furthermore, it is evident that social policy and the law are important agents of social change, so that it is unlikely that any movement concerned with social transformation would ignore the state altogether. Again, it is perhaps not so much that new social movements have introduced new forms of politics since the 1960s, but rather that those forms that did not easily fit the modern sociological paradigm have been overlooked so that they are now taken to represent a radical departure from the norm. New social movements might more reasonably be seen as marking a change of emphasis, both of orientation and in terms of organization and activities, rather than a completely new form of politics.

Social movements have, then, required and contributed to the rethinking of political sociology as a result both of actual changes in politics and also because they have drawn attention to forms previously neglected by the traditional focus on politics at the level of the nation-state. As we will see in section 3.1, this re-thinking is evident in the development of social movement research, even in the case of Resource Mobilization Theory (RMT) which began from very rationalist, instrumental premises. In section 3.2, we look at the competing framework of social movement research, that of New Social Movement Theory (NSMT), which began with an understanding of the centrality of cultural politics to social movements.[1] The work of Alberto Melucci has been especially important in this tradition, dropping the vestiges of determinism which kept it tied to old sociological models. Although RMT and NSMT began from quite different premises, the former in liberal individualism, the latter in Marxism, they have converged in their focus on cultural politics to the point where it is now possible to synthesize the two traditions around a common core of research interests. In section 3.3, we discuss Mario Diani's synthesis of RMT and NSMT in the light of our concern with cultural politics. In section 3.4, we look at what is an increasingly important aspect of social movement studies, their growth and transformation in relation to globalization.

3.1 Resource Mobilization Theory and Beyond

Resource Mobilization Theory (RMT) is based on the liberal view that social phenomena are the result of individual decisions and actions. It was explicitly developed on the premises of rational choice theory, to oppose previous explanations of social movements in American sociology in which they were seen as psychologically motivated, as a more or less irrational response to social conditions. In theories deriving from the work of Le Bon and popularized in functionalist accounts like that of Neil Smelser, collective action was understood as outbursts of uncontrolled behavior as a result of social dysfunctioning. This work was driven by concern to prevent the rise of fascist and authoritarian movements, but by the 1970s, sociologists were much more likely to be sympathetic to the claims of new social movements, if not actively involved in them, and could not subscribe to such a view (Offe, 1987: 81; Scott, 1990: 40–6). The other popular theory against which RMT was developed was that of relative deprivation; it was held that protest is the result of expectations expanding more rapidly than real opportunities, so that groups who experience themselves as marginalized and lacking in influence – students, civil rights protestors, women – will turn to collective action to redress their grievances. Resource Mobilization theorists have a very simple and convincing rebuttal of any theory of social movements in which they are seen as the result of social grievances: since there are always grievances in a society, their mere existence cannot explain participation in collective action (Zald and McCarthy, 1987: 16–18). For Resource Mobilization theorists, what needs to be explained is why individuals are purposefully involved in collective action as a result of rational consideration of their own interests: social action is not caused by structural conditions.

More recently, the premises of RMT in rational choice theory – itself rooted in classical neo-economics – have been subjected to extensive criticism; there has been an awakening of interest in less rational aspects of individual motivation, and theorists sympathetic to the tradition have attempted to develop a more sociologically satisfying account of participation in social movements. This has led to an interest among Resource Mobilization theorists in subjectivity and culture. They have incorporated ideas from the interactionist sociology of Erving Goffman into the approach as a way of enriching its conception of individual decisions. However, Resource Mobilization theorists have somewhat resisted the implications of the "cultural turn" they have taken, simultaneously maintaining the realist epistemology and rationalist premises on which the tradition was founded. This has resulted in inconsistencies in the approach which can only be addressed by recognizing those implications.

It is not only its methodological individualism that makes RMT a liberal approach, but also the way in which it implicitly takes the state as the arena of politics proper. For Resource Mobilization theorists, although social movements may initially have a problematic relation to government insofar as their members do not see themselves as properly represented in dominant political parties and institutions, success for a social movement involves achieving routine access to the political process. This premise is also problematized, however, by the incorporation of concerns with subjectivity and culture into the theory. If participation in a social movement depends on how individuals understand themselves and their situation, there seems to be no good reason for ignoring the contestation of perspectives and the transformation of identities in civil society as if this were not itself an aspect of politics. The extension of RMT to include such issues, however, again points beyond the liberal paradigm, and is, therefore, somewhat difficult for its adherents to accept.

Resource Mobilization Theory: the premises

The contribution to rational choice theory that has been most influential in RMT is *The Logic of Collective Action* (1968) by Mancur Olson. As Scott points out, the theory of social behavior outlined in this book is established on the basis of two premises drawn from neo-classical economics: first, that social choices are to be explained with reference to individual preferences; and, second, that individuals act rationally to maximize their interests and minimize their costs (Scott, 1990: 10). Olson is interested by the idea that there is no necessary connection between collective interests and collective action. On the contrary:

> If the members of a large group rationally seek to maximize their personal welfare, they will *not* act to advance their common or group objectives unless there is coercion to force them to do so, or unless some separate incentive, distinct from the achievement of the common or group interest, is offered to the members of the group individually on the condition that they help bear the costs or burdens of the group objectives. (Olson, 1968: 2)

This is the famous "free-rider" problem of rational choice theorists. It is in the very nature of a public good that no individual in a particular group can feasibly be prevented from benefiting from it if it is enjoyed by others in that group. Because the participation of a single individual makes so little difference to the achievement of a public good, it is more rational to gain it without participating in collective action, unless the group can somehow reward or punish particular individuals in direct proportion to their degree of participation. This is very difficult to do, impossible even, for a social movement intent on changing the very rules and structures by which a category of persons is systematically disadvantaged in relation to others.

Olson was not himself aiming to provide an explanation of the formation of social movements. On the contrary, he was interested in showing
why it is that people *do not* take part in collective action, despite their
individual interests in collective goals. The existence of social grievances
is not a sufficient condition for the rise of a social movement. However,
for Resource Mobilization theorists impressed by rational choice theory
but interested in studying actually existing social movements, given that
people *are* participating in collective action, the question becomes rather
different: how are resources mobilized in such a way as to make that
participation rational for self-interested individuals?

This is the question addressed by Anthony Oberschall, who extended
Olson's theory to explain the historical emergence of oppositional social
movements. Oberschall defines resources widely enough to include material resources, such as jobs, money, and the right to goods and services,
and non-material, including authority, commitment, friendship, skills,
and so on. By mobilization, he means the processes by which groups
manage resources for the pursuit of their goals (Oberschall, 1973: 28).
Like Olson, Oberschall supposes that individuals faced with their own
resource management decisions participate in collective action to the
extent that they rationally choose to pursue their interests in this way.
However, he is able to show that such participation is more common than
one would suppose on Olson's theory by taking into account aspects of
the social situations in which individuals find themselves, something
Olson largely ignored. In the case of movement leaders, he argues that,
although the costs of their participation are very high, as indeed may be
the risks where they are involved in activities which are opposed to vested
interests, so too are the potential benefits in terms of social status and
power within the movement, and a successful career as a result of the
leadership role if it succeeds. This is particularly the case where "normal"
opportunities in the wider society are closed to members of a particular
social group, in which case the benefits to leaders as individuals should
they succeed will be very high, and the costs relatively low. Oberschall
also considers the social context of the rank-and-file members of social
movements, arguing that they do not exist as isolated individuals as Olson
assumes; in fact, they often live in communities in which everyone stands
to gain from collective action so that each individual is under social pressure to participate in a movement working toward common goals. This
is particularly likely to be successful because the costs of that kind of
participation are low. In fact, Olson himself thought that social sanctions
and rewards are among the kinds of incentives that can mobilize a group,
but he believed they only work among small, friendship-based groups

(Olson, 1968: 60–1). Oberschall extends that idea to give a more socio-logical account of individual preferences as shaped by social conditions. He remains clearly committed to Olson's methodological individualism, however, arguing that consideration of action as based on anything other than rationally chosen self-interest is mere speculation (Oberschall, 1973: 118).

RMT was further developed by the sociologists Mayer Zald and John McCarthy, who were the first to coin the term as such, and who developed many of the ideas on which the empirical research program it stimulated has been based. Zald and McCarthy focused particularly on social move-ment organizations, arguing that it was, above all, the fostering of such organizations which was responsible for the exponential growth of social movements in the 1960s. Again, they largely accepted the premises of rational choice theory and Olson's ideas on the fundamental incompatibil-ity of individual self-interest and collective action. For them, any satisfac-tory explanation of social movements would have to be consistent with those premises.

According to Zald and McCarthy, the professionalization of social movement organizations responsible for the increase in social movement activity involves the development of career opportunities for the individu-als they employ. Often experts in social policy, the law, or a "social problem," they move "in and out of government agencies, private agen-cies, community organizations, foundations and universities," committed above all to programs and policies rather than to a particular organization or to their profession (Zald and McCarthy, 1987: 397). These opportuni-ties were linked in the 1960s and 1970s to a growth in funding for "worthy causes" provided by charitable foundations, corporations, churches, and, also, the state.

Zald and McCarthy define resources more narrowly than Oberschall and Olson – setting the terms within which the research agenda of RMT was to develop – as involving legitimacy, money, the labor of supporters, and facilities. In practice, however, the resource with which they are most concerned is money. This is the second important factor Zald and McCarthy see as contributing to an increase in social movement activity: the general increase in wealth of developed societies. The increased wealth of the new middle classes, who are able and inclined to provide such resources, is significant, according to Zald and McCarthy, as it helps to form "the social movement sector," consisting of the total activity and membership of all social movements in a society. Social movement organizations compete with each other to convert what Zald and McCarthy call "adherents," those who are sympathetic to the aims of their movement, into "constituents," those who provide its resources, from within much the same social group. Especially important in this respect are "conscience adherents," likely to have considerable resources and to be receptive to the claims of more than one movement. Zald and McCarthy further distinguish what thy call "potential beneficiaries," those who stand to gain from the movement's activities, who may fall into none of the previous categories. For example, a woman without disposable income who happened to be opposed to rights for women might nevertheless benefit from increased opportunities won by the women's movement.

As Zald and McCarthy see it, their version of RMT, emphasizing as it does the importance of social movement organizations, provides a full response to Olson's claims concerning the lack of rationality of collective action. The free-rider problem does not arise where the participation of most individuals is virtually cost-free, requiring nothing more than an annual subscription and/or occasional donation, while there are considerable benefits in terms of employment and career opportunities for those who do take an active role in the collective action of social movements. According to Zald and McCarthy (1987: 27), their theory turns Olson's thesis on its head:

> Though it may be individually irrational for any individual to join a social movement organization that already fights on behalf of his [sic] preferences, the existence of a social movement made up of well-heeled adherents calls out to the entrepreneur of the cause to attempt to form a viable organization.

In fact, far from being the outcome of individual action to redress social wrongs, Zald and McCarthy suggest that social movement organizations may even create grievances which are not felt as such by members of the population concerned.

The influential work of Zald and McCarthy and their various collaborators (see Zald and McCarthy, 1987, 1988) went some way toward situating social movement organizations in relation to the wider political process insofar as they suggested that, since the sources of funding they identified as contributing to those organizations were established elite institutions, it is likely that there would be difficulty in mobilizing resources in support of radical causes seen as seriously challenging to the existing order. It was the work of Charles Tilly, however, particularly in *From Mobilization to Revolution* (1978), which provided the tools for the investigation of political opportunity structures.

The most important aspect of Tilly's work is the way in which he deals explicitly with what is often implicit in other studies based on RMT: the importance of the state. Tilly argued that, as the most powerful political actor in modern industrial societies, the state selectively represses or facilitates social movements and/or their activities according to the perceived interests of state elites. That the state represses certain movements and organizations is evident: terrorist organizations are to be repressed by definition, for example; those who take direct action in opposition to government policies are not usually tolerated; and even those organizations which act within the limits of the law may find themselves outside it if a change in policy is seen as desirable and practicable (as in the case of trade unions in Britain in the 1980s, for example). By the same token, some social movements are tolerated, even encouraged, to the point where they become part of the *polis*, that is, where they gain routine access to the government. Tilly suggests that the American state creates three main destinations for a social movement: its dissolution (as a result of repression); the merging of organized activists into an existing political party (absorbing it into the polity – this is how the labor movement became established in the corporatism of post–World War II Western Europe); or the constitution of an enduring pressure group working on the government and political parties (the most frequent outcome for social movements in the US). There is a fourth destination common in countries in which there are single-constituency and single-issue parties – where the electoral system is based on proportional representation, for example: the creation of a new, possibly temporary, political party (as in the case of the German greens) (Tilly, 1984: 312–13).

According to Tilly, in comparison with social movements before the nineteenth century, those with which we are familiar today are organized and oriented toward effecting change through the nation-state to an unprecedented degree. In fact, he calls such movements "national movements" to distinguish them from the less organized, more defensive, and more local movements which were particularly prominent during the aggressive expansion of states in the seventeenth century. The rise of national movements is due to the growth of electoral politics and the consequent widening of access – at least in principle – to the political process, according to Tilly: where movements see themselves as having routine access to government agencies, they are likely to take their grievances there; where they do not, they will resort to other means. It is also due to the learning of what he calls "repertoires of collective action." A repertoire of collective action includes all the ways in which a group uses its resources to bring about a common end. In twentieth-century North

America, for example, these include striking, petitioning, and organizing pressure groups, but rarely rioting, machine-breaking, or rebellion – common actions in previous times. Tilly argues that movements learn from each other; the success of a particular tactic on the part of one movement is likely to lead to its adoption by another.

This aspect of Tilly's work fits within the RMT tradition insofar as he is, above all, concerned with how resources are mobilized by social movements to deal with collective grievances. However, it differs from that of Zald and McCarthy in at least two important respects. First, he rejects the premises of the rational choice theory insofar as he adopts the more radical, Marxist view that interests cannot be reduced to the preferences expressed by an individual at any particular moment. It is possible to be mistaken about one's "real interests" and, in fact, part of the task of agencies working on behalf of the status quo is to obscure such interests where their articulation could be threatening to it (Tilly, 1978). Second, the theory of political opportunity structures and repertoires of collective action gives quite a different emphasis to the development of social movements than does Zald and McCarthy's focus on formal organization. It directs attention to the development of resistance in grassroots settings as an important aspect of that development, rather than toward professional organizations as the necessary condition of social movement mobilization.

This difference in emphasis does not necessarily make the two approaches incompatible. It may be rather that, in different instances, different aspects of the development of social movements are prominent (McAdam et al., 1996: 4). Such a view is developed in Sidney Tarrow's influential work on "cycles of protest" (or, as he now calls them, "cycles of contention"). He argues that social movements do not arise individually, but rather as part of a general wave of social unrest, generally precipitated by some unpredictable event and facilitated by changes in political opportunity structures. At the beginning of the cycle, mobilization takes place directly among existing social networks. As it develops, collective action increases and is diffused across a wider range of social groups. Social movement organizations are formed at the peak of the cycle of protest and compete with one another for constituents within the social movement sector. At this stage, they tend to be demanding of members' time and energy and have little to offer in return except enthusiasm, a feeling of solidarity, and the joy of rebellion. They therefore contribute to the escalation of direct action which characterizes this stage of the cycle of protest. The student movement of the 1960s was led, for example, to employ increasingly radical tactics to challenge the authorities, eventually

leading to violent clashes with the police. This escalation actually contributes to the beginning of the decline of the cycle, as participants reject
increasing violence or simply become exhausted, and as the state either
exercises effective repression or, in rare cases, capitulates to the demands
of the protestors. The decline often, however, results in the consolidation
of social movement organizations, which adopt a more measured and
long-term approach, and which act to mobilize resources on this basis.
Moreover, it does not necessarily mean defeat of the protestors' aims.
Often, the effects of the peak of the protest are not felt immediately, but
become apparent later in the agendas of political parties, policy decisions,
and changes in attitudes and values among the general population. The
cycle of protest initiated by the student movement of the 1960s may be
seen as an example. Initiated among groups of friends and colleagues,
reaching its peak with demonstrations and clashes between police and
students and young workers, it resulted in the formation of the "new"
social movements which became prominent in the 1970s, and which are
continuing to have far-reaching, though more diffuse, effects (Tarrow,
1989, 1998: chapter 9).

Tarrow's analysis of cycles of protest is well supported empirically. It
also complements Zald and McCarthy's analyses of the importance of
social movement organizations and Tilly's work on political opportunity
structures. However, both Tarrow's and Tilly's emphasis on grassroots
mobilization has one main weakness from the point of view of RMT. It
returns sociologists working in this tradition to its starting point: why is
it that rational individuals participate in collective action? If, as Tarrow
argues, social movement organizations are only effective once a cycle of
protest is underway, how does it begin? He tentatively suggests that
people revolt when new grievances are heaped on the old, or when new
political opportunities develop (Tarrow, 1989: 51). However, his model
of cycles of protest presupposes that individuals have motivations apart
from their rational self-interest for initiating collective action since, as we
have seen, from a rational choice perspective this is not sufficient to make
participation worthwhile. The question of individual motivation and participation in social movements with which the RMT tradition began is
also the question which has led to its transformation into quite a different
perspective from that premised on rational choice theory.

The "cultural turn" in Resource Mobilization Theory

From the very beginning of the development of RMT, there have been
criticisms of its excessively rationalist and instrumentalist approach to

social movements. The most frequent and extensive criticisms concern the model of the social actor on which it is premised. It is argued that to see individuals acting solely out of rational self-interest ignores how actors are always socially situated. Individuals are not detached and solitary, with merely instrumental relationships to others, but always already members of groups and communities, with feelings, beliefs, ideas, and values about shared, collective identities. As we have seen, Oberschall criticized Olson's view of the individual as essentially isolated very early in the development of RMT, but it is nevertheless Olson's individualistic assumptions which have been dominant in RMT research.

A further criticism related to the assumptions of rational choice theory is the neglect of actors' perceptions; it is assumed that an individual somehow immediately knows what is in his or her most rational self-interest. In fact, even if self-interest is always the dominant motivation in any individual decision – an assumption which is either tautological, assuming that whatever the individual does is necessarily in his or her rational interest, or else doubtful in the extreme – this depends on a calculation of costs and benefits which are themselves socially constructed. It is rational to pursue certain ends only if those ends are of value, and value itself is socially constructed; it is not something decided on by an individual in isolation (Scott, 1990: 117–28; Morris and Mueller, 1992).

In response to such criticisms of the atomistic, over-rationalist model of the individual on which the approach has been premised, those working within the RMT tradition have attempted to develop a better account of subjectivity and culture. The most influential work in this respect is that of David Snow, in association with various colleagues. They draw on Goffman's ideas of framing to analyze how actors negotiate meanings and commit themselves to social movements. This work is intended to supplement RMT, to provide it with the tools to understand how individuals make the choices so difficult to account for from a rational choice perspective and also, to a lesser extent, to understand the "meaning-work" carried out by social movements. However, the attempt to combine a social constructionist approach with the methodological individualism of rational choice theory is actually more problematic than Resource Mobilization theorists suppose. They stop short of accepting the full implications of the understanding of culture they have adopted, which actually brings the development of the approach within the "cultural turn" of contemporary political sociology.

According to Snow and his associates, it is through "frames" that social actors define grievances, forge collective identities, and create, interpret, and transform opportunities in order to bring about social movements.

A "frame" works because "it simplifies 'the world out there' by selectively punctuating and encoding objects, situations, events, experiences, and sequences of actions in one's present or past environment" (Snow and Benford, 1992: 137). Frames enable the interpretation of what would otherwise be a mass of complex data, fleeting impressions, and confusing ideas. It is "collective action frames," in particular, which work to mobilize the members of social movements: they "punctuate" or emphasize the intolerability of some aspect of a group's social condition, defining it as requiring corrective action; they make what Snow and Benford call "diagnostic attributions" – attributing blame to individuals, groups, or social structures – and "prognostic attributions" – suggesting how the problem could be ameliorated; and they "encode" an array of events, observations, and experiences into meaningful "packages" for the targets of mobilization (1992: 137–8).

Influenced by Goffman, Snow and his associates consider mobilization to take place in face-to-face interaction, in what they call "micromobilization." Building on earlier work concerning different processes of recruitment into different social movements, on how movements "solicit, coax, and secure participants," they locate mobilization in the face-to-face interactions of everyday life (Snow et al., 1980: 799, 1986: 464–5). Social movements recruit and secure adherents by linking individual interpretations with those of the movement in an ongoing process which Snow et al. (1986) call "frame alignment." There are four strategies of frame alignment, as they see it, which depend on how far individuals are from the orientation of the movement: "frame bridging" in which "ideologically congruent but structurally unconnected frames" are linked; "frame amplification" in which there is the "clarification and invigoration" of an already existing interpretation; "frame extension" in which the objectives of the movement are portrayed as continuous with the values and interests of potential adherents; and "frame transformation" in which a movement puts forward a radically new set of ideas and must therefore totally reframe old understandings of issues and problems (Snow et al., 1986).

In more recent years, while still focusing on micromobilization insofar as they see framing and reframing as interactive, Snow and his associates have turned their attention to the wider context in which social movements mobilize resources, to look at the "master frames" through which a variety of movements are created and constrained (Snow and Benford, 1988, 1992). This enables them to take a more historical view, and they argue that, using this concept, they can explain the well-documented "cycles of protest" which characterize the activities of new social movements. Like collective action frames, master frames are modes of punctuation, attribution, and encoding, but they are more universal and less context-specific. They are powerful if they make claims which resonate with central ideas and meanings already existing in the population and, as such, they contribute to the escalation and intensity of collective action which characterizes the upswing of a cycle of protest. In fact, Snow and Benford argue that without the construction of an innovative frame there will be no mass mobilization. Similarly, the deterioration of the master frame due to changes in the prevailing cultural climate, or its displacement by a more potent master frame, has a significant effect on the decline of a cycle of protest.

Tarrow sees the American civil rights movement of the 1960s as a good example of Snow and Benford's theory of framing, arguing that its dominant theme of "rights" was resonant with widely shared values, both among black middle-class members of the movement and the white liberal "conscience constituents" who supported it. However, this easy relationship between the movement and American cultural understandings also contributed to the decline of the cycle of protest initiated by the civil rights movement; the rights frame was appropriated by disparate groups across society, including even those who saw affirmative action as an infringement of their rights, while more radical black groups, rejecting the symbols of white liberalism, failed to find resonance in an oppositional subculture and became increasingly isolated and ineffectual. As Tarrow sees it, success depends on "maintaining a delicate balance between the resonance of the movement's message with existing political culture and its promise of new departures" (Tarrow, 1992: 197).

Resource Mobilization theorists have attempted to integrate the framing approach with the more familiar concepts in the tradition: "political opportunities" and "mobilizing structures." In their introduction to an important collection of articles intended to do just that, McAdam, McCarthy, and Zald argue that in order to fully understand social movements it is necessary to analyze the dynamic relations between political opportunities, mobilizing structures, and framing processes, to examine how they condition and constrain each other to shape movements' aims, and activities (McAdam et al., 1996). To further this analysis, they propose the study of social movements through time, over the course of their development. The initial emergence of movements, they argue, is due principally to social changes which make the political order more vulnerable to change. However, the political opportunities created in this way are only opportunities insofar as they are defined as such by a group of actors already sufficiently organized to take advantage of whatever openings the political system might offer. In the case of the revolutions in

Eastern Europe in 1989, for example, the relaxation of state control in the wake of Gorbachev's reforms provided the conditions for mobilization, but it only became a real possibility because already existing dissident groups had defined regimes as illegitimate and were ready to act against the authorities. It is the dynamic interaction between political opportunities, mobilizing structures, and framing processes which produces the emergence of a social movement.

McAdam et al. (1996) further suggest that the form of mobilization, as well as its timing, is affected by perceptions of political opportunities. To take the example of the Eastern European revolutions again, Elena Zdravomyslova argues that in 1988, following relaxation of state control, the Democratic Union was formed in Leningrad/St Petersburg; it exploited the more tolerant policy on public gatherings by staging disruptive demonstrations. In contrast, following a law granting popular elections passed in the same year, the Leningrad People's Front was formed to mount an electoral campaign (McAdam, 1996: 10). The divergent form of these movements was the result of perceived political opportunities available during their mobilization, according to McAdam and his associates. Further, they argue that, as a movement develops, it may create its own political opportunities, again illustrating the dynamic interaction between different aspects of a movement's activities across time. A good example of mobilization *creating* political opportunities is that of the civil rights movement; as a result of electoral access to Southern political structures, and a consequent rise in the number of elected black officials, the political opportunities available to the movement as such, as well as to its beneficiaries, were significantly altered (McAdam, 1996: 36).

In fact, McAdam et al. (1996) suggest that a movement is increasingly the author of its own fate: organizations claiming to represent the movement consciously shape shared understandings of it in contestation with other collective actors claiming to represent it, with the state, and also with counter-movements. However, the degree of control over definitions and opportunities that McAdam and his associates suppose in this respect is somewhat exaggerated. As Tarrow notes, social movement leaders do not have complete control over how the collective frames of action they propose will be received, nor over how far their supporters will be prepared to follow their lead. In his words, "framing is less like a completed symphony than like improvisational jazz: composers provide the initial 'head' for a jam session, but the improvisations depend on a group of players over whom they have little control" (Tarrow, 1992: 191).

McAdam et al.'s mistaken view of the possibilities of controlling framing processes is actually indicative of a wider problem concerning the "cultural turn" of RMT. The understanding of actors' motivations for collective action as socially constructed cannot simply be grafted on to the RMT approach, as if its premises in rational choice theory were irrelevant. The turn to culture implies a radical constructionism which is an unexpected and unwelcome consequence for Resource Mobilization theorists. It can no longer be assumed that participation in social movements is rational, the realist epistemology on which analyses of political opportunity structures is based becomes untenable, and RMT's understanding of politics as centered on the state becomes problematic. These conclusions are avoided because Resource Mobilization theorists tend to see culture simply as a resource, to be manipulated by an actor who is somehow outside it, using it rationally as the best means to reach a given end. However, this is unsatisfactory, even within the RMT tradition, since it means that the question the "cultural turn" was supposed to address – how it is that social actors become involved in collective action – remains unanswered.

McAdam et al. (1996: 6), for example, see framing as "the conscious strategic efforts by groups of people to fashion shared understandings of the world and of themselves that legitimate and motivate collective actions." On this model, framing takes place after the (rational?) decision to undertake collective action on the part of the social movement's organizers. For Snow and Benford, however, whose view of framing McAdam and colleagues specifically commend for its clarity, frames provide the initial *motivation* for individual involvement in collective action. According to Snow and Benford, as we have seen, they do so insofar as they resonate with the ideas, experiences, and values of potential adherents, that is, with already existing frames within which social actors locate themselves. It is on the basis of these existing frames, and their "fit" with "collective action frames," that social actors identify themselves as members of the group for which the movement exists, or as sympathizers with its cause who are prepared to commit their support, and possibly money, time, and energy to achieve its ends. In this case, collective action in the form of the contestation of actors' identities and the framing of cultural understandings is *prior* to the individual calculation of the costs and benefits of collective action.

If McAdam et al.'s view is followed, the question remains unanswered of how it is that the instigators of the social movement come to decide to participate in collective action, if not on the basis of cultural framing. On Snow and Benford's account, there is no need to conclude that the process of mobilization is fundamentally different for leaders and followers: micromobilization may take place in networks and friendship groups, from which social movements grow in momentum. However, if framing processes are seen as fundamental to mobilization, as indeed McAdam et al. themselves suggest in their proposed synthesis of approaches within RMT, this suggests conclusions which are more radically constructionist than theorists within the approach have acknowledged.

First, the implication of framing as fundamental to movement mobilization is that individuals may never act in ways which Resource Mobilization theorists would find rational. If individual decisions to join social movements are made on the basis of the internal validity of the frames within which they are situated as social actors, the link between actual political opportunities and collective action is severed. As Gamson (1992: 69–70) puts it, "A successful theory of framing must be based on an epistemology that recognizes facts as social constructions and evidence as taking on its meaning from the master frames in which it is embedded." The *success of a movement* may be assessed on the basis of the actual political opportunities available to it, regardless of how those involved in it see them; but the *action of those involved* cannot be assessed as rational aside from the terms in which they themselves construct it as such. In fact, Gamson argues that adherents are more likely to act if they make an over-optimistic assessment of the chances of a movement's success; ironically, from a rational choice perspective, they are more likely to act irrationally, without a realistic assessment of the opportunities available to them.

Second, the framing approach suggests that, rather than objectively and scientifically studying social movements as social phenomena "out there" in the world, Resource Mobilization theorists are actually much more implicated in that world than has hitherto been supposed on this approach. The assumptions on which RMT is based are themselves cultural constructions. According to the RMT account, in order to participate in collective action, one must see oneself as having an interest which can only be realized in common with others, as capable of acting with them to bring about change, and as gaining from that activity. In other words, one must frame one's identity as a rational calculator of the costs and benefits of collective action. Insofar as it is the case that social actors *do* frame their identities in this way, then it is not that Resource Mobilization theorists provide a detached *explanation* of social movements; it is rather that both share the same master frame. The implications of this are clear. If, as Gamson has clearly pointed out, the framing approach is based on an epistemology in which "facts" are internal to a particular frame, there is no possible independent verification of the way in which RMT frames social action. Resource Mobilization theorists cannot step outside the cultural frame in which they are situated any more than any other social member. RMT, however, is based on a realist epistemology in which the objects of study are, or have been, real resources and political structures which exist independently of their meaningful construction by social actors. The implications of adopting a framing theory of social action which is incompatible with this realist epistemology have not yet been fully considered within this tradition.

Finally, the cultural framing approach also has important implications for the RMT view of politics. If social action is based on definitions and meanings made from within cultural frames, then there is no reason to see the contestation of definitions and meanings as simply a preliminary to collective action, a mobilizing strategy to enable a social movement to realize the real goals of influencing political structures and effecting socio-economic change. On the contrary, the theory of framing suggests that what is at stake in much collective action is cultural politics: the contestation and transformation of the meanings actors attribute to events, experiences, and perceptions, and the attempt to construct and reconstruct one's view of oneself and others.

Traditionally, RMT has focused on social movements as political actors concerned above all with achieving change to the socio-economic structure through the nation-state. It is important not to neglect the relationship between social movements and the state, nor to ignore the fact that integration into the political process in the way Tilly describes may *facilitate* the realization of a movement's aims, rather than representing its cooption and neutralization (as, for example, Touraine would see it). However, this is very different from the understanding of politics which is the consequence of RMT's "cultural turn." On this understanding, the ongoing contestation of social identities and structures and the broader social change effected as a result must also be seen as political. At this point, the RMT tradition joins "new social movement" theory, to which such an understanding of the cultural politics of social movements has always been central.

3.2   New Social Movement Theory: Conflict and Culture

In contrast to the liberal premises of RMT, New Social Movement Theory has its roots in Marxism, which it rejects but from which it, nevertheless, retains certain presuppositions. It is based on the centrality of conflict to society and, rather than beginning from the starting point of isolated individuals, it takes the collective nature of that conflict as given. In particular, due to the influence of Alain Touraine, the activity of social movements is seen as involving conflict between dominators and dominated which is inherent in all societies and which provides the motor of social change. Theorists of new social movements in this tradition emphasize, therefore, the revolutionary dimension of social movement activity, even if revolution is not seen in Marxist terms. The aim of a true social movement is not to influence the political process, as in the RMT tradition, but to break the limits of the current system and to lead the transformation of society. New Social Movement theorists are often criticized, as we will see, for their utopian ideals, particularly where they are inconsistent with other aspects of their work. However, it is their understanding of cultural contestation as a vital element of social conflict that makes the contribution of this tradition so important.

Alain Touraine: social movements and the sociology of action

According to Alain Touraine, social movements are the central topic in sociology. Since the ordering of social relations is the product of social action, and social movements are the collective agents of social action, social movements are not exceptional and dramatic events, as they are for Resource Mobilization theorists: "they lie permanently at the heart of social life" (Touraine, 1981: 29).

Touraine explicitly develops his view of social movements in opposition to the structural determinism of Marxism and functionalism dominant in European and American sociology respectively in the 1950s and 1960s. According to Touraine, functionalism's neglect of social action means that it suffers from an uncritical acceptance of social institutions and values as they happen to have solidified at any particular moment; functionalists fail to see how the apparent unity of a social system is nothing more than the imposition of a dominant movement over the dominated (Touraine, 1981: 34–5). Similarly, Marxism is flawed insofar as it shares the determinism of structural-functionalism. Although conflict is central to Marxism, it is attributed to underlying structural conditions; a contingent social formation is explained in terms of evolutionary laws of history which again fail to acknowledge the role of social action in the production of society. While Marxism imputes interests and motives to class actors which they themselves might not recognize but which Marxists see as produced by socio-economic structures from which they cannot escape, Touraine argues that the terms in which social movements present themselves as actors must be taken seriously if social action is to be properly understood (Touraine 1981: 57–9).

Nevertheless, despite Touraine's opposition to Marxism, much of his sociology of action has clearly been influenced by the central idea of Marxist theory that all history is the history of class struggle. According to Touraine, every society is formed by two opposing social movements, which he goes so far as to call class movements. He does not see these classes, however, as struggling over ownership and control of the means of production of a society, as Marxists do, but rather over the control of what he calls "historicity." By "historicity," Touraine means the processes by which society is produced as a result of conscious reflection on social action and its conditions.

In every society, according to Touraine, there is one key conflict between opposed social movements: the conflict between the dominant class which has appropriated historicity, changing it into order through organization, and the dominated who attempt to re-appropriate it, to break down the *status quo*, reveal the conflict it conceals, and introduce innovatory ways of thinking, working, and living. Touraine agrees with Marxists that in industrial society the key conflict was between capitalists and proletariat, though he thinks it is a mistake to think of it solely in economic terms since, although it was a struggle over the distribution and control of material resources, this was as a means to the control of historicity rather than as an end in itself. However, he argues that we are now living through the transition to a "post-industrial" or "programmed" society: there has been a shift from manufacturing toward knowledge-based industries in which education, training, information, design, and so on are central to production. In such a society, control over information and knowledge are the immediate stakes of social conflict, and technocrats are the dominant class to the extent that the interests of the society as a whole are identified with the technological development and management of organizations they achieve. For Touraine, this leads to new forms of conflict which are more cultural than economic. The opposing class is not made up solely of workers, but of all those subject to technocratic control; for example, consumers or simply "the general public." According to Touraine, class struggle in post-industrial society is no longer in the name of political or workers' rights; it is not related to economic class struggle, but for people's right to choose and control their own lives.

In Touraine's view, since social movements now struggle directly over the social conditions of self-determination, contemporary society works on itself directly through culture to a greater extent than ever before. His definition of social action makes clear his view of the importance of cultural contest: "Action is the behavior of an actor guided by cultural orientations and set within social relations defined by an unequal connection with the social control of those orientations" (Touraine, 1981: 61). He sees control over historicity as involving control over "the great cultural orientations" by means of which a society's relationships are normatively organized (1981: 26). The conflict between social movements which produces social transformation is principally a conflict over interpretations shared by both sides of the conflict; if actors do not share the same values in the broadest sense – what Touraine calls the "stakes" of the struggle – a conflict cannot be said to be social (1981: 32–3). In Touraine's view, culture not only provides the motivations for collective action in the normative orientation to such issues as "progress against tradition" and "universalism against particularism," it is also the principal object of class struggles.

Touraine does not use the term "cultural politics." He actually restricts the term "political" to activities directed at representative institutions organized at the level of the state. However, he is sympathetic to what he calls Foucault's "denunciation of power" as inherent in all social relations. He sees it as contributing to critical social thought by revealing how apparently rationally organized social relations have actually been established through conflicts and clashes between dominators and dominated. Moreover, although Touraine criticizes Foucault for failing to consider the source of power in society, arguing that it originates in the apparatuses of the ruling class – in post-industrial society, from centers of technocratic domination – like Foucault, he sees power as operating in every social sphere rather than as possessed or produced by the modern state (Touraine, 1981: 21).

For Touraine, social relations are relations of power insofar as they are fixed in certain patterns by class domination. Struggle for the control of historicity takes place in conflicts across the social field, wherever domination tries to impose itself. Touraine's theory of social movements therefore minimizes the importance of the state in the transformation of society. In his view, genuine social movements struggle in the social realm, not through the state. He considers engaging with the political system to be cooption into the status quo and antithetical to the radical changes social movements may achieve. The importance Touraine gives to struggles over interpretations of norms and values in civil society allows us to see much social movement activity as political in the widest sense, not just in relation to the political process narrowly defined.

However, there are also problems with Touraine's approach which limit the development of an understanding of cultural politics based on his work. First, he over-emphasizes ideology in social movement conflicts. This is well illustrated by his study of the anti-nuclear movement in France in the 1970s. Touraine's interest in anti-nuclear protest lay in his hope that it might be the central social movement of post-industrial society, replacing the workers' movement of industrial society. In order to establish whether or not this was the case, he used his unconventional method of "social intervention." The first aim of this method is to study collective action as directly as possibly, by looking at the self-analysis of a militant group in confrontation with its opponents. Second, the researcher actively intervenes to help collective struggle take shape as a force for social transformation by challenging the assumptions with which activists work and raising their action to a "higher level of struggle." It is this aim which has earned Touraine's method the epithet "sociological Leninism" (Cohen, cited in Pickvance, 1995: 127; *cf* McDonald, 2002). Finally, the researcher also tries to get the group to develop an alternative, progressive model of modernity. In the case of the nuclear protestors Touraine found so promising, he hoped that they would develop an anti-technocratic vision of society as a whole for which they could fight. In fact, however, he found that they were unable to fulfil the criteria he specified as those of the central movement of post-industrial society. Motivated above all by fear rather than by a vision of the future, they were unable to identify a concrete enemy – attributing problems to "the system" – and were eventually tempted by the utopian ideal of a retreat into community and withdrew from engagement in the struggle to bring about social transformation (Touraine, 1983).

As several commentators have pointed out, Touraine's methodology, particularly the way in which he attempts as a researcher to bring the movement to the realization of its potential, seems to suggest that the most important aspect of bringing about social transformation is to have the right ideas. This is manifestly not the case; since action takes place in practice and so is subject to constraints and is implicated in modifications and consequences which cannot be foreseen in advance, even the best plans may be thwarted. In Touraine's work with social movements, furthermore, it is not ideas of strategy which are at issue, but rather the "true" definition of the social actors involved in the struggle, and the cultural orientations at stake (Pickvance, 1995: 127). This is problematic, not just because "truth" is relative to perspective, but also because it is counter-intuitive, begging a number of questions about the relevance of "truth" to social movements. It is not that social movements must establish the "true" identities of their opponents, or the "realities" of the situation in which they are engaged. It is rather that they necessarily engage in strategic and persuasive exchanges in which they try to bring others into their project for change, redefining the terms within which the battle lines have been drawn, changing people's views of their real interests, and convincing them to see the world and themselves in a different way. Social change is not achieved by revealing the truth, as Touraine seems to suppose, but rather by challenging received understandings and introducing new frameworks within which change becomes possible and desirable.

Second, from the point of view of this model of cultural politics, Touraine retains some of the problems of the Marxism he rejects, notably – and ironically – its determinism. The problem lies in Touraine's view that there is a single appropriate social movement for every type of society which will bring about the transition to another type of society. As Scott points out, this is at odds with his definition of social action as having no *a priori* direction or foreseeable outcome. The emphasis Touraine gives to actors' interpretations of social action as its cause, rather than underlying structures that work themselves out in a "logic" of development "behind people's backs," is testimony to the idea that social action takes place in an open system, potentially transformable in any direction. On the other hand, his diagnosis of the transition from industrial to post-industrial society depends on a theory of society as moving from one relatively closed system to another. Furthermore, he supposes that what is most important in this transition are changes in techniques of production which produce changes in societies as totalities. It is clear from his discussion of anti-nuclear protestors that, rather than analyzing social action in its own terms, as he recommends, his theoretical commitment to the movement for post-industrial society means that what he actually does is to compare the aims of any social movement with the "higher level" anti-technocratic aims he ascribes to it. Apart from problems of inconsistency in his own theory in this respect, Touraine is therefore bound to ignore the diversity of actual social movements and their significance for less total social transformation (Scott, 1996b).

Alberto Melucci: developments in "new social movement" theory

Alberto Melucci, once Touraine's student, has taken up many of the insights of his approach, while at the same time avoiding its inconsistent and untenable determinism and its idealist excesses. In order to avoid the determinism of structural approaches such as that implied in Touraine's theory, he incorporates some ideas from the RMT tradition concerning mobilization and political opportunity structures. In some respects, then, Melucci is concerned to work out a synthesis of RMT and NSMT, but his emphasis on culture and the importance he gives to struggles in civil society make his work very much closer to the latter tradition than to the former. Furthermore, the way in which he has developed Touraine's ideas brings Melucci explicitly within the terms of the cultural turn. Although he does not use the term "cultural politics," Melucci's view of social movements as engaged in the contestation of collective identity in the practices of everyday life is clearly akin to the understanding of cultural politics developed in this book.

For Melucci, Touraine's theory that there is a single progressive social movement in every societal type is a clear case of the typically mistaken view of social movements as *personages* – unified actors playing out a role on the stage of history. In his view, this idea comes from the workers' movement which was relatively unified in terms of its aims, the spaces in which it operated, and its membership among male manual workers. Contemporary social movements, however, are inherently plural; they consist of different levels of action – from political conflicts, narrowly defined, to defensive reactions and challenges to the codes of everyday life – and also of different groups of actors with different reasons for their involvement in collective action. Melucci gives the example of mobilization against a proposed nuclear power station in a rural area, arguing that for the peasants of the community it may represent a threat to traditional ways of life, while for a group of young people who have returned to it from the city, it may symbolize something quite different, for example, a threat to their right to live autonomously (Melucci, 1989: 203–4).

In Melucci's view, the most important point about collective action is that a more or less stable, composite, collective identity – a "we" – must be constructed out of very different ends, means, and forms of solidarity and organization. It must be understood as an ongoing *process* through which actors communicate and negotiate the meanings that produce the social movement as such. It is, of course, also Touraine's view that social movements are the product of social action; as we have seen; however, he re-introduces structural determinism when he interprets collective action in terms of its capacity for leading the transformation from one type of society to another. In such a case, it seems that the actors do not necessarily recognize the "highest meaning" of their action until it is brought to their attention by the researcher. For Melucci, on the other hand, social actors must know the meaning of their actions, even if they do not know it completely, since collective action is nothing but the multiple meanings they give to it (Melucci, 1995b).

Melucci's emphasis on the construction of meaningful collective action is also a response to Resource Mobilization theorists. In his view, RMT is useful for the way in which it stresses the external relationships of social movements to the field of systematic opportunities and constraints within which action takes place. Its focus on *how* social movements are formed and maintained is a good corrective to Touraine's emphasis on *why* they have become so important in contemporary society. However, in Melucci's view, despite the way in which RMT postulates the construction of collective action as a necessary process for social movements, it, too, takes the unity of social movements for granted and fails to examine it as a process. Furthermore, it is seriously limited in its capacity to do so insofar as Resource Mobilization theorists tend to see opportunities and constraints as "objective" realities. Melucci is opposed to what he calls dualistic thinking, which emphasizes either the objective or the subjective dimensions of social life; for him the goals of action, the means to be used, and the environment within which it takes place are all defined by collective actors in the ongoing process of constructing a social movement. In this respect, his work is in sympathy with those who have used Goffman's model of frame analysis, arguing that the motivation to participate in collective action is produced in interaction (although, as far as I know, he nowhere refers to RMT's appropriation of Goffman's work). However, unlike Resource Mobilization theorists, Melucci follows the logic of this "cultural turn" through to its conclusion, arguing that the reasons for becoming involved in a movement and the calculations of cost and benefits are *only* developed in interaction. Although he thinks – perhaps somewhat inconsistently – that structural explanations of the objective conditions in which social movements have recently risen to prominence are of value, they are relevant to collective action itself only insofar as they enter into actors' perceptions and evaluations and so into the processes of interaction in which it is constructed (Melucci, 1988).

Finally, Melucci breaks with Touraine and with RMT by rejecting the view that it is committed militants or social movement organizations who are the principal actors in collective action. For Melucci, social movements are, above all, sustained in "invisible submerged networks" in which experiments in life are carried on, new experiences created, and collective identities forged in everyday life. In his view, movements appear relatively infrequently as publicly visible phenomena in comparison with their existence in the practices of a largely part-time and floating membership in which they are formed and gain and maintain strength. The consciousness-raising groups of the early women's movement would no doubt be good examples of Melucci's "submerged networks," as would the health food shops, walking groups, conservationists, and self-help building programs of the green movement. Although movements may be invisible to the point where it seems as if they have altogether collapsed, the practices of networks of groups and individuals nevertheless develop alternative ways of living and thinking that quietly challenge society's dominant codes and which are ready to be mobilized for public protest if the occasion arises.

Despite these crucial disagreements with Touraine's work, Melucci does build on his understanding of social movements. Most importantly, like Touraine, he sees social movements as primarily engaged in cultural challenges to the logic of "post-industrial" society. Information is the key resource in contemporary society, the reflexivity of individuals and the society as a whole has been massively increased as a result, and global processes impinge on individual awareness in an unprecedented way. In view of this new social situation, social movements should also be seen as "new," in Melucci's opinion, because the problems to which they respond are different from those of the social movements of the nineteenth and early twentieth century – the main point of comparison being, of course, the labor movement – and so, too, are the responses they make to those problems (Melucci, 1995a).

For Melucci, post-industrial societies are above all concerned with "signs"; even the production and distribution of economic goods are symbolically mediated, through design, advertising, the media, and so on. As a result, according to Melucci, unlike their nineteenth-century counterparts, "new social movements" are not concerned with struggles over the production of material resources, or with their distribution or control through the state in citizenship rights, but rather with access to information (about the hazards of nuclear testing, for example) and the contestation of symbolic resources (such as sexist advertising or the aestheticization of violence in the media). This is also the case, according to Melucci, because, again unlike working-class politics, contemporary movements are concerned with forms of organization and lifestyle which are ends in themselves rather than the means to realize an end in the future. In particular, the split between public and private spheres is lived more as a complementarity than an opposition, as it was in the past: the experiences and meanings of private life are directly linked to publicly expressed commitments and vice versa. The women's movement would again be a good example of Melucci's point here because of the way in which it has provoked the revolutionizing of relations between men and women in the private, domestic sphere and, to a lesser extent, in the private realm of the economy, as well as in legislation and social policy.

In Melucci's view, the struggles of new social movements are struggles over identity: "to push others to recognize something which they themselves recognize; they struggle to affirm what others deny" (Melucci, 1989: 46). Although any conflict might be characterized in this way, he argues that the issue of identity has become more central with the increased reflexivity of complex societies. In Melucci's view, there is an ever-increasing control over every aspect of our lives in such matters as health, sexuality, and our relations with the natural environment. In this respect, he sees Foucault's understanding of power as important. On the other hand, however, the organizations that regulate our behavior also facilitate individual autonomy because they thereby put resources of knowledge and communicative skills at our disposal; without the development of capacities for learning and action, individuals would not be capable of the self-regulation required by the system. Increasingly, therefore, there is a greater emphasis on the capacity to act on action itself; to intervene in the biological and motivational structures of human beings in order to change oneself as an individual. In this respect, Melucci sees Foucault's model of power as one-dimensional; power does not simply involve the administration of subjects, since networks of actors in complex societies may use the resources provided by powerful organizations in ways which were not intended by bureaucrats and managers (Melucci, 1989: 208–9).

According to Melucci, the emphasis on individual identity in complex societies is linked to new forms of collective action in social movements. This is most directly evident in the fact that individuals are motivated to participate in movements only insofar as it "makes sense to them," meeting, as they see it, their own personal needs. As Melucci sees it, however, it is relatively rare that this leads to narcissistic inward-turning groups, since work on oneself is generally seen in these movements as the way to change the world by creating meaningful alternatives to the existing state of affairs. For example, the questions raised by the ecology movement concerning human relations with nature are immensely important for society as a whole as the destructive potential of technological intervention increases. Similarly, women's mobilization raises the general issue of how to recognize and accommodate biological and historical difference without repression (Melucci, 1989: 62). In fact, for Melucci, the definition of such questions as meaningful and the negotiations between individuals that link them to concrete ways of life are precisely the ways in which collective action itself is constructed in interaction. All the cultural innovations made in the process of individuals working on themselves in negotiation or in conflict with others – on the language they use, their sexual customs, affective relationships, dress, eating habits, and so on – constitute collective action that modifies the social order. Moreover, insofar as individual identity requires recognition by others, it is in itself intrinsically social; by its very nature, identity cannot be constructed outside relationships that give it meaning (Melucci, 1996: 29).

For Melucci, as for Touraine, social movements have a tangential relationship to established institutional politics; they cannot be assimilated to the political process because the conflicts they engender break the bounds of the current system (Melucci, 1989: 29). Melucci uses the term "politics" in a narrow sense, defining a political relationship as "one which permits the reduction of uncertainty and the mediation of opposing interests by means of decisions" and arguing that it takes place wherever interests are represented and decisions taken: in national political systems, but also in educational, administrative, and regional institutions (Melucci, 1989: 165). Social movements are principally concerned with solidarity and conflict in the cultural realm for Melucci, and their most important political function is as signs, or messages, which highlight hidden conflicts and problems and make visible the power used to resolve them in apparently rational, technical, decision-making procedures. As he points out, some of the dilemmas of contemporary society cannot be definitively resolved; for example, neither the elimination, nor the free use of nuclear energy is possible. Social movements publicize these "meta-political" dilemmas and Melucci argues that, as a result, they are necessarily ill suited for, and highly suspicious of, the conventional political process. Those, like Resource Mobilization theorists, who look only at the effects they have on politics, in this sense will, therefore, gain a wholly distorted view of their importance in contemporary societies.

In Melucci's view, social movements point the way beyond the limits of the present system, toward a new form of democratization appropriate to complex societies. They embody the need for new public spaces between civil society and the state in which movements can articulate and publicize themes and dilemmas to the rest of society and to the political actors who make the final decisions about how they will be dealt with. Such public spaces already exist to some extent, as Melucci sees it, in knowledge-producing institutions such as universities and cultural foundations, but they should be strengthened in the field of collective consumption – in relation to housing, transport, health, and so on – and also in relation to communications and the media in order to allow public confrontation and negotiation between the various actors involved (Melucci, 1989).

Melucci's work draws our attention to the new forms of cultural politics in contemporary society in which social movements are engaged, even if he himself uses a much narrower definition of politics. Melucci has been influenced in this respect by Touraine's re-thinking of Marxism, particularly by the way in which Touraine puts historicity at the center of his analysis. Both theorists have clearly taken seriously Marx's dictum that "Men make their own history, but not under circumstances of their own choosing." Melucci, however, is clearer than Touraine that it is the contestation of collective identity which is the key activity of social movements in cultural politics; there is no "objective" definition of the stakes of the conflicts in which they are engaged.

This understanding makes Melucci's work especially important for the cultural turn of contemporary political sociology. He sees identity as constructed by the manipulation of symbols which are effective in particular social contexts. There is no clear separation to be made between the way social life is defined and understood and the way it is lived: both are implicated in ongoing social practices. Melucci makes the implications of his work clearer in this respect in his last work, putting forward the view that it is the development of post-industrial society that increasingly makes symbols effective in reality. He argues that to see information as mirroring or representing reality is simplistic; information encoded in language and images increasingly contributes to the construction of social reality:

> Technological power has been accompanied by an exponential growth of symbolic possibilities, by an increase in self-reflective activity: by the heightened capacity to reflect and represent reality through a multitude of languages. This capacity seems to be gradually replacing reality itself, so that we are in the process of coming to inhabit a work constructed out of the images that we ourselves have created, a world where we can no longer distinguish reality from the reality of the image. (Melucci, 1996: 43)

What was previously implicit in Melucci's work – that it is in the manipulation of symbols and signs that collective identity is forged through the production of common meanings – is now made explicit. The question for social movements in contemporary society is, he suggests, "How and for what purpose should we use the *power of naming* which allows us to fabricate the world and to subsume it to the signs with which we express (or do not express) it?" (Melucci, 1996: 131).

Melucci's understanding of the cultural politics of social movements as taking place in everyday life is an important contribution to our understanding of contemporary society. There is no doubt that the way in which he sees social movements as active in civil society, rather than as oriented toward politics at the level of the state, has encouraged the development of his theory in these respects. However, there is an element of dogmatism in Melucci's refusal to consider how "new" social movements as well as "old" have been concerned with politics at the level of the nation-state. As we have seen, his theory illuminates the activities of social movements in civil society in ways which are completely neglected by RMT, focusing as it does on formal political activities. In this respect, it has been deservedly influential. However, social movements have always also engaged with the state to a greater or lesser extent. In particular, emerging in the context of an interventionist welfare state in Western liberal-democracies, "new" social movements have generally been involved in demanding the extension of citizenship rights in various ways. (We will look at this in detail in chapter 4.) This aspect of social movement activity is ignored by Melucci, doubtless because of his utopian view of social movements as "breaking the limits" of existing society.

However, it is not clear that Melucci's theory of cultural politics *need* commit him to ignoring the activities of social movements in this respect. On the contrary, given his emphasis on the internal plurality of social movements and the way in which they work at different levels, his theory would seem to be well designed to encompass the range of political activities in which they engage. It should be possible, as Melucci himself argues, to see social movements working *between civil society and the state*, as engaged in the democratization of everyday life and also in extending citizenship rights. In the next section, we will look at a synthesis of RMT and NSMT to see whether, given the prejudices of each tradition and the way in which they have developed, such a balanced perspective on social movements is now possible.

3.3   Toward a Synthesis: The Definition of "Social Movement"

In discussing the two main traditions of the study of social movements, we have seen that there has been a convergence between them in terms of the importance they give to culture in shaping participants' perceptions of aims and strategies. In fact, despite the very different premises of each tradition, those currently studying social movements are more likely to try to draw on both rather than to see them as incompatible (Klandermans et al., 1988; Johnston and Klandermans, 1995). One of the most thorough attempts to combine them is that of Mario Diani, who argues that the two traditions are now so close that it is possible to begin to synthesize them without doing injustice to either.[2] It is clear that the basis of Diani's synthesis is a sympathy with the work of Melucci, who has already tried to incorporate some elements of RMT's understanding of the importance of mobilizing structures and political opportunities. Here we will look at Diani's synthesis with a view to drawing out the importance of cultural politics to both major traditions in social movement theory.

Diani begins his task by laying out a working definition of "social movement," pointing out that it is striking how little work has been done on actually identifying social movements as distinct from other types of collective action. A social movement is a:

> specific social dynamic. … It consists in a process whereby several different actors, be they individuals, informal groups and/or organizations, come to elaborate, through either joint action and/or communication, a shared definition of themselves as being part of the same side in a social conflict. By doing so, they provide meaning to otherwise unconnected protest events or symbolic antagonistic practices, and make explicit the emergence of specific conflicts and issues … This dynamic is reflected in the definition of social movements as consisting in networks of informal interaction between a plurality of individuals, groups and/or organizations, engaged in a political and/or cultural conflict, on the basis of a shared collective identity. (Diani, 1992: 2–3)

It should be noted that Diani's definition differs in one crucial respect from the understanding of cultural politics developed here. According to this understanding, there is no distinction between "political" and "cultural" as different kinds of conflict in the way Diani suggests. All conflicts necessarily take place in culture and, insofar as they involve struggles to realize only one of various possible courses of action in practice, they are political. It is, however, the case, as we have noted, that social movements engage in cultural politics in civil society and also at the level of the state, contesting exclusionary definitions of citizenship. It is no doubt in this sense that Diani intends his distinction between "political" and "cultural": the first term referring to conventional forms of politics aimed at mobilizing political parties and lobbying to change legislation and the latter referring to the politics of everyday life. He apparently does not recognize both as cultural, although this is clearly the implication of the terms on which RMT and NSMT converge. This will become clear as we work through the synthesis he has constructed.

According to Diani, his definition of social movement emphasizes at least four aspects of their dynamics:

(1)   "A social movement is a network of informal interactions between a plurality of individuals, groups and organizations" (Diani, 1992: 8). Both Resource Mobilization theorists and New Social Movement theorists see the mobilization of social movements as occurring in informal interactions involving individuals, groups, and organizations. This is made explicit in the case of Melucci's definition of collective identity as formed through interaction in "submerged networks," but it is also important among Resource Mobilization theorists for whom "micromobilization" is a key component of social movement activity. There is a difference in emphasis, however, as those in the RMT tradition tend to see networks as providing the preconditions for mobilization which is then orchestrated by social movement organizations, while, for Melucci, they provide the settings for social movement activity proper – the contestation of identities and the practicing of alternative lifestyles. Arguably, this difference of emphasis is rather important, suggesting that the convergence between the traditions has distinct limits. Nevertheless, Diani is clearly correct to point out that both now recognize the importance of informal interactions to social movements.

(2)   "The boundaries of a social movement network are defined by the specific collective identity shared by the actors involved in the interaction" (Diani, 1992: 9). According to Diani, writers in both traditions again acknowledge what is emphasized in Melucci's work: that a social movement requires a collective identity, including both a shared set of beliefs and a sense of belonging. Resource Mobilization theorists have tended to focus on the former to the neglect of the latter. Zald and McCarthy, for example, see social movements as "sets of opinions and beliefs," which do not necessarily imply shared feelings of belongingness. However, Diani sees the more recent work in the RMT tradition on "micromobilization contexts" and "frame alignment processes" as emphasizing the collective negotiation of individual commitment, as opposed to individuals' solitary reflections on their reasons for joining collective action, and so at least implying the construction of solidarity. He, therefore, insists on the importance of the process of symbolic definition and redefinition of events, issues, activities, and other social actors in both traditions.

In Diani's view, both Resource Mobilization theorists and New Social Movement theorists must now take seriously the terms within which social actors themselves see the movements in which they participate: the collective identity of a social movement *is* that movement – it is nothing but a meaningful construction created in social action. Cultural politics is crucial, then, to the understanding of social movements in both traditions. Structural or causal explanations of members' participation have been ruled out as inadequate: the negotiation of individuals' reasons for participating and the collective identities which are constructed as a result are what creates social movements as such.

(3) "Social movement actors are engaged in political and/or cultural conflicts, meant to promote or oppose social change either at the systemic or non-systemic level" (Diani, 1992: 11). As Diani notes, the idea that social movements aim at social change through conflict is central to NSMT. For Touraine especially, but also Melucci, one of the core components of a social movement is that it is engaged in conflict with an adversary who interprets the same values in an antagonistic way. However, Diani argues that, although the RMT tradition is ostensibly more concerned with processes of social change, conflict is implicit in their understanding of social movements insofar as they acknowledge that social change is achieved only through conflict with other actors, whether institutions, other social movements, or counter-movements.

The main difference between the two traditions is, as we have seen, that while RMT is concerned above all with the way in which social movements effect change through the mainstream political process, New Social Movement theorists see activity at this level as that of a "public interest group" or even a political party, not a social movement. They see social movements as active in culture, as engaged in challenging shared meanings, and, in the case of Melucci, in self-transformation. Diani plays down this difference, clearly seeing it in terms of the difference between formal political activities and conflicts in civil society and arguing that it is a matter of emphasis rather than of fundamentally incompatible understandings of social movements. However, his reading of both traditions is rather selective on this point. In order to reach consensus on the different orientations of social movements, adjustments have to be made both to RMT and NMST.

RMT has, above all, been concerned with political change at the "non-systemic" level, that is, through the institutions of the state. In order to engage fully with cultural change, it would be necessary for Resource Mobilization theorists to give less emphasis to social movement organizations as the principal actors in social movements and more emphasis to the negotiation of collective identity and social action in processes of interaction. It is true that this is possible within the terms of RMT but, as we have seen, it would also mean giving up the commitment to objectivity and scientific neutrality on which the tradition has been based. It would mean RMT following the implications of the more cultural understanding of politics it has developed to a conclusion which would bring it much more fully within the "cultural turn."

NSMT, on the other hand, has been exclusively concerned with cultural change at the "systemic level." This is explicit in Touraine's work, and also in Melucci's: both see social movements as "breaking the limits" of the existing social system. For a complete synthesis between the traditions and an integrated social movement research program to be possible, New Social Movement theorists would have to drop their commitment to complete "systemic" transformation.

In fact, the idea of "system" is inconsistent with other aspects of Melucci's social theory. First, as we saw in chapter 2, the transnational flows of globalization undermine the idea of a strictly bounded society with distinct limits. Second, insofar as collective identities are seen as nothing but unstable composites of different meanings continually in the process of renegotiation, it is again difficult to see society as having fixed limits. Melucci's commitment to the idea of system is at odds with his idea of increased reflexivity in contemporary society which is more readily understood as giving rise to a permanent state of relative fluidity rather than the transformation of one "system" into another. As we have noted, Melucci's understanding of social movements as inherently pluralist and working on several levels would otherwise allow him to accommodate the way in which they engage in formal political activity, without compromising his understanding of the ways in which they engage in the democratization of everyday life in civil society. It would seem quite reasonable to adopt such an understanding, while giving up the romantic commitment to "systemic" transformation. Melucci's theory is potentially the more comprehensive in this respect, then, allowing an understanding of the way in which social movements engage in cultural politics both to realize social change through the state and also in the practices of civil society.

(4) "A social movement is a network of informal interactions between a plurality of individuals, groups and/or organizations, engaged in a political or cultural conflict on the basis of a shared collective identity" (Diani, 1992: 13). As Diani sees it, it is important to distinguish between social movements and other types of social and political action, such as interest groups, political parties, or religious movements. This is sometimes difficult given that social movements involve such a wide range of practices. However, he argues that it is precisely in this way that we should see social movements as distinctive forms of collective action; they are not simply organizations, however informal and non-hierarchical, but rather networks between different actors in which more or less formal organizations may sometimes play a part. Such citizens' rights groups as Common Cause in the US and interest groups such as the Child Poverty Action

Group in Britain are not social movements. Nor are religious sects such as Nichiren Shosh (studied as such by Snow et al., 1980, in terms of their recruitment techniques). The unique characteristic of a social movement, according to Diani, is a collective identity which exceeds the boundaries of any single group of organization, while nevertheless maintaining a limited specificity. This definition would seem to be acceptable from within the terms of both the RMT and NSMT traditions.

Diani's analytic synthesis is useful for the way in which it clearly brings out the important insights of both the major traditions in the study of social movements. In particular, it brings out the importance of cultural politics to both RMT and NSMT. The understanding of social movements as involving the negotiation of collective identity, the contestation of definitions and meanings in conflict with other social actors, and social action carried out in accordance with those shared meanings are all aspects of cultural politics theorized by both traditions.

However, Diani himself does not entirely acknowledge this importance insofar as he seems to suppose that some social movements are engaged only in political action narrowly defined. In this respect, he fails to acknowledge what NSMT theory has always insisted on, and what the appropriation of Goffman's ideas on "framing" in RMT is designed to illuminate, that the conflicts in which social movements engage are always, at the most general level, conflicts over cultural meanings. Social movements are often engaged in activities designed to influence governments, political parties, and policy-makers, and it is possible that some may not be concerned with politics in this sense but solely with conflicts in civil society. They are, however, always engaged in the politics of cultural contestation. It is the understanding of social movements as continually engaged in cultural politics which makes them so central to contemporary political sociology.

3.4   Global Social Movements

The assumption of most social movement research has been that mobilization, organization, and action take place within a bounded national territory, even if they are not necessarily addressed to the nation-state. In fact, however, social movement networks and exchanges across borders are not new; the anti-slavery movement, the women's suffrage movement of the nineteenth century, and the international labor movement were all involved in campaigns and exchanges which aimed at nation-states but which were not themselves confined within national borders (Tarrow,

1994: 52–3). Moreover, it is still the case that social movements differ within national contexts in terms of styles of mobilizing, the relative visibility of different causes, the actors involved, and the conflicts in which they are engaged (Tarrow, 2005; Della Porta, 2007). However, the possibilities for exchanges between activists across borders and for the awareness of global problems have been enormously increased in recent years by the explosion of new technologies that have facilitated other aspects of globalization. New media and communications bring individuals and groups news of distant events and problems and possibilities of action in other places, whilst, at the same time, they facilitate cooperation across borders.

In the last decade, the growth of transnational activism has been such that Donatella Della Porta and Sidney Tarrow, probably the most prominent scholars of social movements in the US and Europe today, argue that we are now seeing a new "cycle of protest," a general wave of the formation, growth and expansion of multiple and overlapping social movement activities (Della Porta and Tarrow, 2005: xiv). Della Porta defines global social movements as "transnational networks of actors that define their causes as global and organize protest campaigns and other forms of action that target more than one state and/or international government organization" (Della Porta, 2007: 6). There are a number of movements today that can be considered global, including: the women's movement (Eschle, 2001; Moghadam, 2005, 2008; Naples and Desai, 2002; Ferree and Tripp, 2006); the environmental movement (Chasek, Downie, and Brown, 2005; Lipschutz, 2004; Rootes, 2005); and the global justice movement (Moghadam, 2008; Della Porta, 2005; Della Porta, 2007; Smith, 2008). The human rights movement may be considered as part of the global justice movement (Blau and Moncada, 2007, 2009; Gready, 2004; Stammers, 2009). The movements of this globalizing "cycle of protest" differ in some respects from those of the last century. Here I will outline the differences globalization is making to social movements, and social movements are making to globalization, under the headings of Diani's synthetic definition, looking at networks, identity, and conflict.

Networks

In terms of networks, there is no doubt that use of new media technologies plays a crucial role in enabling activism across national borders (van de Donk et al., 2004). Where social movements tended to be based on face-to-face personal relationships above all, with printed media used to recruit, persuade, and challenge those not involved in such networks, use of new media technologies facilitates and alters social movement activity today. In the first place, use of the Internet contributes to recruitment, to publicizing social movement causes and activities. It also makes some kinds of participation in a movement very easy; on the Internet, social movement sympathizers may be just a click of a mouse away from joining in an action by adding a name to an e-petition, or, with very little effort, joining a discussion linked to a social movement website, blogging, or posting pictures and videos. New media technologies also enable sharing of knowledge about a movement's concerns, expertise, and strategic thinking to an unprecedented extent. The Internet can be used to disseminate information that is not covered, or that is actively suppressed, by the mainstream media, so involving people who would not otherwise be addressed by particular issues. And use of new media technology, including mobile phones, also facilitates the organization of protest events, enabling large numbers to coordinate their convergence at particular times and places (Scott and Street, 2001). In this respect, the transnationalization of movements is facilitated by cheap air travel, too. It is virtually unimaginable that such large numbers of people should come together in different cities around the world to protest at the G8 summits, for example, before the Internet and cheap flights. Similarly, setting up the World Social Forum as a global meeting place for activist discussions is unthinkable without cheap forms of transport. In general, then, use of new media technologies and cheap air travel enable the diffusion of social movements, which was already going on across national borders, to be speeded up and extended geographically. They make sharing frames of understanding, forms of organizing, and repertoires of action much easier and quicker across wider geographical areas.

Collective identity

As we have seen, collective identity is a crucial aspect of social movement activity. In fact, the formation of a collective "we" and its extension to include those who are indifferent or opposed to "our" vision *is* the principal political action of the movement. Social movements work by persuasion: making injustices or problems visible, creating knowledge and persuasive arguments, and effectively constructing social reality in such a way that ignoring those injustices or problems becomes impossible. In this respect, and rather oddly perhaps, a social movement actually aims to dissolve itself; it is successful when it becomes "a way of seeing" generally, rather than a bounded, if loosely networked, group of activists who share a common perspective (see Rochon, 1998).

The new modes of global social networking complicate the formation and extension of collective identity, which was always a highly complex undertaking. The Internet facilitates more individualized participation in social movements than was previously the case. Although credible information and authoritative debate is generally channeled through the websites of social movement organizations, the web enables individuals not only to interpret a movement's aims and means for themselves, but also to communicate easily and widely with other people. An expansive, virtually infinite, variety of individual perspectives potentially makes for a much more diffuse sense of commonality amongst those who see themselves as members of a movement. In addition, the fact that individuals' particular views are so much more visible on the Internet also facilitates multiple links between and across different causes. Global social movements like the global justice movement are remarkably diverse, linking a range of issues including human rights, the environment, and poverty that were addressed by quite distinct networks of activists before the Internet (Bennett, 2005). Della Porta argues that, in comparison with previous movements, the global justice movement is also much more diverse in terms of participants, too, with different generations, people with a wide variety of conditions of employment, and roughly equal numbers of men and women participating. She argues that the global justice movement favors "tolerant identities," stressing the importance of diversity and dialogue, openness and fluidity, with the simultaneous expression of multiple identities (Della Porta, 2005: 180–6).

"Collective identity" is further complicated insofar as individuals' search for meaning and value for their own lives is prominent in the mobilization of global social movements. This may not be in such marked contrast to previous social movements, but perhaps it is of increasing significance. "Subjectivity," the way activists think and feel about themselves as individuals, is itself of immense symbolic importance in these movements (Della Porta, 2005: 198–9; McDonald, 2006: 32–3). Kevin McDonald argues that the search for meaning, the way in which individual activists are trying to make sense of their own lives through collective action, is evident in the immense value that is put on embodied experience in global social movements: in participation in the expressive protest events of the global justice movement, for example, and the embodied politics of occupying space to protest against environmental damage (McDonald, 2006).

The relative ease with which activists switch between issues, targets, and messages, which is facilitated by the use of new media technology, certainly raises important questions about whether membership of global social movements is sufficiently united and stable to develop coherent political positions and common goals (Bennett, 2005: 208). But forming "collective identity" was never simple in social movements. It invariably involved huge and often bitter debate across different perspectives, leading to factions and conflicts that were irresolvable, not just intellectually but personally, because they were embodied and emotional, for the people involved. This is nowhere more evident in debates over identity in the movements that came to be characterized as exclusively concerned with "identity politics" in the 1970s and '80s. It is not because feminists, for example, *agreed* on the identity of "women" that the feminist movement was so actively and creatively engaged in this issue. Nevertheless, the fact that the feminist movement debated the question of "women's identity," raising crucial questions about the relationship between biology and destiny and the diversity of women's lived experiences, forged not only recognizably common reference points for those who identified as feminists, it also brought the issues into public debate more generally.

Della Porta argues that, diversity and individualism notwithstanding, there is a concern with solidarity and how to achieve it in the global justice movement. It is for this reason that dialogue across differences is so important, as exemplified by the World Social Forum (WSF) set up to facilitate debate amongst members of the global justice movement across the world. Solidarity is a recurring topic at the WSF. It is self-consciously pluralist according to the Principles of its Charter. Principle 1 states that the WSF is an

> open meeting place for reflective thinking, democratic debate of ideas, for-
> mulation of proposals, free exchange of experiences and interlinking for
> effective action, by groups and movements of civil society that are opposed
> to neo-liberalism and to domination of the world by capital and any form
> of imperialism, and are committed to building a planetary society directed
> towards fruitful relationships among Mankind and between it and the
> Earth.

Nevertheless, debate over whether the WSF should produce a manifesto or a declaration of purposes comes up regularly, leading, for example, to the "Porto Alegre Manifesto – Twelve Proposals for Another Possible World" in 2005. Similarly, ongoing debates on the Internet – easy to access and to participate in – over what to call this movement, whether "anti-capitalist," "anti-globalization," or "global justice," are reminiscent of debates concerning who "we" are, and what we stand for, of previous social movements. As we have learned from Melucci, the collective identity of a social movement is never settled once and for all; on the contrary, who "we" are is formed through ongoing disputes, and conflicting perspectives do not in and of themselves prevent solidarity.

Conflict

What is also crucial, however, for the formation of a sense of "we," is conflict with "them," with a concrete embodiment of the ideals to which the movement is opposed which make it clear that conflicts within the movement itself are between "us." This opposition may be with another organization, a network, or an authoritative policy-making institution. Transnational movements, operating in a world in which many organizations, including states, are networked into global governance, have a range of such interlocutors at different scales, from the local to the global. For the most part, social movements aim to achieve change that is rooted in national contexts. Globalization makes strategic "scale shift" easier: "scaling up" to extend activities to include a wider range of actors and sites of conflict with opponents; and "scaling down," where the range of actors and sites is reduced (see Tarrow, 2005). There are two main ways in which transnational movements shift scale in order to bring about domestic change. In "externalization," movements "scale up" to bring domestic causes to the attention of international organizations, especially IGOs. As Margaret Keck and Kathryn Sikkink have shown, in the case of the campaigns against violence against women, for example, advocacy organizations put pressure on states from below, at the domestic level, and from above, at the international level, in order to try to shame them into acting to deal with issues within their own borders (Keck and Sikkink, 1998). Alternatively, social movements may "scale down," to "internalize" or "domesticate" conflicts that have their basis in policy made at a supranational or international level (Tarrow, 2005). Tarrow argues that the global justice movement in the US has largely now internalized protest again global economic policy, focusing on issues, such as racism and police brutality, that activists see as especially relevant within their states (Hadden and Tarrow, 2007). Similarly, protests against economic policies of the European Union within member states are now quite common (Imrig and Tarrow, 2001). Examples from elsewhere include protests across the world at the IMF-imposed austerity, especially in Latin America and Africa (Della Porta and Tarrow, 2005: 4–5). It was these protests that began the global justice movement (Moghadam, 2008: 92).

In fact, and despite the spectacular high-profile protests at G8 summits over the last decade, it seems that social movement activity directly targeting IGOs in order to bring about change is relatively rare. Jackie Smith argues that, in the case of activity specifically centered on the UN, it has actually declined in recent years (Smith, 2008: 97–8). This is also somewhat surprising given, as we have seen, the significance of NGOs and INGOs in global governance at every scale. As Margaret Keck and Katherine Sikkink have shown, transnational advocacy networks, which are made up of professional organizations and expert individuals, are certainly active internationally (Keck and Sikkink 1998). However, the relationship between these networks and those of social movements is inherently hard to assess. Whilst, as we have noted, use of new media technologies may make virtual participation in both types of networks quite easy, there tends to be mutual suspicion between those who engage with elite organizations and grass-roots activists. Members of NGOs, especially at the international level, tend to be treated with suspicion by movement activists as lacking awareness of realities, as naïve about the possibilities of bringing about change "from above," and as uncreative with regard to political possibilities. By the same token, activists tend to be seen as undisciplined and ineffective by members of professional political organizations (see Bennett 2005: 215–16). In this respect, members of global social movements are true to the values of social movements developed much earlier: social movements not only deliberately differ from interest groups and political parties in style and organization, but they are committed to creating new forms of political action that give greater emphasis to informal and inclusive ways of participating, contesting "official" definitions of events and processes, and, in the process, remaking the identities, not just of those directly involved, but of everyone. The main difference is that, whereas in the past, it tended to be assumed that "everyone" lived in nation-states, in the case of global social movements, as we shall see in chapter 5 when we consider democracy and global civil society, the inequalities and injustices of the way in which the planet as a whole is governed may be as much in question as anything else.

Notes

1   It is worth noting here that at least some of the theoretical differences between RMT and NSMT are related to the national contexts in which they were formulated and to national differences in social movement activity. Historically,

party politics in the US has been much less dominated by the labor movement than European politics; government has been characterized by a more open, non-corporatist style of politics in which movements tend to try to adapt to and influence the political process through organized lobbying. It has also been preoccupied with constitutional interpretation and litigation so that social movements have been very much concerned with legal contestation. In contrast, Western European politics has been characterized by a more rigid corporatism to which movements have tended to respond in a more radical, anti-systemic way. In some part, these differences account for the emphasis of US-based RMT on social movement mobilization through professional organizations, and European-based NMST which emphasizes mobilization in civil society.

2   Diani's schema actually includes four main trends which he sees as important within social movement analyses since the 1960s: collective behavior (Turner and Killian), RMT (Zald and McCarthy), political process (Tilly), and new social movements (Touraine, Melucci). The collective behavior approach has not been considered here because it has not been very influential in recent years, and the "political process" approach has been categorized with RMT, as is more usually the case. These differences do not affect our assessment of Diani's synthesis.

Chapter 4
Citizenship

Social movements concerned explicitly with identity and equality have been transforming citizenship. The sociological study of citizenship is relatively recent, although as a concept, social status, and set of political practices, it goes back to the ancient world. The model of citizenship outlined by T. H. Marshall in the late 1940s, now regarded as the classic starting point of any discussion of the topic, did not achieve widespread influence until relatively recently (Rees, 1996: 1; Somers, 2008: 162–8). It is especially since the 1980s that citizenship has become a topic of extensive debate in political sociology. This is undoubtedly linked to the growth of social movements which have challenged the traditional form of citizenship as it has developed in liberal democracies.

As we will see when we examine Marshall's model of citizenship in more detail in section 4.1, his account of the historical development of citizenship focused on the extension of citizenship rights as a feature of the progress of modern society. He represented this as the achievement of universal citizenship, of identical rights for all citizens regardless of socio-economic class. Focused on citizenship in relation to the occupations of male heads of households, Marshall neglected other dimensions of social inequality. This is unsurprising, as Marshall was writing in Britain in the late 1940s, when society was seen as stratified only in terms of class, and the labor movement was prominent in campaigning for the expansion of citizenship rights, particularly the social rights of the welfare state. Class inequalities were the main focus of attention in society and in sociology. Increasingly, however, as "new" social movements like the civil rights and anti-racist movements, feminism, and the gay liberation movement gained in strength and directed campaigns at inequalities in the rights of different categories of citizens, both Marshall's optimistic model of "universal" citizenship rights and the idea that social inequalities are essentially class inequalities have come to be seen as less relevant.

Sociologists are interested in how formal citizenship rights are related to non-formal criteria of inclusion in what Alexander calls the "civil sphere," the space of citizenship between the state and the market (Alexander, 2006). Formal rights are granted by the state, but citizenship entitlements depend on informal criteria that are decided on in the civil sphere. In the first place, the civil sphere involves the construction of shared understandings concerning which individuals are entitled to the status of citizen. It is inherently normative; inclusion in the civil sphere depends on the recognition by others that an individual deserves to be included within it. It depends on the assessment and valuation of a particular individual as the kind of person who, along with others in the civil sphere, should enjoy the "right to rights," as Hannah Arendt puts it (Arendt, 1968: 298). These criteria of inclusion are invariably mediated, however, by identification and self-identification of individuals with different social groups.

Social movements challenge informal criteria of citizenship that define some individuals as "Other," as belonging to a group that makes them unworthy of equal rights in the civil sphere. Although social movements are generally directly engaged in making demands for formal citizenship rights, they are even more fundamentally engaged in the cultural politics of identity formation. The identity of those who "belong together" in the civil sphere must be altered to make it more inclusive of previously stigmatized groups, as well as commonly shared definitions of those groups who are excluded or who are included only in ways that are unequal. The state ultimately guarantees citizenship rights, but it is the way in which citizenship identities and entitlements are settled between the civil sphere and the state that creates different historical forms of citizenship. It is how citizenship is defined in the cultural politics of social movements that matters.

The main theme in the cultural politics of citizenship inspired by social movements is that of "difference." It is always, however, closely linked to "equality." Historically, the cultural politics of social movements has involved challenges to assumptions that "normal" citizens are white, heterosexual, male heads of households, on the basis that others should enjoy the *same* formal rights. This was, for example, the main theme of first-wave feminism in the nineteenth and early twentieth centuries. In contemporary society, however, challenges to inequality rarely involve the simple claim that members of particular social groups are not treated like "normal" citizens. It is much more common now that cultural politics contest and displace what is "normal" as just one of a range of possibilities. In this respect, social movements challenge the idea of citizenship as consisting of individuals enjoying identical rights and imply a more open, pluralist model of society.

Indeed, the risk that group-differentiated rights themselves may produce "Otherness" in relation to a norm tends to be taken very seriously in social movements concerned with difference and equality. The identities and positions represented by social movements are never homogeneous. It is impossible, for example, to simply be a woman; women are always also socially positioned in terms of ethnicity, sexual orientation, marital status, occupation, age, geographical location, and so on. Furthermore, contemporary society changes fast, partly as a result of the activities of social movements themselves. Social groups contain within them, therefore, a range of more or less traditional or "de-traditionalized" identities. This is evident, for example, where young people have been brought up in a society that is quite different from that of their parents – whether as a result of migration or simply of social change. The heterogeneity and fluidity of social identities is very important to a consideration of citizenship rights intended to promote more progressive and egalitarian ideals. Another way of putting this is to say that "freedom" to create new identities is just as important as "equality" between groups. But this raises very real difficulties. The aim of social movements is not just to equalize citizenship rights but also to avoid constraining the development of new ways of life. We will discuss these issues particularly in relation to sex and sexuality in section 4.3, and racialized ethnicity in section 4.4.

Social movements have typically addressed civil spheres in relation to nation-states, even if, as we saw in the previous chapter, they have also long shared ideas, resources, and tactics transnationally. Similarly, sociologists have understood the civil sphere as a space between the nation-state and state-regulated markets. It is important, however, not to see the civil sphere as literally a geographical space; the civil sphere is not necessarily national. Indeed, people living within the same national territory may be excluded from the civil sphere by "internal borders," as Margaret Somers argues that people in poverty are today (Somers, 2008). By extension, the civil sphere might include those living outside a national territory. Though given that, as we have noted, rights are ultimately guaranteed by states, it is harder to imagine how this might develop.

Marshall's thinking on citizenship epitomizes "methodological nationalism" in that he assumes that society is confined within national borders and that the state is the ultimate power over citizens. Since that time, however, globalization has called a number of the features of the bounded society into question. In the first place, in accordance with conventional understandings of his time, Marshall assumed cultural homogeneity amongst citizens. In fact, the ideal of the nation-state as consisting of a singular, unified, and self-determining nation has rarely been realized historically; there have almost always been large cultural minorities in nation-states, whilst "countries of immigration" have long received people from different societal cultures. In the late twentieth century, the enjoyment of cultural rights to difference came to be seen as an ideal in societies oriented towards multiculturalism. In addition, there has also been mobilization for changes in the rights of long-term residents who are not citizens, and for states to respect the human rights of migrants fleeing persecution. We will look at these issues in section 4.4, on multinational citizenship rights, and in section 4.5, on post-national citizenship rights. Finally, debates over citizenship at the beginning of the twenty-first century also concern concrete possibilities for global environmental citizenship, which we will consider in section 4.5.

Before looking at the politics of social movements around citizenship, however, we will look at how citizenship has changed since Marshall was writing with respect to issues of wealth and poverty. At more or less the same time that social movements began to make an impact on citizenship rights, from the 1970s onwards, the neo-liberalization of welfare states began in response to the crisis created by the rigidities of the Keynesian management of capitalism. Neo-liberalization involves an emphasis on freedom *from* the state, traditionally associated with classical liberalism and given new life by the New Right, especially in Britain and the US with Thatcherism and Reaganomics. From these origins, neo-liberal policies have become part of the toolkits of governments across the world; to a greater or lesser extent in different cases, securing economic growth now involves cutting business taxes to attract multinational corporations, cutting state costs, and trying to pass the costs of social reproduction onto citizens. Social movements, on the other hand, typically come from the Left, and emphasize equality and freedom *to* realize one's full potential. They generally aim at expanding state regulation and expenditure. It is difficult to defend and extend citizenship equality in a context in which markets and consumer choice are promoted as the best way to deliver public services. The expansion of the market is the context within which social movement definitions challenge hegemonic understandings of membership and identity in the civil sphere, with consequent limitations on claims for rights to equality and difference from the state.

4.1   T. H. Marshall: Citizenship, Social Class, and the Nation-State

The classic starting point for a discussion of citizenship is the historical-sociological analysis of Thomas Humphrey Marshall. It is very much a product of its time and place, written at the peak of optimism concerning the post-war welfare state in Britain, and it is therefore of limited relevance for an understanding of contemporary society. Nevertheless, the analytic framework Marshall provides, in which citizenship is seen as comprising civil, political, and social rights, is useful and widely adopted. Furthermore, a number of the deficiencies of Marshall's model clearly illustrate the directions in which the new political sociology of citizenship has developed in relation to the cultural politics of social movements and processes of globalization.

Marshall analyzes citizenship as consisting of three types of rights: civil, political, and social. Civil rights involve the protection of individual freedoms, including "liberty of the person, freedom of speech, thought, and faith, the right to own property and to conclude valid contracts, and the right to justice" (Marshall, 1992: 8). Associated with the modern institutions of the civil and criminal courts of justice, Marshall sees civil rights as developing in the eighteenth century. Political rights involve the right to "participate in the exercise of political power as a member of a body invested with political authority or as an elector of the members of such a body" (1992: 8). Already existing for some, according to Marshall, they became citizenship rights only in the twentieth century with the extension of universal suffrage to all adults. This established the principle that they depend on personal status rather than on economic means. In terms of institutions, they involve the development of parliament and the councils of local government formed in the nineteenth century. Social rights Marshall sees as developing in the twentieth century in their modern form, with the institutions of the welfare state, including the national system of compulsory education and those of health and social services. Marshall's definition of social rights is more abstract than his definition of civil and political rights, reflecting the wide view he takes of them:

> By the social element I mean the whole range from the right to share in a modicum of economic welfare and security to the right to share to the full in the social heritage and to live the life of a civilised being according to the standards prevailing in the society. (1992: 8)

Marshall linked the historical development of citizenship to the development of capitalism. In particular, he was interested in the coincidental development of citizenship rights as a system of *equality* with capitalism as a system of *inequality*. In conjunction with civil and political rights, he saw the slow development of social rights as contributing to the development of a parallel system of substantive equality which mitigates, and is in contradiction with, the economic inequalities of capitalism. As Marshall (1992: 33) puts it:

> The extension of the social services is not primarily a means of equalising incomes ... What matters is that there is a general enrichment of the concrete substance of civilised life, a general reduction of risk and insecurity, an equalisation between the more and the less fortunate at all levels – between the healthy and the sick, the employed and the unemployed, the old and the active, the bachelor and the father of a large family. Equalisation is not so much between classes as between individuals within a population which is now treated for this purpose as though it were one class. Equality of status is more important than equality of income.

Although the only existing inequalities Marshall pays attention to are class inequalities, at the same time, it is clear from his understanding of the inter-relationship of capitalism and citizenship rights that he actually sees class conflict displaced with the development of citizenship. In fact, Marshall goes so far as to predict that citizens will become less interested in earning high wages, not only because of high levels of taxes in a welfare state, but because money will itself become less relevant where the essentials of life – including pensions, unemployment benefit, good education, healthcare, and so on – are provided equally, by right, to all citizens (1992: 47–8).

The details of Marshall's prediction have not been borne out, but arguably, the development of citizenship rights is one of the factors that has contributed to the decline of class politics. Citizens orient their political struggles and claims for greater equality toward the state, while workers' struggles with employers have become less important. Of course, class inequalities in welfare provision could have remained the main object of citizens' concern, as they were in Marshall's time, but in fact, this has not been the case. It is not only that class struggles at the economic level have been displaced by the system of status equality constructed in terms of citizenship rights Marshall analyzed; it is also that class is no longer the principal identity around which demands for greater equality are organized.

Limits of Marshall's account of citizenship

Marshall's account has several problems that are relevant to our consideration of citizenship in relation to the cultural politics of social movements and the consequences of globalization. We will deal explicitly with these topics in following sections, but for the moment, we will look at the deficiencies of Marshall's theory of citizenship more generally.

First, Marshall's model is criticized for the way in which it tends to ignore politics. It is argued, notably by Anthony Giddens, that Marshall's treatment of the extension of citizenship rights is implicitly evolutionist; it is as if there is a natural progression from civil to political to social rights as part of the development of modern industrial society. Giddens argues that Marshall fails to give enough consideration to how each of the three sets of rights has only been achieved after protracted struggle (Giddens, 1982: 171). Not all commentators on Marshall's work agree with Giddens. As Barbalet (1988) notes, some actually take quite the opposite view, arguing that Marshall's model shows how citizenship rights are extended through conflict. Such divergent understandings stem in large part from Marshall's own ambivalence on the question. He is certainly much more interested in the sequence of development of citizenship rights than in how this development has been achieved, and he gives an unresolved and even contradictory account of it. In *Citizenship and Social Class*, he says that the growth of citizenship "is stimulated both by the struggle to win those rights and by their enjoyment when won," but then almost immediately goes on to say that "the familiar instruments of modern democracy were fashioned by the upper classes and then handed down, step by step, to the lower" (Marshall, 1992: 24–5). Barbalet's interpretation seems the most reasonable: although Marshall does speak of conflict, what he means by it is the conflict of principles between capitalism as a system dependent on inequality and citizenship as a system of equality rather than struggles between actual social groups. Barbalet argues that it is not possible to judge from Marshall's sparse comments on the issue whether he saw the working out of this conflict as a matter of bargaining and conciliation or of struggle and violence. However, as he notes, an emphasis on the development of new sets of rights out of existing ones, combined with Marshall's lack of interest in the actual conditions of their development, does incline his model toward evolutionism (Barbalet, 1988: 30–1).

From Marshall's point of view, on the crest of the wave of post-war welfare state creation in Britain, evolutionism would presumably not have seemed as inadequate as it does to most sociologists in these less expansive times. From our vantage point in the twenty-first century, it is clear that citizenship rights are an important object of cultural politics. Continually contested, they can never be finally secured and they certainly do not develop according to an inherent logic.

The implicit evolutionism of Marshall's account is linked to another problem: he apparently assumed that the development of citizenship rights took the same form in all countries. Marshall's history of the development of citizenship rights is a description of British society. However, he is, at the same time, proposing a general model of the development of the relation between citizenship and class in capitalist societies. It is implicit, therefore, that the British case is not unique, but representative of all capitalist societies. This is an unwarranted assumption which is not borne out by the development of citizenship in other countries (Turner, 1990). In the case of the US, Michael Mann argues that because political rights were granted to the working class much earlier than in Britain, before the labor movement was strong enough to offer a real challenge to the ruling class, workers formed interest groups within the political constitution and party system (Mann, 1996). As a result, social rights were already underdeveloped in the US before neo-liberal globalization. Scandinavia is at the other extreme, where welfare provision has been much more comprehensive and generous, shaped by a strong socialist party, trades unions, and farmers' organizations early in the twentieth century (Stephens, 1996).

From the point of view of social movements, there is a still more important aspect of Marshall's universalism: he assumes that citizenship rights within a society *are* genuinely universal and confer equality upon citizens. The most theoretically elaborated challenge to this view has come from feminists. It is not that Marshall ignores the differences between the sexes altogether; in his account of the historical development of rights, he does mention the way in which women's citizenship advanced at a slower rate than men's – in relation to winning the vote, for example. However, as Sylvia Walby (1994) has argued, Marshall's analysis of citizenship rights is so imbued with gender-specific assumptions that he fails to notice that the development of women's rights has actually followed quite a different trajectory from men's, in some respects to a different end point, even in the British case. As an example, she points out that women had very few civil rights until they were gained as part of the wider struggle for political rights in the nineteenth and early twentieth centuries: the right to own property, to professional employment, not to be beaten by a husband, to terminate a marriage, and so on. Some were not won until after political rights, thus reversing the development Marshall proposes for all citizens. Furthermore, Walby argues that some still have not been won today – the right to abortion, for example, she sees as a fundamental civil right to control over one's own body – while social rights to difference and equality are, as we will see in section 4.3, inherently problematic for women where the male norm continues to be taken for granted. Similar points may be made in relation to all those who do not conform to the norm of citizenship. A striking example is the black civil rights movement in the US, campaigning for freedom of the person, equality before the law, and economic freedom for Southern blacks about a hundred years after they had been formally accorded American citizenship with the ending of slavery (Morris, 1993). As we will see in section 4.4, it is arguable that the lack of seriousness with which the judicial system treats racial harassment means that black citizens still do not have freedom of the person.

Marshall's assumptions concerning the normal citizen and the universalism of citizenship rights have also increasingly come to be seen as problematic in relation to culture. What is meant by "culture" in this context is highly complex, but, assuming homogeneity amongst citizens in terms of life-style choices, national origins, history, and language, Marshall simply collapses cultural into social rights. For Marshall's contemporaries, the enjoyment of rights to "live the life of a civilised being" included a cultural component, rights to public museums and heritage sites, state subsidized arts, and perhaps most importantly in Britain, the BBC, the public broadcasting service paid for by viewers and listeners that expanded massively in the post-war period. "Culture" is multifaceted here, including national culture, the memorialization of the nation's history; high culture, "the works and practices of intellectual and especially artistic activity" (Williams quoted in Jordan and Weedon, 1995: 6–8); and, to a lesser extent, popular culture, too: the BBC's ideal was to "inform, educate, and entertain." In Britain and virtually everywhere else, any secure sense of cultural value has been disrupted, as absolute distinctions between high and low culture have come into question (Is Bob Dylan's poetry as good as Keats? Is an unmade bed really Art?), and globalization brings people, images, and ideas from different places and "societal cultures" together in multicultural societies. As a result, in commonsense terms, "culture" has become virtually indistinguishable from notions of "cultural difference" (and, critics would say "cultural relativism," the view that cultural norms are of equal value). The most concrete effect of debates around cultural difference in relation to citizenship rights has been the remaking of national identities as multicultural, and the understanding that different groups in society may need different "cultural rights." Marshall's schema of civil, political, and social must, therefore, be supplemented with rights to cultural difference (Pakulski, 1997; Rosaldo, 1999; Stevenson, 2001, 2003).[1]

Finally, Marshall seems to have understood citizenship as evolving towards the end point at which he analyzed it in Britain in the mid-nineteenth century. He neglected to consider how closely it was linked in this respect to the expansionary post-war economy, apparently assuming that Keynesian corporatism would lead to unending economic growth. Marshall saw a fundamental tension between citizenship, which reduces inequalities, and capitalism, which produces them. He was optimistic that the tension would be resolved in favor of citizenship. In the light of boom and bust economics since the 1970s, and neo-liberal restructuring of relationships between states and markets, the social rights Marshall apparently assumed were the end point of the evolution of citizenship have come much more seriously into question.

4.2   Citizenship, Wealth, and Poverty

From a descriptive analysis of the evolution of citizenship in the twenty-first century, Marshall's model has now become something more like an ideal. Marshall saw social rights as ameliorating the worst inequalities produced by capitalism, which inevitably affect some more than others. Social rights include what is commonly thought of as "welfare" in the US, and increasingly elsewhere: help from the government to those who are not engaged in paid labor to meet basic needs. For Marshall, however, social rights were much more than "welfare." He saw citizenship rights as producing a system parallel to capitalism, a sphere of life in which market logics of competition and profit would become irrelevant. In Europe, the greater part of the welfare state was made up of "universal" services, available to everyone, of which free education and healthcare were the most important in the post-war context. Citizens would spend most of their lives in this parallel sphere, to the point where inequalities produced by the capitalist labor market would become largely irrelevant. For Marshall, social citizenship introduced a fundamental tension into capitalist societies. Capitalism does not just produce inequality between citizens; the market requires that citizens are unequal: that they have incentives to sell their labor to earn money and compete to consume what is produced. In retrospect, Marshall's view of the compromise between citizenship and capitalism looks extremely optimistic (Turner, 1986).

Most importantly, since Marshall was looking forward to the consolidation of citizenship in 1948, states have all been involved, and restructured to different degrees, in processes of neo-liberal globalization. It is not so much that the state has lost control of economic processes with the end of the Keynesian management of capitalism, although this is often the way globalization is represented in the rhetoric of politicians. Neo-liberalism is an economic project, but it has been facilitated by states (Scott, 1997b). Although the ideal of neo-liberalism is the free market, the reality is market-driven government (Somers, 2008: 93-5). In relation to social citizenship, neo-liberalizing states have been involved in rolling back their *own* frontiers, to paraphrase Margaret Thatcher, especially in relation to the costs of social rights. In Marshall's terms, they have been involved in extending the market and narrowing the sphere of public life in which citizens were supposed to enjoy equality. In actual fact, this has led to complex new arrangements between states and markets rather than a reduction in state intervention altogether (Crouch, 2001).

"Market fundamentalism" has been most advanced in the UK and the US, where it originated in the policies of the "New Right" and has now been taken over to a greater or lesser extent by political parties on the center-Left. Although there have been some attempts to redraw the boundaries between states and markets elsewhere in Europe, including Scandinavia, incursions into social insurance and rights to education and healthcare have been much more energetically resisted there, as elsewhere in Western Europe, and have not advanced to anything like the same extent (Cochrane et al., 2001; Harvey, 2005: 112–15).

In the UK, there have been a range of reforms aimed at reducing the cost of the welfare state which have had direct impact on citizens' access to social rights. The most prominent of these effectively re-create citizens as consumers. In some cases, there is a kind of quasi-marketization, as when, in the UK, parents are encouraged to choose a local state school for their children (when previously, they would have been expected to attend the one nearest their home) or – if they can afford it – to send them to private, fee-paying schools. Similarly, although healthcare remains universal in the UK, those who can afford it are now encouraged to supplement treatment in the National Health Service with private medical insurance. State pensions are so low they must be "topped up" by paying into private schemes, and so on. Not only does this mean that citizens receive different treatment according to their income, it also reduces commitment to "universal" citizenship rights and results in the stigmatization of those who have only access to inferior services. Similarly in the

US, where social rights were already far less developed than anywhere in Europe, cuts in state spending have led to reduced levels of social insurance and access to medical care for the poorest. Cuts in the federal budget to help people in the case of emergencies were responsible for the way poor people in New Orleans were left to deal with the devastation caused by Hurricane Katrina, which made the realities of life beneath the poverty line shockingly visible to US citizens, and to the world (Somers, 2008).

The emphasis of neo-liberalism is on freedom rather than equality. Individuals should be free to choose the best provision for themselves and their families. In practice, this means that citizens are encouraged to see themselves as consumers of goods and services, rather than as citizens with rights to a certain standard of public provision. The language of "incentives" is especially important here; the ideal of marketization is that standards of all goods and services will be raised when competition between providers undercuts state monopolies. In both the US and UK, marketization has been accompanied by an emphasis on developing "human capital" through education, skills development, and training to increase people's chances of bettering themselves in the labor market. In this respect, where citizenship was previously understood to involve social insurance against the risk of unemployment, it is now redefined as an obligation to make oneself fit for the labor market (Roche, 1995). The emphasis on paid employment has been accompanied by real cuts in benefits to those without work. In the most extreme case of "incentivization," the US government introduced "workfare," a social program introduced to inculcate work-discipline in welfare recipients (King, 1991). In practice, of course, however disciplined and highly motivated, not all citizens can earn high wages and become consumers of private services. But one of the main effects of the restructuring of citizenship is that failure to become a good consumer is also privatized: it is constructed as a matter of personal responsibility, the failure to make the right, intelligent, and informed choices. In a consumer society, the poor are "flawed consumers" rather than citizens, deficient in the skills and know-how to exercise freedom and to compete with others in the market (Bauman, 1998).

It is not surprising, then, that neo-liberal policies have been accompanied by a polarization of wealth. Britain and the US are now in the bottom four of the most unequal societies in the developed world (with Portugal and Singapore), and inequalities in income have increased dramatically since the mid-'70s (Wilkinson and Pickett, 2009). This is a measure of growing citizen inequality in a straightforward sense in that it indicates growing numbers of people on welfare support and receiving low pay. It is also, however, an indication of even wider citizenship inequality, as those with higher incomes increasingly opt out of public services, while those who are not able to make the right life-style choices find it difficult to get out of poverty.

Defining and measuring poverty is itself political. The definition closest to Marshall's ideal of society is that of Peter Townsend. As we have seen, in Marshall's conception of citizenship, social rights are related to the idea that all citizens should be able to participate in a common standard of "civilized" life. On this understanding, citizenship and poverty are antithetical. In fact, in the years following the institution of the welfare state in Britain, it was assumed that poverty had been virtually eliminated; only poverty among the old, sick, and disabled remained a problem, and it was understood that it would soon be remedied by continuing economic expansion. Notoriously, Townsend re-discovered poverty in the 1960s. He opposed the definition of poverty on which previous assessments had been made, the "absolute" or "subsistence" definition. According to this definition of poverty, only those who do not have enough for the necessities of life are in poverty. Townsend argued that it was too restricted: the necessities of civilized life go beyond those required simply to meet animal needs. He defined poverty in relative terms, as the lack of goods which enable people to participate in everyday life:

> Individuals, families and groups in the population can be said to be in poverty when they lack the resources to obtain the types of diet, participate in the activities and have the living conditions and amenities that are customary, or are at least widely encouraged or approved, in the societies to which they belong. Their resources are so seriously below those commanded by the average individual or family that they are, in effect, excluded from ordinary living patterns, customs and activities. (Townsend, quoted in Scott, 1994: 78–9)

Although Townsend does not use the term "citizenship" in his work, his definition of poverty is complementary to Marshall's view of citizenship rights: poverty has consequences for citizenship where citizenship involves the rights to full participation in society.

Townsend's definition of poverty is used quite often in research carried out for NGOs like the Joseph Rowntree Foundation in Britain. It is difficult to use as a measurement of poverty because it is necessary to decide what should be included as customary, and exactly how much money is needed to live according to these standards. Both change over time; what is normal now would have been a luxury 50 years ago (a TV, or a phone, for example); and costs of items change relative to each other as well as rising with inflation. Townsend himself set the figure at 150 percent of the British unemployment benefit rate, after taking housing costs into account, and this was confirmed by a subsequent large-scale study of poverty in Britain in 1985. This means that all those on welfare benefits or state pensions in Britain are in poverty, as is a high proportion of those on low incomes. Evidently, then, since the numbers of unemployed and those employed on low wages have increased, so too have rates of poverty.

Governments prefer to use their own national poverty line definitions, which result in much lower figures. In member states of the European Union, the most common definition used is the European Poverty Line, which defines households as at risk of poverty if they have an income of less than 60 percent of the national average. This is a very crude measure, but easy to use in collecting survey data. In 2006/07, around 13 million people in the UK were living in households below this low-income threshold. This is around a fifth (22 percent) of the population. This proportion was rising for two years before this, after a number of years in which it had decreased (see The Poverty Site www.poverty.org.uk). In the United States, poverty continues to be defined in terms of absolute poverty. US citizens are poor when they have insufficient income for subsistence. The official poverty line is the level of income that allows for the provision of the necessities of life and is set each year for different states. However, the amount per a year that is supposed to meet basic household needs is too low, as the "basket" of goods it covers has not changed since it was developed in the 1950s. Schwarz argues that the official poverty line should be set much higher as it has lost touch with the actual needs of American families, which are very different now, and we should, therefore, be skeptical about statistics purporting to represent the extent of poverty in the US (Schwarz, 2005: 49–50). Even using this measure, however skewed to keep numbers low, roughly 12.5 percent of Americans were in poverty in 2008 (US Census Bureau: www.census.gov/hhes/www/poverty.html).

As Ruth Lister points out, people in poverty have long been "Othered" as moral lines are drawn between "us," the deservedly well-off or non-poor, and "them," who are inherently different. Historically, discourses of the "undeserving" poor and the "dangerous classes" have identified the poor as diseased and criminal (Lister, 2004). Contemporary understandings of the poor, even when well-intentioned, are entangled with such evaluations.

The most controversial term used to refer to the poor is "underclass." In the US, it both distinguishes the poor from the rest of society and, at the same time, sums up the behavior that keeps them in poverty. People who are poor over the long-term, it is argued, reproduce a "culture of poverty," using welfare to avoid working in paid employment and lacking motivation to integrate with the rest of society. The underclass is seen as made up of single mothers dependent on welfare and semi-criminal men who do not work, and is associated with a supposedly black lifestyle in which women have children by many fathers who do not provide for them. The large numbers of black people living in poverty in the ghettos of American cities are seen to make up an "underclass." In actual fact, most of the poor in the US do not live in urban areas and most are not black (Fainstein, 1996). Nevertheless, theorists of the "underclass" see it as reproducing poverty. In the US, young, unmarried, or childless men have no automatic right to state benefits; they have the right to insurance-based unemployment benefit, but growing numbers do not qualify for it because they have worked too little and made too few contributions. It is practically only single mothers who are eligible for the means-tested welfare benefit, Aid to Families with Dependent Children. Charles Murray, one of the most important proponents of the New Right view of the "underclass," argues from a rational choice perspective that welfare benefits make dependence on the state a more attractive possibility for many women than marriage or paid employment (Lister, 1996). The solution is to alter the rational choices of poor mothers by making them work for welfare.

In the 1980s, William Julius Wilson tried to produce a different understanding of the "underclass," arguing that it should be seen as an economic and social phenomenon rather than the result of rational individual choices. He argued that the "underclass" is synonymous with "the ghetto," the result of the black middle-classes moving out of the inner cities and the worsening economic prospects for the deprived African-Americans who remain there. In Wilson's view, the most important problem for members of the "underclass" is social isolation; many families in poor areas of the city experience long-term unemployment, and, because they have few contacts with those in steady jobs, welfare dependence becomes a way of life (Wilson, 1987). However, despite Wilson's stress on structural causes, his use of the term "underclass" is seen as too close to the moral terminology of the New Right to challenge their interpretation of urban poverty. As a result, he has abandoned the term, preferring "ghetto poor" (Silver, 1996).

In Europe, the term "socially excluded" is more commonly used to distinguish the poor from the rest of society. "Social exclusion" came to prominence in France in the mid-1980s to refer to growing unemployment, marginalization, and perceptions of a general increase in the precariousness of many people's lives (Lister, 2004: 75). Much of this was seen as a result of new social conditions: "the rise in long-term and recurrent unemployment and the growing instability of social relations ... family break-up, single-member households, social isolation, and the decline of class solidarity based on unions, workplaces and social networks" (Silver, 1996: 113). "Social exclusion" does not have the moral resonance of terms like "underclass." Indeed, it is quite closely linked to definitions of poverty as relative deprivation, delineating a group that is excluded from social norms rather than excluding themselves. It is widely used in EU policy documents and in Britain (a rare example of the UK adopting a European rather than a US policy discourse, Lister notes) (Lister, 2004: 76).

Nevertheless, many of the criticisms made of the term "underclass" have been applied also to "socially excluded." In the first place, it is argued that it still suggests that the poor are somehow fundamentally different from others in society. Norman Fainstein argues that the poor are not qualitatively different from the rest of the population; it is not their characteristics as a group we should consider in order to understand growing poverty. He argues that the whole family of terms – "underclass," "ghetto poor," and "excluded" – work "to deflect attention from the dynamics of economic and political processes which generate and reproduce the very populations and places which appear to lie under or outside of capitalist systems" (Fainstein, 1996: 154–5). Similarly, Giovanna Procacci argues that "social exclusion," suggesting as it does that the poor are "outside society," displaces and contains the problem of inequality. While "exclusion" suggests a static division of social space, with citizens inside and the poor outside, the idea of inequality points to the possibility of achieving equality. It, therefore, implies a more dynamic analysis of social institutions and the way in which they produce poverty (Procacci, 1996).

Second, although "social exclusion" does not refer exclusively to exclusion from the labor market, in the UK government policies to combat social exclusion have focused on ending poverty by getting people into paid employment. This has involved a mixture of incentives, including income support for households on low-wages as well as welfare-to-work schemes for single parents. The emphasis on paid work as the basis of citizenship is not new; it is a feature of all insurance-based systems in which welfare is tied to employment status. As Lydia Morris argues, however, the emphasis on paid work to end poverty is problematic because it does not take into account wider social changes that impact on social rights. Citizenship in the welfare state was premised on full, male employment and the nuclear family, consisting of a male breadwinner and female carer at home. For many people, the nuclear family is no longer a possibility (though it remains the ideal for most), and there are high rates of unemployment, particularly in areas where migrant workers were brought in to do the most insecure and poorly paid jobs. In such circumstances, it is unsurprising that single mothers and men in racialized minority groups are over-represented in poverty statistics. To stigmatize women for dependency on welfare in a context in which childcare facilities are still too often inadequate or too expensive is unjust. Similarly, when unemployment is high, even the jobs that white workers prefer not to do may not be available to men and women from racialized minorities (Morris, 1996).

Welfare-to-work schemes are premised on the assumption that well-paid jobs exist that welfare recipients refuse to take. Predictions that new technology would lead to massive unemployment as more jobs became redundant have not been borne out. Nevertheless, the idea that anyone can get a well-paid, secure job is also a dream. Neo-liberalization is, in part, a response to what were perceived as the labor market rigidities of Keynesian economic policy in the 1970s. As employers found it hard to get rid of or to redeploy workers protected by strong trades unions and strict employment law, it was difficult for firms to take a flexible approach to taking on new workers. This led to high rates of unemployment. Where resistance to neo-liberalization has been strong, while those in paid employment have good wages and social insurance packages, the long-term unemployed have little chance of joining them. Neo-liberal marketization is directed at the labor market, to introduce flexibility of labor contracts and low-wages to stimulate economic growth which should lead to low rates of static unemployment. A relatively high level of cyclical unemployment is considered necessary, however, in this type of system: firms make use of the available pool of workers, hiring and firing as necessary, and people go in and out of the labor market (Potužáková, 2007). Neo-liberalization leads to the creation of what are sometimes called "Mc-jobs": low paid, insecure, and with little expectation of job satisfaction or commitment. Paid work for everyone is not a solution to social exclusion, either in states that have subjected labor markets to neo-liberalization, or in those where it has been resisted; low wages and intermittent employment is a route to poverty as surely as long-term unemployment.

John Scott has proposed an imaginative strategy of social integration around differences in wealth. He argues that if poverty is seen in Townsend's terms as relative deprivation, it is, by definition, related to privilege. If people can be deprived by being excluded from public life,

they may also be *privileged* in relation to public life. Citizens may be
excluded, but they may also exclude. He suggests that a privilege line
could be drawn, at an income level above which it is possible to exclude
others from advantages by withdrawing into private benefits unavailable
to the majority of citizens (Scott, 1994). Policies aimed at ending social
exclusion should target the wealthy at least as much as the poor, using
taxation on income above a certain level to redistribute resources to a far
greater extent, and ending private education and healthcare. Such policies
would require global coordination; governments are reluctant to levy high
taxes on the wealthy and on corporations for fear that they will discourage investment, and encourage the rich to deposit their money in tax
havens out of the state's reach.

Unlike other types of citizens we will look at in this chapter, the poor
are not organized into a social movement. The labor movement is still
important to workers in certain sectors of the economy, and unions have
adapted to a changing workforce that no longer consists predominantly
of white, male heads of households. Traditionally, however, unions have
been concerned with workers' rights, not with poverty and exclusion. In
addition, the labor movement has been very much weakened by globalization, as its coordination across national borders has not matched the
growth of multinational corporations and flows of capital (Sklair, 2002).
It is very difficult for the poor to organize specifically around ending
poverty as citizens – in fact, historically, poverty has been associated with
the *removal* of civil and political rights (Lister, 2004: 164). In part, Lister
argues, these difficulties are related to identity; the very idea of admitting
that you are poor is shameful, especially where the poor are seen as
responsible for poverty. Combined with the fact that, by definition, poor
people have fewer resources than others, and that, divided by gender,
ethnicity, and age, they may find little in common, it would require an
extraordinary political will to turn being identified as "poor" from a
source of shame into a mark of political activism.

4.3   Citizenship, Sex, and Sexuality

The women's movement and the gay and lesbian movement have been
among the most prominent of social movements contesting the traditional
model of citizenship rights and trying to work out more inclusive models.
Although, as social movements, they developed quite separately, the issues
they raise are analytically linked. Both women's citizenship and rights in
relation to homosexuality problematize traditional roles for the sexes and

demonstrate how existing citizenship, far from affording rights to individuals as such, depends on the position people occupy in relation to the nuclear family.

The women's movement

The most important point of the recent feminist critique of liberal citizenship is that, developed from a male perspective, it has institutionalized a male norm. Contemporary feminists see women as incorporated into liberal democracy in a paradoxical and unjust way. As a result, they are continually faced with what is known as "the sameness–difference" dilemma. Should the women's movement focus on rights for women to be treated the same as men or on gender-specific rights, enabling women's differences from men to be valued and taken into account as the means of gaining genuine equality between the sexes?

As it is, there are three, quite contradictory ways in which women are excluded from full citizenship rights. First, women are discriminated against when they should have the same rights as men. Second, on the other hand, they are treated the same as men when only differential treatment would make genuine equality possible. In such cases, physical and historical differences are ignored which prevent women from actually participating in institutions and practices developed to suit men, even though they have the formal rights to do so. Third, however, some citizenship rights, notably social rights, are accorded differently to women and men and, in such cases, women are treated as inferior citizens. As feminists see it, the paradoxes and inconsistencies of women's citizenship are linked to the way in which they have developed secondarily to men's. Historically, until very recently, citizens have been male heads of households and women's citizenship has developed within the framework set by rights developed on this basis.

The first and second cases are exemplified by civil rights. In the past, feminists have put a good deal of energy into campaigns for equal rights for women to be treated as identical to men, to remove the barriers to women's participation in public life, and to try to ensure their protection in the private sphere. In the US in particular, many feminists continue to see equal rights as the most important aim of the women's movement. An example is maternity rights. Until the 1960s, many American employers had rules which compelled a pregnant woman to leave her job at a set time and forbidding her to return to work before a certain date. Maternity leave with pay was not provided and the right to return to work was not guaranteed. The initial impetus of feminist campaigns was to overturn such rules as discriminating against women. In the 1970s, they were found to be unconstitutional on the grounds that they infringed freedom of personal choice; it was decided that women should not *have* to go on maternity leave when pregnant. The current situation is that employers are bound to treat pregnancy and maternity no less favorably than any other illness or disability, or states of ill health which may also be suffered by men. Many feminists see this as unsatisfactory: pregnancy is specific to women and to describe it in such terms in order to make it gender-neutral is to capitulate to the male norm. Furthermore, in most states, paid maternity leave is covered only by insurance schemes which employers are under no obligation to provide, so that women who get pregnant are being discriminated against as women. However, "equal rights" feminists support the ruling, against "difference" feminists, on the grounds that to insist on special treatment for women would prevent them from competing on equal terms in the labor market and force them into economic dependence on men (Bacchi, 1990: chapter 5).

As Bacchi (1990) argues, the position of "equal rights" feminists in the US often seems extreme to feminists elsewhere. To a large extent, it is due to a lack of social rights; where women have a statutory right to paid maternity leave, the same problems do not arise. In such countries, the "difference" feminist position is much less risky for women, and it has become increasingly important. Feminists are now concerned that treating men and women as the same in law is ineffective as a means of realizing real equality between the sexes. The anti-discrimination rights gained in Europe and North America in the 1960s and 1970s, for example, now tend to be seen as ineffective precisely because they fail to take into account women's particular embodiment and the way in which their historically specific circumstances differ from those of men. Equal pay legislation, for example, which stated that all workers should get equal pay for doing the same jobs, was of little use because men and women tend to do different kinds of jobs. In the British case, the European Court of Justice ruled against this law and it has now been changed: comparison must now be made between work of equal *value*. However, it remains the case that the basis of comparison is the male norm insofar as women must show the work they do to be of equal value to the better-paid work done by men. Unsurprisingly, perhaps, the job evaluation surveys on which judgments of equal worth are based generally reproduce the undervaluation of women's work that already exists in society (Frazer and Lacey, 1993: 86).

The third case is exemplified by gender-differentiated social rights. Women are disproportionately represented in welfare states, both as beneficiaries and also as workers in the health, social, and education services. Women are often employed intermittently in paid work in order to care for their families when children are young; they sometimes work part-time as families are growing up, and even when they work full-time, they are almost always paid less than men. As a result, women face a higher risk of poverty than men throughout their lives. This is especially true of female-headed households. Single parents, usually women, who cannot afford childcare, and older women who often do not have occupational pensions and who have outlived or separated from their husbands are especially likely to be in receipt of welfare payments (Lister, 2004: 55). Feminists see what is sometimes called the "feminization of poverty" as the consequence of taking men as the norm. Social rights are linked to a male norm of continuous, full-time employment in the labor market, intended to be interrupted only, in the worst cases, by unfortunate accidents or illness against which the worker has insured himself. However, this type of work depends on unseen and unpaid work in the domestic sphere, which is mainly done by women.

Feminists have linked women's inferior social rights to their inferior political rights. Women, it is argued, have less power in society than men. It is for this reason that some feminists argue that the welfare state is patriarchal. A number of Scandinavian feminists in particular, writing in a context in which social rights for women are more extensive than anywhere else in the world, have argued that women's inferior citizenship is due to their lack of decision-making power, both within welfare institutions themselves and also in the institutions of representational government. Although women are employed in large numbers in the public sector, they occupy positions similar to those they occupy in the private sector, low in the bureaucratic hierarchies, so that they do not make decisions about how institutions are organized. It is also argued that, although women have the same formal political rights as men to vote and to stand for election, in practice very few women participate in "high politics." This is seen as due to straightforward discrimination on the part of political parties who propose members for election and of electors themselves, and also to the fact that it requires long hours which are incompatible with women's domestic responsibilities. It is argued, therefore, that although social rights are valuable in allowing women to escape subordination from individual men in the home, if women then become dependent on a state over which they have no control, they have done little more than exchange private patriarchy for public patriarchy (Hernes, 1984; Siim, 1988).

In recent years, then, the focus of the women's movement has been on political rights, both on the part of feminist theorists and movement activists. This represents a significant shift on the part of the second-wave feminist movement which, unlike that of the nineteenth century, was rather suspicious of the state. Second-wave feminism was dominated by socialist and radical feminists who have tended to see the state in functionalist terms as reproductive of capitalism and patriarchy, and who have preferred to direct their activities elsewhere. In many respects, this strategy has proved very fruitful. The success of the slogan "the personal is political" is indicative of the politicizing of subjectivity and personal relations, for example, and many of the institutions set up by the movement, such as the centers dealing with rape and domestic violence, have had a significant impact on perceptions and practices. Arguably, as we saw in chapter 3, these forms of politics are as important to women's citizenship as formal rights to political participation. It has, of course, also been the case that some second-wave feminists have been engaged with issues of law and public policy, often working through trade unions in Europe, or through interest groups such as the National Organization for Women in the US. It is, however, relatively recently that the issue of women's representation as such has been raised.

The discussion of political rights for women, however, exemplifies another prominent dilemma in recent feminist thought and action, that raised by the issue of essentialism. It is useful to distinguish two different types of essentialism used in this debate. Following Diana Fuss (1989), the first may be identified as "real essentialism." Derived from Aristotle, it indicates that the essence of something or someone is what is irreducible and unchangeable about it or them. It is also the most common use of the term in feminist theory. It is used to describe the belief that women are intrinsically and unalterably different from men. The most obvious difference in this respect is in reproductive capacities and there is considerable discussion concerning the intrinsic importance of this aspect of sexual difference. However, the term is also applied – pejoratively – to those who agree with Carol Gilligan (1993) that women have a "different voice" from men in relation to moral issues: context specific and relationship oriented rather than based on adherence to universal moral principles. The second use Fuss calls "nominal essentialism." The essence of someone or something here consists in what remains the same across the different uses of a term, a classification made in language. She argues that social constructionists, those who take as their starting point the view that there are no intrinsic, fundamental differences between women and men, may be nominal essentialists where they focus on historically and socially specific differences between the sexes, on "the production and organization of differences" (Fuss, 1989: 2). In relation to reproductive capacities, for example, they argue that what is important is the way in which perceived differences are used to make a *social* difference between the sexes as stereotypical mothers and fathers of children. Furthermore, social constructionists contend that there are social differences between women in this respect which are as important as those between men and women. Linda Nicholson (1983), for example, discusses how white women in nineteenth-century America were excluded from public activities and confined to the home in order to maximize their capacities to bear children, while, as soon as they were no longer commodities to be bought and sold, black children were much less valued and black women were socially positioned as menial workers. As a result, she argues, the orientation toward care analyzed by Gilligan as specific to women would more appropriately be applied to white women in a particular, historically specific situation; women, as such, do not have a "different voice," since women do not speak with a single voice at all (Nicholson, 1983). Nevertheless, as Fuss argues, although social constructionists oppose "real essentialism," the perspective retains a degree of – unacknowledged – "nominal essentialism" insofar as they continue to classify the world as divided into "men" and "women." As she puts it, "Some minimal point of commonality and continuity necessitates at least the linguistic retention of these particular terms" (Fuss, 1989: 4). Although "women" are treated as a heterogeneous social group, rather than as a "natural kind," there is, nevertheless, the assumption that such a group can, and should, be seen as sociologically relevant.

The importance of Fuss's distinction becomes evident when we look at the issue of political rights. It has been argued by feminists that, given the under-representation of women in political institutions, women need special rights in order to achieve equality with men in this respect. Anne Phillips, one of the most prominent proponents of this view, puts forward the argument that there should be quotas to increase women's presence in the political process in order to enable them to influence policies affecting women (Phillips, 1991, 1995). Phillips actually explicitly rejects essentialism on the grounds that women are not all the same and do not share the same interests. Furthermore, her argument is not that women in political institutions should be seen as *representing* women. As she points out, representation in liberal democracies is based on geographical area or, in the case of proportional representation, on promises of action, not on the direct representation of social groups. In fact, such representation is impossible if the category "women" is seen in pluralist terms, as a heterogeneous group of cross-cutting and even conflicting identities: speaking in the name of "women" could only mean favoring some and excluding others. Nevertheless, her most compelling argument for the presence of women in the political process is that, because women share certain experiences, they will articulate views which would not otherwise be heard. This argument makes little sense without the assumption that women share a certain perspective which makes them different from men, even though Phillips qualifies her argument by saying that there are no guarantees that this is the case (Nash, 1997). She is, then, arguing for special political rights for women on the grounds that there *may* be a real, though not necessarily natural, difference between the sexes.

The essentialist assumptions of Phillips's argument for political rights are clear in contrast to the more resolutely anti-essentialist position of Judith Butler (1993). In her view, *any* use of the term "women" to designate a social group is misguided. In terms of the distinction articulated by Fuss, she argues against real *and* nominalist essentialism. Butler maintains that "women" does not exist outside performances which bring the identity into practice. Any representation of women as an existing social group, in feminist debates and in the campaigns of the women's movement, just as much as in more obviously repressive instances of the use of the term, is actually productive of that categorization rather than the representation of a given reality.

According to Butler, the reification and regulation of gender relations produced in discourse are precisely what feminists should militate against. Far from arguing for political rights for women, since "the feminist subject turns out to be discursively constituted by the very political system that is supposed to facilitate its emancipation ... an uncritical appeal to such a system for the emancipation of 'women' will be clearly self-defeating" (Butler, 1990: 2). Feminists should be concerned rather to disrupt and problematize the use of the term "women" wherever possible in order to overturn the "heterosexist matrix" which requires the duality of the sexes. Butler's work has been as influential in queer theory as in feminist theory and we will return to this point in the following section. For the moment, however, it is important to note that, for Butler, and for other post-structuralist feminists, the invocation of "women" for political purposes makes such a goal impossible. It contributes to the rigidity of the sexual division by foreclosing in advance the emergence of new identities which could transform or expand existing sexual differences. In this way, feminism is part of the problem because it contributes to the reification of sexual difference rather than to the dissolution of the problem itself.

Phillips's proposals and Butler's arguments against any feminist representation of women as a social group illustrate the polarity of feminist views in the current debates on essentialism. There is no obvious resolution to the conflict. However, in practical terms, it is also the case that the women's movement is, and arguably always has been, involved in politics of both kinds. Not only in Scandinavia but in other liberal democracies like Britain, there have been campaigns for quotas for women MPs, for example. At the same time, there has been continual resistance on the part of women to be subsumed under a particular categorization of "women." This resistance may sometimes result in demands for rights to "sameness," but if this is done in a context in which there are institutional structures allowing for differences between the sexes in specific contexts – such as the right to maternity leave, for example – while there may be a tension between the two strategies, they are not necessarily incompatible. Group rights for women may be necessary in specific cases, but it is also necessary to disrupt assumptions about how individual women live as individuals who happen also to be identified as women. Otherwise, group rights "freeze" identities, and prove too constraining, both for those who do not easily fit the group identities available, and also in terms of the wider social change for which the women's movement has always aimed (Riley, 1988; Nash, 1998).

The gay and lesbian movement and queer politics

There is an obvious connection between campaigns for rights for women and rights for sexual minorities insofar as both challenge the way in which citizenship has historically been rooted in patriarchy. Both the feminist movement and the lesbian and gay movement demand rights for individuals to live on equal terms outside the traditional nuclear family which has structured citizenship rights in the past. It might be expected, therefore, that feminists and lesbians and gay men would have a common cause against "compulsory heterosexuality" which relegates those who do not conform to inferior citizenship rights. However, although both movements have used the term to analyze society, in practice, the relationships between the three groups have been much more complex. There have been conflicts between gay men and radical feminists who have opposed what they take to be a masculine, libertarian lifestyle; gay men and lesbians, who often have very different lifestyles and sexual practices; and between "political lesbians," who see themselves as the vanguard of feminism, and other lesbians, who may or may not be feminists and who resist the de-sexualizing of lesbianism by political lesbians (Edwards, 1994). These differences have meant that it has generally proved impossible to present a united front. In recent years, however, feminists and those who identify as "queer" have come together to some extent, at least theoretically.

Paradoxically, however, what makes it possible for individuals to unite under the "queer" banner is the way that queer politics challenges the very identities on which the older movements were based.

The struggle for gay citizenship rights began in the 1960s, alongside other social movements of the time. The gay liberation movement was founded in the US in 1969, following the Stonewall riot, in which the regulars of a gay bar in New York fought back after years of being raided by the police. Similar movements were established a little later in most Western European countries. Proposing a revolutionary anti-capitalist, anti-family, and anti-medical analysis of gay oppression, the movement was short-lived and soon gave way to more moderate organizations campaigning for reform. Campaigns for the extension of citizenship rights enjoyed by the majority to be extended to sexual minorities began to be well supported (Evans, 1993: 114–17; Weeks, 1993: 198). Lesbians, often involved in the initial impetus of the gay liberation movement, were less involved in the campaigns for legal rights and against police harassment which became the main themes of the gay movement. Historically, lesbians have suffered more from invisibility than from legal repression, since lesbianism has never been illegal, though it has been stigmatized. They have, however, participated in the important cultural politics of the movement which have made gay and lesbian lifestyles visible and viable. There is no doubt of its success in this respect. Every city now has gay bars, many have a gay neighborhood, and the impact of the movement on the media, popular culture, and fashion is evident everywhere. "Lipstick" lesbianism, in particular, has been seen as contributing to the recent fashion for gay images. However, with less disposable income than men, women have not been able to exert "consumer power" to the same extent as men and lesbians tend to be less visible in commercial spaces, too.

In terms of citizenship rights, for the most part, the gay movement has focused on equalizing civil rights between heterosexuals, gay men, and lesbians (to the extent that they share the same legal interests). The age of consent to sex, different everywhere but consistently higher for gay men in most countries until recently, has been targeted as blatantly discriminatory. Following a European Union ruling against Britain in 1997, the age of consent is now equal in most countries of Europe. In the US, it varies across different states. There have also been campaigns to legalize gay marriages, which would also bring a number of other rights from which gay partners are otherwise excluded, including immigration rights, pension benefits, and the possibility of legally adopting children. Same-sex partners may now marry in some European countries, including Holland, Spain, and Sweden, and in some of the states of the US. In the UK and elsewhere, including France and Portugal, couples who are united in a "civil partnership" have the same rights as married couples, but there is no religious component to the ceremony. Another continuing injustice is employment rights. In Britain and elsewhere, there are no laws protecting against discrimination for sexual orientation. This leaves gay people open to hiring and firing discrimination, harassment or unequal pay, and dismissal for reasons of sexual orientation. In the US, this issue came to the fore in the 1990s with the question of whether gay men and lesbians should be allowed to serve in the armed forces. The highly unsatisfactory solution of "don't ask, don't tell," while admitting that there are gays and lesbians in the military, gives them no legal rights should they ever publicly affirm their sexuality. Finally, among the most serious cases of the continuing exclusion of gay men from civil rights is the harassment by the police to which they are subject, and the failure of the police to protect them from harassment and violence by other men. There are laws, for example, to which only gay men are subject, although they are supposed to be applicable to all citizens, regardless of sexual orientation. Only gay men, for example, are prosecuted for sodomy, as an "indecent act."

Andrew Sullivan (1995) neatly summarizes arguments for equal citizenship rights for lesbians and gay men. It would mean, he argues, quite simply extending the same civil rights to homosexuals as those enjoyed by other citizens:

> an end to all proactive discrimination by the state against homosexuals. That means an end to sodomy laws that apply only to homosexuals; a recourse to the courts if there is not equal protection of heterosexuals and homosexuals in law enforcement; an equal legal age of consent to sexual activity for heterosexuals and homosexuals, where such regulations apply; inclusion of the facts about homosexuality in the curriculum of every government-funded school ...; recourse to the courts if any government body or agency can be proven to be engaged in discrimination against homosexual employees; equal opportunity and inclusion in the military; and legal homosexual marriage and divorce. (Sullivan, 1995: 171–2)

It is probable that no gay activist would disagree with such a list of rights. However, there is considerable debate about the compatibility of campaigning for citizenship rights with other, potentially more radical, aims to which the gay and lesbian movement might, and arguably should, aspire. Again, as in the case of the women's movement, the question turns on the issue of essentialism.

The problem is that in order to gain citizenship rights, gays and lesbians have, quite reasonably, adopted the strategy of describing themselves as a "sexual minority." This is seen as the only realistic way to gain a hearing for the extension of citizenship rights in liberal democracy. They are claimed as "minority rights," to be granted to those who are not responsible for their sexual orientation and who should not, therefore, be persecuted and oppressed for it. This strategy depends, then, on the essentialist view that homosexuality is an innate disposition. It fits with the conservative, medicalized view of gays and lesbians as born, not made. Although this is certainly the belief of most self-identified gays and lesbians, it is at odds with the arguments of sociologists. They are much more likely to see homosexuality, like heterosexuality, as a historically and culturally specific identity rather than an innate disposition: we learn to see ourselves as having a "sexuality" only when such a view is socially available (Weeks, 1986). This anti-essentialist view is also more likely to be held by the younger generation of "queer" activists, who reject the fixity of the "sexual minority" claim in favor of a more disruptive challenge to the status quo.

From a queer perspective, claims for "minority rights" actually contribute to the dominance of an understanding of different sexualities as "normal" or "abnormal." This means that, at best, gays and lesbians can only ever be tolerated, since they will always be the abnormal minority (Herman, 1993: 251). What queer activists agitate for is rather the disruption of all fixed identities: lesbian, gay, bisexual, transsexual, and "still searching." This challenge extends to the naturalized links between reproductive capacities, gender identity, and sexual desire prescribed as normal by "the heterosexist matrix" in which masculine males must desire feminine females and vice versa. Queer practices may disrupt, as Judith Butler (1990) argues, by parodying and subverting gendered sexual identities, showing that they are not the expression of innate, natural tendencies but are nothing but performances. To quote a letter from a debate in the San Francisco *Bay Times*, "There is a growing consciousness that a person's sexual identity (and gender identity) need not be etched in stone, that it can be fluid rather than static, that one has the right to PLAY with whomever one wishes to play with (as long as it's consensual), that the either/or dichotomy ('you're either gay or straight' is only one example of this) is oppressive no matter who's pushing it" (quoted in Gamson, 1996: 406).

In practice, queer activism is associated with "in your face" demonstrations such as "kiss-ins" which "mimic the privileges of normality" (Berlant and Freeman, quoted in Gamson, 1996: 409), the return of camp styles and other forms of irony, "mixed" venues for men and women, and "gender-fuck" aesthetics like the photography of Della Grace in which lesbians are shown using the paraphernalia of gay male desire (sometimes even including facial hair) (Mort, 1994). Older self-identified gays and lesbians who find "queer" problematic are concerned about the blurring of boundaries it promotes. The inclusion of bisexuals, transsexuals, and even heterosexuals who feel confined by conventional sexual expression, as "queer" removes the solid political ground they have struggled to mark out as a minority, and which provides the basis from which rights claims are made. This is indeed a problem as liberal democracy accords right to groups only if their membership is clear. A judgment in Colorado, for example, found that there was no case for outlawing discrimination against gay men, lesbians, or bisexuals since "We don't have a group that is easily confinable" (the Colorado solicitor-general, quoted in Gamson, 1996: 410).

As Steven Seidman (1993: 132) has argued, anti-essentialist queer activists tend to see identity itself as the main axis of domination. This is problematic insofar as the assertion of collective identity is necessary to militate against institutional forms which exclude lesbians and gays from full citizenship, so perpetuating violence and injustice. In this sense, the conflict between essentialist and anti-essentialist strategies is similar in the case of feminist and queer politics. However, it is not so easy to see how the two strategies can be reconciled in practice. If, as Sullivan (1995) argues, equal citizenship for lesbians and gays requires nothing more in principle than the extension of existing rights to all individuals, it is not clear that this commits those individuals as individuals to any particular sexual identity indefinitely. It is clear, then, that it is possible to affirm the stable identities with secure boundaries the political system requires, without individuals necessarily feeling bound by such identities. However, it is also clear that the public disruption of fixed identities is problematic so long as citizenship rights have not been extended to gays and lesbians. So while both strategies are currently being pursued in practice, given the dangers each one presents for the other, the outcome is far from assured.

4.4   Citizenship, Racialization, and Ethnicity

The themes of exclusion and inclusion in relation to a citizenship model premised on a white male norm are continued in debates around citizenship, "race," and ethnicity. In these debates, however, the social identities in question are highly contested and the very terms used to discuss the issues are controversial in contemporary society.

In this text, and commonly elsewhere, "race" is in "scare quotes" because it is so closely implicated in racism. Developed in a quasi-scientific biological discourse in the nineteenth century, it referred to different species of persons, hierarchically ordered as naturally superior and inferior. This use of the term is now discredited. It is generally held, among sociologists and biologists at any rate, that humans are of the same genetic stock and that there is a continuum of individuals in terms of any of the features used to distinguish them – color, size, intelligence, and so on – rather than distinct groups which exist as "natural kinds." Nevertheless, claims about "race" are still used to distinguish people in social life more widely. It is therefore important to study how individuals are assigned to different "races" and the inequalities which are produced as a result. The difficulty then becomes how to avoid confusing the concept "race" with its referent while studying groups distinguished in this way. A common solution for sociologists is to think in terms of "racialized" groups, to which characteristics are socially attributed on the grounds of race. It is then possible to examine differences between groups of citizens in terms of common social position and treatment, without supposing that the individuals who make up such groups actually possess the racial characteristics attributed to them.

The term "ethnicity" is somewhat less commonly used, though its contestation in cultural politics is increasing. Although it is, therefore, less "dangerous" than "race," the two terms are often closely connected. In Europe, "ethnicity" is used to denote cultural difference, but only those groups distinguished by color are normally referred to as "ethnic groups." Italians, Poles, and Ukrainians are rarely designated in this way (Mason, 1995: 15). In this respect, ethnic minorities are racialized groups. In North America, where immigration is much more established as the norm, this is not always the case: it is more common to refer to white people as belonging to ethnic groups. The question of the interrelation of "race" and ethnicity is further complicated because what is called "new racism" calls for the exclusion of minorities from the nation on the basis of their unassimilable cultural difference, without grounding this in biological difference. At the same time, "ethnicity" is increasingly mobilized in political struggles as a self-descriptive term to represent cultural identity. In many countries, arguments concerning the need for culturally differentiated citizenship rights are now made as the only way in which racialized ethnic minorities can be assured of respect on the part of the majorities with whom they must live.

In this section, we will briefly analyze the history of citizenship with regard to "race" and ethnicity, charting in particular the shift from assimilation to differentiated citizenship rights. Assimilation as a model of integrating immigrants into mainstream society is far from obsolete. On the contrary, it has continued to be favored by policy-makers in some European countries, and it is becoming increasingly popular again everywhere as multiculturalism comes into question. Nevertheless, it now coexists alongside demands for group rights in the name of equal respect for all citizens in multicultural societies.

Immigration, assimilation, and "new racism"

"Racial" or ethnic minority groups take many different forms in relation to the majority society of which they form a part. Some societies define themselves as multicultural. In India, for example, the criminal law is uniform, recognizing only individuals, while each religious community is governed by its own civil laws. The Indian citizen has, then, a kind of dual identity as a member of a religious community and as an individual (Parekh, 1993). In the West, however, the mono-cultural nation-state is the dominant model. In such societies, citizens are supposed to enjoy identical rights as members of a common national culture. Marshall certainly saw citizenship rights in this way: on one hand, they enable citizens to participate in the common standards of civilization; on the other, they contribute to social solidarity, unifying the nation in a shared sense of community (Marshall, 1992). As Will Kymlicka (1995: 236) points out, Marshall's understanding of citizenship rights is somewhat paradoxical: he sees them not only as fostering a common culture, but also as presupposing it. In fact, many European countries have always contained large cultural minorities: Bretons in France, Catalans in Spain, and so on. Some Western European countries, such as Britain, Belgium, and Switzerland, may well be described as multinational, where "nation" means "a historical community, more or less institutionally complete, occupying a given territory or homeland, sharing a distinct language and culture" (Kymlicka, 1995: 11). New World nations, such as Australia, Canada, and the United States, are undoubtedly multicultural since they are made up of immigrants from different cultural and linguistic backgrounds, and, since they all contain native First Nations, they are multinational, too. Despite the fact that it has virtually never been realized, however, the dominant model of a culturally homogeneous nation has nevertheless posed problems for the minorities who live and work in these countries.

The very issue of whether or not immigrants are entitled to citizenship is linked to the homogenizing nation-state. There are two ideal-typical ways of attributing citizenship rights at birth. Some states traditionally grant citizenship to all those born within the state's territory (*jus soli*). Others grant it according to the citizenship of the baby's parents (*jus sanguinis*). In practice, countries now have complicated criteria for grant-ing citizenship, so that these ideal-types are not so clear cut. It is also possible to achieve citizenship as an adult through naturalization. All countries allow naturalization, though some encourage it, while others actively discourage foreigners from applying for citizenship and decisions are discretionary. In all cases, applicants have to prove their commitment to the country of choice. As a minimum, this almost always involves real or effective residence in the state's territory (*jus domicili*) (Hammar, 1990: 72–7).

New World states are often described as "countries of immigration" because a large proportion of citizens were born elsewhere or are descended from people who came to the country relatively recently. "Countries of immigration" typically grant citizenship to all babies born within the ter-ritory of the state, as the US does, as well as to the children of citizens born abroad, and they also have relatively easy procedures for naturaliza-tion. Western European states all now contain large minorities from elsewhere, but they differ in their attribution of citizenship according to the model of the relation between nation and state they embody. Colonialism has been an important factor in labor migration since many people have come from ex-colonies to the over-developed metropolitan centers. In the British case, those who arrived before 1962 from ex-colonies had the full citizenship rights attributed to all those born on British territory. Since then, however, British citizenship has moved closer to *jus sanguinis* and it is now limited to those with a parent or grandpar-ent born in the country – mostly whites. Immigrants who arrived after the 1970s have a status closer to that of migrant workers in other European countries: short-term contracts as workers and no long-term rights of settlement. Citizenship in France, which has long been seen as exemplary of civic nationalism in Europe, although still based on *jus soli*, has also become relatively more closed. Until recently, second-generation migrants were all attributed French citizenship at birth and naturalization was actively encouraged as a policy to assist assimilation and to increase the French population. In recent years, however, rights of automatic citizen-ship have been brought into question in relation to second-generation Algerians, apparently because of the difficulty of assimilating Muslims into a secular society (Oommen, 1997: 165). In contrast, Germany has been taken as exemplary of an ethnic nation and citizenship has been traditionally based on *jus sanguinis*: traditionally, it is blood rather than the law that makes the German nation. This led to the anomalous situa-tion in which Eastern Europeans of German descent were legally citizens of the Federal Republic of Germany even before unification of East and West in 1990, while people of Turkish descent born and bred in Germany had to apply for naturalization. In recent years, however, naturalization, which was very difficult, has been liberalized, and the principle of *jus sanguinis* has been supplemented with that of *jus soli*: children born to foreign parents may now be attributed dual nationality, and they may choose to become German citizens when they reach adulthood (Kivisto and Faist, 2007: 119). European countries, it seems, are converging around citizenship criteria to include some racialized groups, where individuals have shown commitment to the state, whilst retaining tight control over immigration (Brubaker, 1992, 2002). The fact that dual nationality has been growing, as a legal possibility allowed by states and as a status that is increasingly taken up in practice, is further evidence that citizenship is increasingly seen as a civic status: states are allowing the links between citizenship and ethnic nationality to be loosened (Kivisto and Faist, 2007).

This is a relatively new departure. Citizenship always involves more than simply a matter of legal rights. Assimilationism is the name that is commonly used for the "melting pot" ideal of incorporation into the civic nation that was such a prominent ideal of immigration into the US since as early as the eighteenth century. In the "melting pot," immigrants are supposed to give up distinctive cultural identities so that everyone converges on the norms of the civic nation. In fact, however, civic norms are never abstract: they are always concretized in particular cultural forms. Furthermore, dominant forms of the civic nation are those with which elite groups are most at home. In order to assimilate, people do not learn norms of civic life in the abstract; they learn how to express civil competence in new concrete ways: "as Protestants rather than Catholics or Jews, as Anglos rather than as Mexicans, as whites rather than as blacks, as northwestern Europeans rather than as southern or eastern ones" (Alexander, 2006: 422). As a result, there have long been contestations of this ideal in the US, especially as it has grown more diverse with waves of immigration from different parts of the world. An alternative image of the American nation is that of the "salad bowl," in which migrants retain distinct identities as "hyphenated" Americans. According to Alexander, however, this remains close to the older model of assimilation insofar as "the center" of American life, to which "hyphens" attach, is not really questioned. The dominant culture takes up some of the "flavor" of other contributions – for example, the way in which Jewish writers like Saul Bellow and Phillip Roth have contributed to creating America's own image of itself. But hierarchies in the valuation of the cultural traits of racialized groups, especially those who identify as "African-American," make the "salad bowl" as problematic as the "melting pot" (Alexander, 2006; Kivisto and Faist, 2007).

When Western Europe states invited immigration to re-build economies after World War II, they adopted a model of assimilationism that closely approximated the ideal of the "melting pot." This model has had two interrelated elements in this context. First, it has been closely linked to the control of numbers of immigrants. This has been a feature of the recent histories of all Western states, including "countries of immigration" which now have tight restrictions and quotas for the admission of migrants to live and work within their territories. In the words of Roy Hattersley, a British politician, speaking in the 1960s, "Integration without control is impossible, but control without integration is indefensible" (Solomos, 1993: 84). The rationale behind this view is that the national majority will not accept large numbers of immigrants, so that in the interests of social and racial harmony there must be restrictions. Second, the latter half of Hattersley's phrase makes clear the further connection between assimilationism and race relations policies in legislation against racism. Most Western states have laws banning discrimination against individuals on the basis of race, color, or ethnic origin. They were passed with the explicit aim of defusing conflicts between white and black and to promote the integration of immigrants into the fundamental institutions of the wider society. However, where such legislation exists, it has not ended either racial discrimination or the systematic disadvantage suffered by racialized groups. Although there is diversity in the socio-economic situations of ethnic minorities across Europe, in general, non-whites are more likely to be disadvantaged in terms of pay, unemployment, and welfare provision (Lister, 2004: 61–3).

At the very least, then, the assimilationist model of immigration has failed to ensure equal rights for all citizens of the nation-state. However, the more serious charge against it is that it may actually contribute to racism. In supposing that racial harmony can only be achieved by absorbing minority groups into the wider society, it contributes to the view that each nation has its own cultural values and way of life such that it cannot tolerate sharing its territory with those of another culture. The view is actively promoted in "new racism," explicitly promoted by neo-fascist groups across Europe. Unlike older versions of racism, it is not premised on the supposed biological superiority of one race over another. What is at issue is cultural difference: it is held that all ethnic and racial groups are equal, but it is "natural" that members of different cultures should feel threatened if they have to share their territory with those who live according to incompatible cultural norms (Barker, 1981). In practice, "new racism" legitimates violence against members of racialized groups who do not belong to the majority nation and may lead to calls for their repatriation – a genuine, if impracticable, possibility where minorities are not citizens. Although assimilationism differs from "new racism" by calling for tolerance on the part of the white majority, it mirrors it by supposing that it is only insofar as members of ethnic minority groups are few in number and indistinguishable from the white majority that they can be tolerated. Like "new racism," assimilationism makes racialized minorities the "problem" in race relations, not racism.

Multiculturalism, group-differentiated rights, and "new assimilationism"

From the 1970s, increasing criticisms of assimilationism, whether "melting pot" or "salad bowl," led to adoption of multiculturalism as an ideal in many countries. It began in Canada and spread from there to the US, Australia, and New Zealand and also to some Northern European countries like Britain, Scandinavia, Holland, Belgium, and Switzerland. At the turn of the twenty-first century, however, multiculturalism itself is under serious strain as an ideal model for the integration of recent migrants into mainstream society. Criticisms of multiculturalism have grown, especially following the terrorist activities of Muslim fundamentalists since 9/11 because it is seen as fostering segregation rather than the integration of all citizens into civic culture, as working against social solidarity, and as facilitating the oppression of women. As a result, there is now a return of arguments for assimilationism, but this time for a "new assimiliation-ism" which encourages respect for diversity as well as for common values and national solidarity.

As a prominent advocate of multiculturalism, Will Kymlicka has argued that it is the only justifiable liberal policy. This is important since citizenship rights in the West are based on the liberal tradition. It is also surprising since liberals have generally held that the public sphere, including state institutions and the law, should be value-neutral and that cultural identity should be relevant only in the private sphere. However, the presence of cultural minorities who come from significantly different backgrounds to those of the majority makes it obvious the public sphere is not neutral: legal rights premised on the individual, assumptions concerning children's education, the role of the family in society, the language that is used in public institutions, the celebration of public holidays, and so on are all culturally specific. In fact, it is not possible to be neutral in such matters. Supposed universality, therefore, is a mask for the dominance of one culture over others. As Kymlicka sees it, there is an impeccable liberal argument for individual freedom which follows as a consequence of acknowledging the cultural specificity of liberal institutions. The central liberal tenet is that individuals should be free to choose their own lifestyles. It is this premise that makes liberals view cultural rights with suspicion, since they are opposed to forcing any individual to conform to a set of group values. However, as Kymlicka points out, in order to make choices, there have to be valuable ways of life to choose from. It is culture – traditions, history, and language – which gives choices meaning, makes them comprehensible, vivid, and desirable to us. Therefore, in the name of individual freedom, cultural differences should be upheld and protected (Kymlicka, 1995).

Kymlicka analyzes multiculturalism into two kinds, each of which is now a somewhat different issue with respect to group-differentiated rights in liberal democracies. The first he calls "multinationalism." Multinational societies contain within them minorities which, under different circumstances, might have retained or established their own sovereign governments, but which have been incorporated into a single state, either voluntarily through federation, or as a result of conquest. The US, he argues, is of this kind, containing American Indians, Puerto Ricans, the descendants of Mexicans (Chicanos), Hawaiians, and others (Kymlicka, 1995: 11). Typically, demands for rights from these groups are for rights to some kind of self-government as a separate nation. Quebec has achieved such status in Canada, for example, through the federal division of powers which gave the province extensive powers over language, education, culture, and immigration. Native peoples in North America have also gained considerable rights to self-determination through the system of reserved lands within which they have increasing control over health, education, family law, policing, criminal justice, and resource development (1995: 29–30). Legitimate multinationalism, in Kymlicka's view, results in virtually parallel sets of citizenship rights which overlap only to some extent in common rights for all.

The second type of multiculturalism he calls "polyethnicity." Societies into which there has been migration are of this type. Polyethnic societies are those in which immigrants participate in the public institutions of the dominant culture, but maintain some distinctive ways of life in terms of customs, religion, language, dress, food, and so on. Again, the US is a good example. Immigrants have been expected to conform to the English-speaking institutions of the public sphere and, although tolerated in private, it is only since the 1970s that the expression of different cultural heritages has been encouraged in public. Kymlicka argues that these groups do not require such extensive group-differentiated rights as nations. Their main aim is to be integrated into the multicultural society of which they are a part and to enjoy equal respect with other citizens. Minority groups in a polyethnic society will generally enjoy those rights common to all citizens, in his view. They should also, however, have *some* distinctive rights, in order to avoid disadvantages suffered as a result of their difference from the dominant culture and to combat racism (Kymlicka, 1995: 30–1).

To a limited extent, distinctive rights have been granted to ethnic minorities in some countries. In Britain, for example, Jews and Muslims are exempt from laws which would make it impossible for them to slaughter animals in accordance with their traditional methods, and Sikhs may wear their turbans instead of the crash helmets required by law. In addition, in recent years, Muslims, Seventh Day Adventists, and Hindus have won the right, already enjoyed by Christians and Jews, to government funding for schools in which the curriculum will be organized around these religious faiths. This has been very controversial because of the importance given to education in forming personal and social identity. Indeed, multiculturalism in mainstream education is perhaps the most highly developed aspect of multicultural policies around the world. It involves the recognition of the history, literature, and religion of cultural minorities, and often the celebration of different festival days. Although it is not actually a legal right as such, multicultural education is seen as offering children from minority groups genuine equal access to educational opportunities, as well as encouraging tolerance, if not understanding, from the majority population. In a sense, then, and paradoxically, faith schools are seen as opting out of multiculturalism because they have much more control over the curriculum and the intake of pupils than do mainstream schools. Most controversially, the possibility of institutionalizing Shari'a law has been proposed and debated in Canada, which already allowed Jewish and Catholic organizations to set up arbitration tribunals to regulate family disputes. The issue was resolved in this case when the government decided to equalize the communities, not by allowing Muslim courts, but by closing down Jewish and Catholic ones instead. There are ongoing campaigns both for and against introducing Shari'a law in Canada and elsewhere, including the UK, and it will surely become an issue again (Phillips, 2007: 170–6).

The most prominent example of a state that has resisted adopting multiculturalism as official policy is France. Interestingly, anti-racists as well as those sympathetic to the anti-immigration rhetoric of the National

Front Party, the largest of its kind in Europe, have been against multicul-turalism. This resistance is constructed in terms of a fundamental com-mitment to French republicanism as historically involving universal equality for citizens. That is to say, in France no difference amongst citi-zens should be recognized by the state: all individuals are treated equally insofar as they are treated the same. As a consequence, it is maintained that the French state should not even gather statistics on ethnic minorities – to know, for example, the extent of racism and discrimination in employment and state services – far less accord different groups different rights. In fact, it has been shown that the construction of French univer-salism as dating back to the French Revolution is a myth: it was actually promoted by right-wing intellectuals in the media and taken up by policy-makers as part of the rise of racist nationalism with the emergence of the National Front Party led by Jean Le Pen in the mid-1980s (Favell, 2001; Brubaker, 2002). It is a myth that is, however, now very well-established and difficult to challenge, even if it is coming under increased pressure as a result of growing unrest amongst young French people.

As multiculturalists see it, recognizing cultural differences in group-differentiated polyethnic citizenship rights enables genuine integration, while the assimilationist model results in exclusion for those who do not fit, or who are seen as not fitting, the dominant culture. Kymlicka (1995) argues that, far from encouraging the fragmentation of society, as assimi-lationists fear, demands for culturally specific rights enable minorities to participate fully in a multicultural society.

Nevertheless, it is important to recognize that "culture" itself is a term which may be used to different effect in different situations. There are certainly cases where it is inappropriate to think of unequal citizenship as primarily a matter of cultural differences. In some cases, indeed, this may be a way of de-legitimizing claims for greater equality. Perhaps the best example of the difficulty of thinking of citizenship in this way is the position of African-Americans in the United States and the way in which the New Right has suggested cultural differences as the reason for their predominance in "the underclass."

Since the civil rights movement of the 1950s and 1960s, the chief issue for African-Americans in terms of citizenship has been integration through desegregation. The striking separation of black and white in the US invari-ably works to the advantage of whites: poor housing, neighborhoods with high rates of crime, poor schools, low pay, and limited job oppor-tunities restrict the realization of full citizenship rights for black Americans in comparison with whites. The role of culture in segregation is, however, far from clear. As Kymlicka notes, African-Americans fit neither the category of multinational nor that of polyethnic group. They were brought to the continent involuntarily, from different African cultural and linguistic backgrounds, and for a long time they were actively discouraged and even prohibited from trying to develop a common culture. They have no homeland nor distinctive social forms in America as national minorities do, and yet they have been kept physically segregated from the mainstream white culture (Kymlicka, 1995: 24). Multiculturalism has played some part in the movement against segregation, challenging the ethnocentrism of the liberal arts canon in American education, for example, with black history, literature, and so on. But the main claims for cultural difference have come from those who argue that poor black Americans reproduce their poverty as a result of inappropriate attitudes to work and family life. In this case, as we saw in section 4.1, a discourse of cultural difference reinforces segregation and legitimates inequalities rather than articulating claims for more equal citizenship rights and the genuine participation of all. We will look at these claims with respect to the racialized underclass in more detail in section 4.4 below.

The movement against African-American segregation, although not calling for group-differentiated rights on the basis of *cultural* differences, has called for "special rights" for black people in order to redress historic disadvantage. According to Kymlicka and others, such arguments are also justified in liberal terms insofar as they are designed with the aim of bringing about a color-blind meritocracy. The best known of these involves the use of quotas in universities, companies, and the public sector to bring the prospects of employment for black Americans closer to equivalence with whites than they would otherwise be as a result of imposed historical segregation, poorer living conditions, and disadvantage in the labor market. "Affirmative action" takes many forms, from "active non-discrimination" in which the employer tries hard to recruit minority applicants before deciding which candidate to employ for the job, to "reverse discrimination" in which preference is given to applicants from minority groups which have been discriminated against in the past. Affirmative action programs have always been extremely controversial and highly politicized. They have been criticized from the left on the grounds that they have benefited some black people while failing to address the problem of black poverty as such. However, it is the right-wing criticism which is currently dominant: that affirmative action is unfair to white individuals who may not be chosen for jobs or university places in competition with black people. The counter-argument that white people have only lost what they gained through past discrimination no longer has the resonance it once had. While affirmative action continues in the US, it is increasingly under threat and has been outlawed in recent well-publicized court cases involving selection for university places. For African-Americans in US, it is individual rather than group-differentiated rights that are in the ascendant (Omi and Winant, 1987).

"Special rights" remain important, however, with regard to rights to representation in the political process. Multiculturalists, like feminists, are concerned with the way in which minority groups are under-represented in the legislatures of Western liberal democracies. Claims for political representation take different forms according to the group in question. As Kymlicka notes, claims for political representation are not synonymous with demands for self-government or for group-differentiated rights on the grounds of cultural difference. It is rather that they involve giving minorities a fair hearing in a situation in which their views would otherwise be systematically ignored. This is consistent with liberal understandings of democratic representation in which, as a bare minimum, it should provide for the protection of individual interests. In a more elaborated liberal version of democratic participation, political representation does more than this, facilitating citizens' individual development in accordance with their recognition of the common good. In either case, it is unfair that individuals who are members of minority groups are not represented. Increasingly group-differentiated political rights are an important issue in multicultural liberal democracies.

In the US, the most prominent attempt to reform systematic imbalances in representation has been "redistricting" – redrawing the boundaries of electoral districts to create black-majority or Hispanic-majority districts. Ironically, however, although instituted as part of the campaign against segregation, it is only effective insofar as residential segregation is the reality. In response, the Supreme Court has ruled that redistricting involving "segregating" races for the purposes of voting is to be regarded with suspicion. Like other affirmative action programs designed to redress systematic disadvantage, it should be seen, Kymlicka (1995) argues, as a temporary measure. In fact, it is reviewed regularly to assess how well it is working and whether it is still required.

However, there are cases where societies seem to be divided more permanently along religious or cultural lines. In such cases, it may be argued that requirements for group representation are not temporary. This is clearly the case where there are claims for a degree of self-government, as in federal systems, or where groups live on their own land, as Native Americans do. In other cases, however, group political rights are designed to accommodate differences within common decision-making procedures. This is, for example, the case in what is known as "consociational democracies," like those of Holland and Belgium, in which religious cleavages are represented by different political parties. In such cases, political stability is supposed to depend on sharing decision-making power so that the cabinet will be composed of leading figures from all parties, there will be minority veto over socially divisive issues, and so on (Phillips, 1995: 14–15). The system in New Zealand is similar in that Maoris select candidates from a specific electoral list so that they are guaranteed representation in parliament as a group, though there is no Maori party. However, there are no examples of special political rights for racialized minority groups in Europe. Although consociational democracies are apparently more open to the possibility of fitting Muslim representation into the existing pluralist framework than other political systems, this remains no more than a possibility at present (Phillips, 1995: 15).

The whole issue of group-differentiated rights might be considered highly contentious in relation to the critique of essentialism which has been so important, as we have seen, in relation to citizenship for women and "sexual minorities." It is, however, less well developed than in these cases. In some respects, this is surprising. The anti-essentialist case against the concept of ethnicity as a way of distinguishing actual groups of persons *is* highly developed. Anti-essentialists argue strongly that we should see culture as *process* rather than as a set of attributes possessed by a particular group. Culture is not fixed in eternal forms; it is constantly being made and re-made in historical processes. It is on these grounds that theorists of race and ethnicity have argued that cultural identities are "hybrid": they are always constructed by drawing on a multiplicity of cultural symbols and identifications which are re-combined in ways such that there are no "authentic" ethnic groups (Hall, 1990, 1991a, 1991b; Gilroy, 1993).

In addition, individuals identify in a range of ways: why should they be identified with the cultural belonging their parents, or even their grand-parents, may have inherited (Hollinger, 2000)? Multiculturalism is, there-fore, seen as problematic insofar as it contributes to what Gilroy calls "ethnic absolutism," the construction of rigid and supposedly unchanging distinctions between cultures in ways that constrain creativity, individual-ity, and challenges to the *status quo* (Gilroy, 1993).

In recent years, concerns about the dangers multiculturalism raises for reifying cultural differences have been linked much more to questions about social cohesion and civic values than to the problems of balancing equality, diversity, and freedom for members of minority groups. David Hollinger (2000) criticized multiculturalism along these lines, as well as on anti-essentialist grounds, before 9/11, arguing for the political importance of a sense of commonality amongst Americans, but critical voices have grown louder since the attacks on New York. Especially in Europe, critics of multiculturalism link it to the involvement of young Muslims in terrorist networks, arguing that – ironically, given the liberal roots of multiculturalism – it fails to foster a political culture in which toleration and respect for different ways of life are valued. Instead, multiculturalism is seen as promoting what is effectively community segregation as different ethnic and religious groups live together in the same districts, speaking their own languages, and often maintaining close links with "home" through minority media and social and religions organizations. Multicultural policies, it is argued, have failed to bring immigrant groups into mainstream society and they have therefore given support to extremists to whom that society is anathema. The fact that three of the young Muslim men who carried out the bombings in London in 2005 were born and brought up in Britain is taken as evidence of the failure of multiculturalism to create a society in which diversity is valued rather than hated and feared.

These criticisms do not only come from the Right. Some critics on the Left go further still in their arguments that multiculturalism undermines social cohesion. In a magazine article that was very much debated in Britain, David Goodhart argued that the more diverse a population is in terms of religion and ethnicity, the more difficult it becomes to build and sustain national solidarity. This has serious consequences for security, as community segregation leads to racial violence, the growth of racist right wing political parties and riots by disaffected young people who see no future for themselves in Western societies. But it also has serious consequences for the quality of citizenship itself. In particular, Goodhart sees diversity as undermining the grounds on which the redistributive policies of the welfare state were founded, as a sense of belonging together and sharing a common fate associated with nationalism is eroded (Goodhart, 2006). A parallel argument is that of Nancy Fraser, who has argued that the focus on the Left with cultural recognition has tended to lead to the neglect of concerns with redistribution. Fraser is not against multiculturalism as such, but she does see it as limited in comparison with the anti-essentialist transformations that are needed to cultural identities as well as in patterns of inequality if society is to become more egalitarian. Multiculturalism is not an end in itself, she argues: the politics of recognition should not lead to neglect of commitments to the politics of redistribution (Fraser, 1997, 2008).

However, it is concerns with social cohesion that now dominate debates over multiculturalism in the twenty-first century, whilst questions of justice and equality in relation to racialized minorities are exclusively focused on the rights of individuals *within* groups. In his advocacy of multiculturalism, Kymlicka argues that not only is it rare for ethnic minority groups to demand "internal restrictions," the legal power to impose cultural norms on their members, but it is unacceptable from a liberal point of view, since they undermine individual freedom rather than protecting it (Kymlicka, 1999a). The enforcement of cultural norms that impose traditional restrictions on women and children which are not legal in liberal democracies, such as arranged marriages which violate existing laws regarding informed consent, clitirodectomy, and so on, are not acceptable in liberal multiculturalism. Nevertheless, the distinction between lifting "external restrictions" on group members and imposing "internal restrictions" is highly complex, as Kymlicka himself now admits. Although, as we noted above, multiculturalism does involve some group-differentiated rights, they are actually quite minimal in the West. However, it is not really the law that is at issue here. The legality of practices that are radically different from the Western norm has mostly been due to an *absence* of law. Polygamy, for example, was legal in France until 1993 simply because there was no law against it. And although it is now illegal, many West African families continue to practice it. Clearly, traditional practices are not eradicated simply by making them illegal where they are important to the identities and social relations of people who have grown up with them. Critics of multiculturalism argue that it promotes a political culture in which customs that are antithetical to modern progressive ways of life are tolerated out of a misguided cultural relativism, the view that each culture has its own values and that all are worthy of equal respect.

The claim that multiculturalism promotes oppressive practices raises particularly difficult issues for feminists, as it is invariably women and girls who are portrayed as its victims. On the one hand, as Anne Phillips argues, it is hardly news to feminists that gendered practices disadvantage and oppress women. On the other hand, however, many feminists have been reluctant to criticize minority practices to avoid themselves contributing to the victimization of women who are vulnerable members of minority communities in societies in which racism and Islamophobia is endemic. As Phillips puts it, in regard to the public outrage around practices of Muslim women's dress, for example: "People not previously marked by their ardent support for women's rights seemed to rely on claims about the maltreatment of women to justify their distaste for minority cultural groups, and in these claims, cultural stereotypes were rife" (Phillips, 2007: 2). The question is even more complicated because women are often responsible for safeguarding cultural difference within communities, so that as well as being subjected to repressive practices, they are also actively engaged in perpetrating them. It is older women who are responsible for ensuring that girls become eligible for a "decent marriage" by arranging and carrying out female genital cutting, for example. Criminalization of these practices often, therefore, falls particularly hard on women who are effectively carrying out their duties as wives and mothers (Dembour, 2001; Gunning, 2002). As a consequence, although feminists are now quite routinely seen as complicit with racism, if not racist, and arguments about women's equality are used to discredit the ideal of respecting cultural diversity, at least in the English-speaking world, feminists themselves are actually much more likely to *support* multiculturalism (see Phillips, 2007; Schachar, 2001; Volpp, 2001; *cf* Okin, 1999). The multiculturalism feminists tend to support is, however, what Phillips calls "multiculturalism without culture." It is, in other words, anti-essentialist multiculturalism.

Phillips follows Kymlicka in arguing that multiculturalism is valuable because people are cultural beings: everyone is shaped by the norms and practices that have made us who we are. She departs from Kymlicka's reasoning, however, by arguing that it makes no sense to think in terms of cultures as if they were bounded, unified "things." In doing so, she argues, we bundle together sets of norms and customary behaviors which do not invariably go together, and which are, anyway, continually changing (Phillips, 2007: 52). In addition, people themselves differ in terms of the importance they give to cultural norms: while some endorse them, others celebrate the superiority of their way of doing things, and others resist thinking in terms of culture at all. In fact, it is very common to think: "I" have moral values; "they" have cultural traditions (Phillips, 2007: 31). In all these respects, she argues, women are effectively no different from men. Whilst it is certainly true that women are frequently identified as the "guardians" of culture, and they may lack resources that would enable them either to leave close-knit communities or to speak out against community leaders, what follows is support for women's rights as *individuals* – to refuges to protect them against family violence, for example, or to education and training to improve their social status, expertise, and economic situation. In addition, however, women also need individual rights that have long been taken for granted, but which are now in question for those whose choices offend the cultural norms of the majority: for example, the right to dress according to cultural and religious codes that is now treated with such suspicion and contempt in the case of some Muslim women.

Phillips's arguments are couched as a defense of multiculturalism, but in shifting the emphasis from group rights to individual rights, she brings it very close to what is sometimes called "new assimilationism" (Brubaker, 2002). In dissolving the "groupness" of cultures, in order to emphasize diversity and fluidity, she has changed what "multicultural-ism" stood for in Kymlicka's version of group-differentiated rights. However, "new assimilationism" is not the assimilationism of the "melting pot." What is emphasized above all is belonging to a civic nation of liberal rights and obligations. It is solidarity and belonging across all groups that critics of multiculturalism believe should be fostered (Modood, 2007: 146–54). In Britain, for example, the government has introduced citizenship ceremonies for residents who become naturalized, in order to symbolize pride in joining the British nation, not just the acquisition of citizenship. Citizenship should be experienced as more than simply an abstract bundle of rights that are provided by the state. It should be felt as the expression of common values, to which everyone feels commitment and loyalty, not just acceptance and far less active resistance. This need not mean that immigrants give up their own sense of cultural belonging. Immigrants must become "like" the majority only to a degree and over time, and only to the extent that their values and practices are incompatible with mainstream values (Brubaker, 2002; Joppke, 2004; Kivisto, 2005). In this sense, the "new assimilation-ism" is a form of "hyphenation": there may be a variety of ways of belonging to the nation, as long as they are not in tension with its core commitments.

Nevertheless, there is a difference between Phillips's argument for mul-ticulturalism "without culture," and that of the "new assimilationists." Phillips argues that it is important to retain multiculturalism as an ideal, while "new assimilationists" see that ideal as one of the main reasons for the crisis of civic nationalism. In a climate in which "cultural difference" is under attack, it is important to remember its importance to an egalitar-ian society. If, as we noted earlier, "new racism" finds cultural difference problematic, a commitment to multiculturalism is a clear demonstration of its value. To some extent, as Phillips notes, the term "cosmopolitan" may now be replacing multiculturalism in this respect, as in thinking of particular cities as "cosmopolitan," for example. "Cosmopolitan" does not, however, carry the same implications in terms of public policy. Phillips's arguments also give far more attention to individual rights com-pared to "new assimilationists," who are concerned, above all, with social cohesion. In focusing on rights, it is easier to avoid the slippage between civic and ethnic nationalism that has been such an important feature of the exclusion of "foreigners" from enjoying equal, or even fundamental, rights. Instead of civic nationalism, Tariq Modood suggests rather that "civic multiculturalism" might be a good term for the balance between solidarity, cultural difference, and individual rights that is needed in contemporary Western liberal-democracies (Modood, 2007). Ideals of "equality" and "difference" are rather abstract, not least because they have such a variety of meanings and applications. On the other hand, it seems that nationalism must itself become more abstract if feelings of solidarity are to be forged more around the civic than the ethnic pole on the continuum of nationalism. Creating new names like "civic multiculturalism" to describe the realities of a country of which we might be proud, and as an ideal to which we might aspire, is surely necessary to guide collective life within and beyond the nation. And, no doubt, it will be necessary to invent new names again in the future.

4.5 Post-National Citizenship?

A further challenge to settled assumptions about citizenship comes from the way states now grant rights to non-citizens. The paradigm case of non-citizens who are entitled to rights as long-term residents within state territories in Europe is "guest-workers." Originally invited and given temporary work visas, there are guest workers who have been resident now for decades in Western Europe, especially Germany and France, and many of them now have children born in their new home states. Other non-citizens with entitlements in Europe and North America include asylum-seekers and refugees who, with illegal migrants, make up the majority of the most recent wave of migration. As a result of successful rights-claims on states by non-citizens, it is argued that citizenship itself is changing: it no longer involves rights for nationals to the exclusion of all those who do not have nationality. As rights are extended to residents and others who make claims on the state on the grounds of universal human rights, membership of the civil sphere is also extended to include persons as human beings.

In addition to changes *within* states, the European Union, which now confers European citizenship on individuals within its borders, is seen as a manifestation of the development of post-national citizenship *between* states. The EU is not a state; it has not developed into the United States of Europe, and the prospect of it doing so is in many ways as remote as ever, despite the hopes of European elites (Kivisto and Faist, 2007: 125).

It is a unique supranational institution, which shares sovereignty with member states. It is in this respect that (as we noted in chapter 2), Europe is sometimes seen as prefiguring the political institutions of a more cosmopolitan world. Unless the problem of Europe's "democratic deficit" can be solved, however, it is rather a tarnished flagship for cosmopolitan democracy.

Possibly the most far-reaching vision of citizenship is raised by the environmental movement. Global citizenship may not seem the obvious way to develop environmental politics, with its focus on rights for human beings. Although rights always entail obligations, discussions of environmental citizenship are unusual in giving more weight to obligations than rights. It has in common with other discussions of citizenship raised by global social movements, however, an emphasis on the importance and value of public goods – the environment itself being chief amongst them, and questions of global justice are similarly to the fore in models of citizenship developed by environmentalists.

Migration and rights across borders

Section 4.4 of this chapter, on citizenship, racialization, and ethnicity, was concerned with settled populations in Western states. Until the 1980s, there was a general belief amongst sociologists and others that mass migrations had ended, and debates over citizenship rights in relation to discrimination, racism, and multiculturalism took place on the basis of this assumption. In fact, while immigration into the US was restricted from the 1920s, and European countries ended systematic labor migration from the mid-1970s, migration continued in other forms. There were the families of migrant workers who were granted rights of settlement on the grounds of "family reunion." This form of migration was particularly important in European countries like Germany with its "guest-worker" system. In the US, it actually led to an *increase* in immigration in the 1960s and 1970s, and it also meant more visible immigration with the entry of Asians and Latin Americans rather than the Europeans who had previously made up the majority of migrants. There was also a significant migration of managerial, professional, technical, and scientific workers who moved between advanced capitalist countries. These privileged workers are usually ignored in discussions of migration.

Since the late 1980s, there has been political alarm in all Western countries about illegal immigration and asylum-seekers, because they are understood to threaten nation-states' control of their borders. These migrants are also, no doubt, seen as particularly problematic because they involve migrants from the developing world. In the US, it is over the increase in illegal immigrants from Mexico that the alarm has been raised. In fact, restrictions on entry by Mexicans into the US have never been closely enforced and employers have long made use of low-skill, low-wage, agricultural workers from south of the border. Indeed, until quite recently undocumented migrants in the US were entitled to gain legal residence if they could prove they had been in the country and of "good conduct," for several years (Sassen, 2006: 295). However, due mainly to worsening conditions in the Caribbean Basin, there has been an increase in illegal immigration in this region since the 1970s. As a result there have been increased restrictions on crossing the border into the US and new limits on illegal migrants gaining legal residence. In Europe, illegal immigration is seen as a problem especially in relation to opening up national borders within the European Union. Unskilled manual labor has been recruited to build up service industries in Spain, Italy, Portugal, and Greece, until recently providers of migrant labor for elsewhere and now the destination for illegal immigrants from North Africa. Other European countries are concerned because they see the opening of national borders as allowing the spread of illegal immigrants throughout the Union. Numbers of asylum-seekers in Europe and North America have actually dropped since the steep rise in the 1980s because of restrictive measures. But, as Castles and Miller point out, much migration is simply unrecorded, and, in general, it is likely to grow with inequalities of living standards between the global North and South, and conflicts and wars that mean people have to flee their homes. Furthermore, working against the restrictions, there is the fact that international migration, like other processes of globalization, is made easier with networks of digitalized communication and transportation across borders (Castles and Miller, 2005: 4–5).

As a result, all states have taken measures to discourage new forms of migration. In the US, there have been attempts to control illegal immigration, by penalizing employers who knowingly hire unauthorized aliens and by stricter policing of the border with Mexico. In Europe, immigration measures have been linked to the institutions of the European Union. While to some extent travel across borders within the Union has been made easier, increased resources have been made available for surveillance of the external borders and the policing of migrants and asylum applicants, including a computerized database of criminals and deported and unwanted persons. There is also growing international cooperation between the countries of Europe, North America, and Australasia to facilitate harmonization of immigration policies and to combat illegal immigration. Measures include the use of detention camps where migrants are held, sometimes for years, in overcrowded and poor conditions whilst waiting for asylum cases to be heard. Such measures are often described as constructing "fortress Europe" or "fortress America," political units which put up barriers to those outside. On the grounds that these are at the same time barriers to maintain racial segregation, Anthony Richmond has described this new world order as "global apartheid." He argues that immigration controls involving work permits, segregated housing locations, restricted travel, and deprivation of political rights are used against illegal immigrants and asylum-seekers in order to protect privileged access to health, education, and welfare services, just as the South African government used such measures to control and exploit the black population when apartheid was enforced (Richmond, 1994; see Balibar, 2004; 120–3).

An alternative, much more optimistic, assessment of global migration processes sees them as significant for the way in which they have prompted a form of post-national citizenship. According to Yasemin Soysal, migrant groups who are resident but not citizens in Europe (most notably "guest-workers") have won human rights to a wide range of benefits within European states. They have been able to do so because international human rights have been incorporated into national law in Europe. Organizations representing migrants have won civil rights to appeal against deportation, political rights to vote in local elections, cultural rights to translation services in public institutions, and a range of social rights to healthcare, education, housing, and welfare. As a result of global migration and developing regime of international human rights, Soysal argues that rights are now based on universal personhood, not membership of a particular nation. Nationality and rights are disarticulated as the absolute distinction between "citizenship" and "foreigner" is eroded within nation-states, at least in terms of formal legal rights (Soysal, 1994).

Similarly, David Jacobson (1996) argues that in the US, individual rights are no longer directly tied to nationality; the individual now has a status in international law, and in many cases, rights attached to this status are equivalent to the rights of citizens guaranteed by nation-states. The US has adopted quite generous interpretations of international human rights law covering asylum-seekers, including for women fleeing gender-specific violence to which much of Europe remains closed. It is also the case that, over many years, resident aliens in the US have won rights through the courts, including social rights to children's education and welfare. However, US state officials are notoriously reluctant to introduce international human rights law into domestic law, and the rights of resident aliens tend to be based on "activist" interpretations of US law itself. Bosniak argues that US law is inherently schizophrenic, separating out questions of who is and can be a member of the society, which is covered by immigration law, from questions of the rights of individuals within the territory, which may include those of non-citizens. She argues that constitutionally resident aliens are entitled to virtually the same rights as citizens in US law, and the courts have accepted this to some degree (Bosniak, 2006). On the other hand, as Rainer Baubock points out, where resident aliens have recourse only to national law, with no direct appeal to international human rights in US courts, those rights are particularly vulnerable to changes in the political regime. Indeed, from 1996, resident aliens were denied federal welfare benefits through government legislation (Baubock, 2002: 134).

Theorists of post-national citizenship are much more optimistic than Richmond because they do not see the state as acting in a singular and unified fashion with regard to migration processes. Nor do they see a homogeneous global order emerging. It is rather that there is often a void in national law with respect to detailed provision for non-national residents and asylum-seekers. Under these conditions, associations, organizations, and individuals maneuver to try to gain a measure of security and well-being when non-citizens would otherwise be without rights – with some degree of success. As Soysal puts it, states are caught between competing claims to legitimacy: bound on one hand to respect human rights, and we might add, domestic law where it may be interpreted to cover non-citizens, and on the other, to regulate immigration as an expression of sovereignty. Their activities are not always consistent (Soysal, 1994: 7–8).

Jacobson argues that post-national citizenship erodes the principle that a state should, above all, be concerned to protect its national interests (Jacobson, 1996). This is far from evident, however, even in Europe. First, states have withheld rights to vote in national elections from non-citizens; although in most European states they have the right to vote in local elections. In this respect, then, they deny non-nationals the right to determine the laws and policies under which they live that is considered the defining feature of democratic citizenship. Second, especially since heightened security fears after 9/11, the precariousness of even the formal rights of resident non-citizens has become much more visible, especially where accusations of involvement in terrorist activities have resulted in the infringement of basic civil rights. In the UK, several non-citizens were detained without trial for a number of years following 9/11, without even being allowed to see the evidence against them, before the policy was ruled illegal under the European Convention on Human Rights. At the same time, individuals thought to be dangerous to the state have lost their citizenship status, as in the case of the "accidental citizen" Yasser Hamdi who was detained by the US authorities, similarly without charge and without access to lawyers, before being persuaded to give up his US citizenship (Nyer, 2006; Nash, 2009b). In fact, such practices are consistent with the thesis of post-national citizenship insofar as *removing* citizenship may indicate that nationality no longer counts as it once did in terms of securing, or losing, citizenship rights. Nevertheless, Hamdi was headed for Guantanamo Bay when it was discovered that he was a US citizen, and in comparison with those detained there, he enjoyed privileged treatment.

Insofar as post-national citizenship is developing, then, as rights are granted to non-citizens, it is resulting in the growing *proliferation* of citizenship statuses. The formal equality of rights once only afforded to citizens is just one aspect of citizenship. Post-national citizenship does not simply involve resident non-citizens gradually winning approximately the same rights as citizens. Throughout this chapter, we have been looking at how, even when marginalized groups are successful in winning formal rights, inequality continues in their actual enjoyment of rights in practice. Similarly, in post-national citizenship, the actual enjoyment of formal rights depends on other conditions, including not belonging to a minority about which the majority population has suspicions. In effect, post-national citizenship means quite different things to different groups. Post-national citizenship involves a proliferation of citizenship statuses: from the "super-citizens" of the global elite; to "quasi-citizens" who have formal rights but who may find themselves in anomalous situations because they are unable to demonstrate that they "belong" to the majority culture or that they are loyal to the state; through to "un-citizens," who may be long-term residents in a state, but who, without legal rights to remain, face deportation if they come to the attention of the authorities (Nash, 2009b). In practices of post-national citizenship, the state does not act in a unified and homogenous fashion. Possessing nationality, and therefore "full" citizenship status, still makes a difference in relation to state authorities, though for some people, even that may not be enough to ensure respect for their rights.

It is not, then, that the proliferation of citizenship statuses undermines the state. On the contrary, in some respects, it may be that the legitimacy and scope of the state is strengthened in the multiplicity and variety of citizenship claims. It is states that are called on to guarantee human rights. In the case of refugees, for example, it is because states have the duty to protect and further the well-being of the population residing within their territories that asylum-seekers may legitimately claim to be stateless when they are in danger of persecution in their homeland. Furthermore, it is not obvious either that post-national citizenship undermines nationalism. On the contrary, it may be rather that, as Soysal argues, claims to nationality, cultural distinctiveness, and self-determination that were previously linked together in nation-states are now disarticulated and re-articulated as core elements of what it is to be human. As she notes, "The universalistic status of personhood and postnational membership coexist with assertive national identities and intense ethnic struggles" (Soysal, 1994: 159). Nowhere are these dialectics more evident than in the political institutions of the European Union.

European citizenship

The word "citizen" has only recently been used to refer to those who live and work in the countries making up the European Union. Before the Maastricht Treaty was ratified in 1993, the main reference was to "workers," economic cooperation being the chief concern. The language of citizenship represents a further step toward a supranational European state with an explicit focus on political union. The Maastricht Treaty created citizens of Europe, stating, "Every citizen holding the nationality of a member state shall be a citizen of the Union." It further stated that the four fundamental freedoms – of movement of goods, persons, services, and capital – previously attached to citizenship of a member state were to be rights of citizens of the Union. They remained the same as they were before in virtually every other respect, though the treaty also created some new citizenship rights. The most important are undoubtedly political rights; those citizens of the Union who are resident in a member state of which they are not a national now have the right to vote and stand for election in local elections and for the European Parliament. Significantly, they still have no rights with regard to national elections. There are also new rights for all residents of the EU, including non-citizens, to petition the European Parliament concerning maladministration of its institutions (Guild, 1996). Social rights remain minimal at the EU level. Previous attempts to standardize benefits and rights for workers across nations are continued in the Maastricht Treaty, but social rights are extended very little beyond participation in the labor market. The emphasis on ensuring the free movement of workers remains and there is no attempt to harmonize national welfare systems (O'Leary, 1995).

The question of the extent to which citizenship of the European Union may be described as post-national is not a simple one. Citizenship rights remain clearly national in some respects. EU citizenship is granted only to those who are nationals of member states and the decision about who to include is made at the national level. Nation-states retain the power to divide those who are resident in their territories into European citizens, with all the freedoms of the Union, and non-citizens, who will not have the automatic right to travel or work in other countries within Europe. The link between nationality and citizenship is reproduced rather than undermined in the current conception of European citizenship (Mitchell and Russell, 1996: 63). Furthermore, rights will continue to be assured by nation-states, and the European Union has only limited power to make member states comply with its rulings. The European Union has an integrated legal system but, as Elizabeth Meehan (1997) has pointed out, there is a plurality of legal instruments within the common legal order, each of which works differently at different levels. The European Parliament, Council, and Commission act jointly to make regulations which are directly applicable in member states. However, most common policies are not the object of regulations but of directives which "direct" states to act to bring about a common objective expressed quite abstractly and without detailed instructions. Directives are intended to allow divergences in national procedures with respect to policy implementations, resource allocations, and so on. Furthermore, new directions in policy cannot be made without the consent of the Council of Ministers, an intergovernmental body made up of representatives of member states rather than a supranational institution. In some cases, states are permitted to opt out of commonly agreed objectives on the basis of distinctive national traditions. The UK, for example, is exempt from introducing workers' rights to consultation in the workplace. The rights of the citizens of the European Union continue to be determined to a large extent, then, by the nation-state within which they happen to reside (Meehan, 1997).

On the other hand, it is clear that in some respects the new citizenship rights instituted by the Maastricht Treaty are post-national. They are, however, post-national in two rather different ways. First, a number of the rights ensured by the European Union are post-national in the sense that they are universal human rights, attached to persons rather than to citizens. For many years, the European Court of Justice (ECJ) has been guided by the European Convention on Human Rights (ECHR) in order to make its judgments. In most of the member states of Europe, the ECHR is not only recognized as international law but is directly incorporated into domestic law-making. The judgments of the ECJ are binding on member states. In addition, individuals – citizens or non-citizens – and member states may also bring cases to the European Court of Human Rights, which produces rulings to which states are obliged to respond with new legislation if necessary. The nation-states that make up the European Union have, therefore, been incorporating international human rights law into their statutes for up to 25 years before the Maastricht Treaty created European citizenship. In this sense, at least, post-national citizenship in Europe was not created by the explicit declaration that Europeans are citizens of the EU.

Second, however, European citizenship may be said to be post-national in that the European Union is increasingly a supranational state, sharing the sovereignty of member states. This is evident in the fact that, as we have noted, law is made in the institutions of the Union which overrides that made by the member states. In addition, the EU now has policing powers, border controls, a common currency over much of its territory, and even the beginnings of a cooperative foreign policy.

The main issue that arises with respect to post-national citizenship as a result of shared sovereignty is what is called "the democratic deficit": the EU is seriously inadequate in terms of political rights. At the level of the nation-state, democratically elected governments are losing the power to make policies and legislation that are binding on their citizens, as member states give up sovereignty to the institutions of the EU. At the level of the EU, however, elected officials have very little influence over the legislative process. The European Parliament is the only democratically elected institution of the EU and it has only a consultative role in policy-making. The European Commission draws up legislation which is then debated by Parliament and voted on by the Council of Ministers before it becomes law. Officials on the Council are chosen by their respective national governments, not elected. In addition, some argue that the EU results in a strengthening of the judiciary within member states that is undemocratic, as European human rights law is made binding on states without necessarily being made by legislatures (Jacobson and Ruffer, 2003). The Maastricht Treaty took certain measures to address the "democratic deficit" of the EU by strengthening the powers of the European Parliament; for example, the Commission and its president are now subject to Parliamentary approval. However, it is clear that in order to prevent a lack of democratic accountability as a result of the transfer of powers from the member states to the EU, all the political institutions of the EU need reform (Newman, 1996).

The issue of "democratic deficit" has been raised very starkly by attempts to decide on a European Constitution over the last decade.

Following the enormous expansion of the EU with the accession of Eastern European states in 2004, it was decided that a formal constitution was needed. A 300-page document, which apparently aimed to improve the transparency and efficiency of EU structures, was completed in the same year, and it was left to member states to decide how it should be ratified. Most opted to vote on it in their legislatures; several decided to hold referenda amongst their citizens. Almost half the legislatures of the member states had approved the new constitution when voters in France and the Netherlands rejected it in 2005. Although this meant an end to this form of the constitution, as member states had to be unanimous in its approval before it could be adopted, what is more important is that, whilst the constitution was being drafted, the majority of European citizens appear to have been completely unaware that it was in process at all (Beck and Grande, 2007: 228). What this indicates is a complete lack of interest and debate about the EU amongst ordinary people across Europe. European citizens may identify as European to some extent, but insofar as they are interested in current events, they are oriented far more towards national media – which generally take little interest in EU procedures and policies, except when national interests are in question – and national political institutions. It is unclear now what will happen to the European constitution. In 2008, Irish voters rejected its successor, the Lisbon Treaty, despite the fact that virtually all the Irish political parties were in favor of it and the EU is generally very popular in Ireland. Whatever happens, however, it is clear that without a European-wide debate on the necessity for a constitution, what form it should take, and how the political procedures of the EU might be made more transparent and relevant to European citizens, it will have no effect whatsoever on the EU's "democratic deficit" (Beck and Grande, 2007: 230).

Europeans do have a form of post-national citizenship assured by the EU as an emerging "supranational state," then, but it is problematic insofar as it has eroded some of the political rights they enjoyed as the citizens of sovereign nation-states. This is not to suggest that the EU is inherently undemocratic. On the contrary, lack of democratic accountability at the supranational level must presumably be weighed against the potential gain in control by national governments over processes that cannot be contained within national borders. It must also be weighed against the success of the EU in coordinating the peaceful existence of states that have been at war with each other, on and off, throughout their history, and in institutionalizing cosmopolitan law that gives individuals living in Europe, including non-citizens, some legal leverage over their fundamental citizenship rights.

Nevertheless, the EU vividly illustrates the problems for the democratization of global political institutions which we will look into more fully in the following chapter. Unless these problems can be solved in the European Union, there is little prospect that other regional bodies might develop along similar lines. The only possible candidate, currently, is the North American Free Trade Agreement, an economic pact linking Canada, Mexico, and the US. There are a number of reasons why it is unlikely that it will evolve, as the EU did, from linking states purely through economic relations to building political structures – especially, perhaps, the disproportionate size and wealth of the US (Kivisto and Faist, 2007: 128). But unless the EU can overcome its "democratic deficit," which appears to be very difficult indeed, there are good reasons to be skeptical about the desirability of the EU itself as an ideal that others might choose to emulate.

Citizenship and the environment

What difference might sensitivity to the natural environmental make to citizenship? In many ways, there is no obvious connection between environmentalism and citizenship. On one hand, citizenship is organized nationally, and environmental processes do not respect the artificial boundaries of nation-states. It is in this respect that environmentalism is linked to aspirations for global citizenship. On the other hand, many of the practices of the environmental movement involve care for local resources. How might the environmentalist slogan "think global, act local" work in practice for the extension of citizenship? In addition, the very notion of extending rights would seem to be at odds with at least some aspects of environmentalist thinking. The Keynesian welfare state, for example, was premised on the possibility of continual economic growth, and, therefore, of infinite natural resources. Might expectations of citizenship rights themselves need to be restricted as a result of our awareness of the potentially devastating effects of economic growth? Indeed, environmentalists do tend to be at least, if not more, concerned with citizenship obligations as with rights. Finally, democracy and environmentalism are not always obviously compatible. If state planning is needed to deal with climate change, for example, as Giddens argues, since policy changes across society are needed, what room is there for democratic decision-making that might result in the "wrong direction," potentially with catastrophic consequences (Giddens, 2009)?

In the first place, then, thinking about the relationship between the environment and citizenship raises a number of challenges to Marshall's understanding of citizenship rights. First, there is the issue of who should be included as a citizen. Environmentalists argue that future generations should be included as having citizenship rights. In some ways, this is not as controversial a proposal as it might initially seem. To some extent, the rights of future citizens who are now children are already considered: rights to education, for example. Furthermore, there is the expectation that citizenship will be awarded to those as yet unborn insofar as the relevant conditions are expected to continue in much the same way. The Norwegian Constitution seems to have formalized such an expectation in relation to the environment in an amendment which states that:

> Every person has the right to an environment that is conducive to health and to natural surroundings whose productivity and diversity are preserved. Natural resources should be used on the basis of comprehensive long-term considerations whereby this right will be safeguarded for future generations as well. (quoted in Christoff, 1996: 165)

More controversially, animal rights activists argue that rights should be extended to animals, on the grounds that they, too, suffer, and also that they have moral value equal to that of human beings (Van Steenbergen, 1994). There are obvious difficulties with this argument, however, since animals, unlike humans, will never be able to exercise citizenship rights on their own behalf, nor respect the rights of other citizens, nor carry out the duties expected of citizens. It, therefore, seems more reasonable to think of the protection of animals and other non-human species as a matter of *responsibility* on the part of citizens, rather than as a matter of citizens' rights.

Second, environmental citizenship is often seen in terms of responsibility for nature, or "environmental stewardship" as it is sometimes called. This emphasis on responsibility rather than rights marks a difference, and perhaps potential for conflict, between environmentalism and other social movements. The idea of citizenship responsibility is not new; in fact, it has always been intrinsic to the enjoyment of citizenship rights. For example, the right to vote implies also the responsibility to elect political leaders, and in some countries, citizens are legally required to participate in local and general elections. More minimally, obligations to pay taxes and to obey the law (except under very particular conditions where civil disobedience may be more important) are also part of citizenship. Social movements have, however, generally campaigned for the extension of citizens' rights, not for redefinitions of citizenship obligations.

There may be a tension between environmentalism and other social movements over the balance between citizenship rights and obligations.

The extension of rights has been linked historically to the expansion of the capitalist economy. While some representatives of the green movement see concern for the environment as compatible with capitalism, all agree that economic growth is unsustainable in the long-term interests of the environment. There is, then, uncertainty over whether states could meet demands for expanding social rights (given the political will to do so), for example, at the same time as environmentalist demands to curb capitalist exploitation and despoliation of environmental resources. Developing alternative measures to GDP that would include assessment of environmental damage is crucial to beginning debates over the changes that are needed for a sustainable economy and how they are to be managed for the good of all (Giddens, 2009: 65–7).

On the other hand, however, the environmental movement does share appreciation of the importance of public goods with other social movements. Of course, the most important of these are the natural goods we enjoy in common in living on Earth, but it is the way in which they are managed that is important for citizenship. In keeping with neo-liberalization, market solutions to environmental problems are now prominent. It is possible, for example, to pass on the costs of sustainable development to the consumer. A simple example is the decision taken by all large supermarkets in the UK in recent years to stop giving out free plastic bags to shoppers. The main problem here is that, although this is virtually guaranteed to change *behavior*, it may not do much to change long-term *attitudes* to the environment. The same supermarkets, for example, continue to sell goods wrapped in huge amounts of plastic, paper, and cardboard. It is true that most of this wrapping can be recycled, but creating, transporting, storing, and then recycling such a mass of packaging is hardly energy efficient. There is, however, no public campaign against this practice. Although market incentives have a role to play in creating a sustainable economy, then, they do not necessarily generate fundamental changes in how we live (Dobson and Bell, 2006). In skepticism about the role of markets, and in seeking to bring more social and economic life within the domain of public, rather than private decision-making, environmentalism is consistent with the cultural politics of other movements for expanding citizenship.

Third, although there are certainly potential tensions between democracy and environmental responsibility, in practice greater participation in political life is currently needed in order to make environmental citizenship a reality. Steward (1991) suggests that citizens should be involved with experts in assessing the environmental risks that directly affect them, and how they should be tackled. This is already practiced in the environmental justice movement, based primarily in the US, which involves people trying to take control of local conditions that are unhealthy and unsightly, but also socially and economically damaging. Often these actions are linked to social and economic regeneration of a local area. In this respect, environmental citizenship is human-centered: it is rights to a decent, healthy, pleasant, and socially vibrant environment that are important. Although the model of the environmental justice movement remains well within existing understandings of citizenship rights in its concern with the equality of peoples' rights, it could have a huge impact around the world. Many people whose livelihoods depend on agriculture or fishing, or who rely on the local environment for firewood, water, or food, are well-aware that the conditions of their lives are directly at risk from environmental damage and are ready to take action to prevent it (Dobson, 2003: 92–4; Agyeman and Evans, 2006).

There is already European Union policy that is supposed to extend local participation in determining the direction of sustainable development. In principle, it extends power, responsibility, and influence to local government on the basis of subsidiarity, the democratic principle of the EU that political decisions should be make as at the smallest possible scale. It follows the Local Agenda 21 rules agreed at the UN Summit in 1992 of devolving responsibility to local governments to develop their own definitions of sustainable development in consultation with local citizens. At the moment, environmental action at the local level generally involves similar tactics to those of the environmental movement more broadly: lobbying government; investigating the activities of corporations and industries that are damaging the environment; and media campaigns to raise awareness, and to educate and inform other citizens. Use of the Internet may be especially promising in broadening consultation on environmental issues (Schlosberg et al., 2006). Agyeman and Evans argue, however, that there is comparatively little evidence of activity at the local level in the UK as a result of these initiatives: they doubt that top-down, procedural approaches can generate the kind of bottom-up grassroots movements that have become typical of actions for environmental justice in the US (Agyeman and Evans, 2006).

Ultimately, responsibility towards the environment can only be generated and sustained by changes of attitude towards environmental issues at all scales, from local to global; and by policies to end the rapid rate of environmental damage. Andrew Dobson takes the view that what he calls "ecological citizenship" involves non-territorial responsibilities. It is the responsibility of those who are causing environmental damage to stop, as they are affecting the rights of others, including those who live in other

countries and those who are not yet born. In Dobson's view, such responsibilities go far beyond any solutions that might be created at the local
level; they involve a concrete sense of global citizenship. Dobson's ideas
for global citizenship duties are actually very practical. He argues that
responsibility for the environment should be addressed by national governments putting in place policies to reduce a country's "ecological footprint": its impact on the environment in terms of various elements,
including carbon emissions, use of finite natural resources, and pollution.
This idea can itself be applied at different scales: it is possible for a person
to calculate their own personal ecological footprint (there are many calculators on the Internet), but it can also be done for a household, a town,
an organization, a region, or a country. Measuring an "ecological footprint" is a very graphic way of showing how natural resources are being
used and damaged. The "footprint" is the amount of the Earth's surface
that is needed to sustain the person or organization measured. The great
majority of people in the West are taking up far more than their share of
the planet's surface. In effect, what Dobson is proposing as the basis of
ecological citizenship is a development of what was agreed in the 1997
Kyoto Protocol: that countries must each take responsibility for reducing
a quota of carbon emissions to reverse climate change (Dobson, 2006;
see Greene, 2005: 471).

Writers on environmental citizenship tend to see the emergence of
global civil society as offering the best hope for its future. Evidently,
globalization in the widest sense – the growth of transnational economic
and social processes and the setting up of international political institutions – does not necessarily mean an increase in environmental awareness.
On the contrary, economic globalization may result in a more extensive
and effective exploitation of the Earth's resources and more widespread
environmental degradation. Of course, environmentalists believe that the
planet's inhabitants will, by the same token, be increasingly exposed to
ecological disasters as a result. However, this will not in itself lead to
informed measures to safeguard the environment. People may ignore
"nature's warnings." Anthony Giddens argues that this is especially likely
because, although people may believe that environmental damage will be
catastrophic, if they do not actually experience its effects, they will prefer
not to change their way of life until it is too late (Giddens, 2009: 2). Nor
will a greater degree of democratic participation lead automatically to a
greater sensitivity to the environment. Indeed, it might equally well lead
to greater destruction if citizens embrace a productivist, consumer
identity. Global environmental citizenship requires an increase in
public awareness of the issues and the construction of the will to act in

such a way as to ensure a healthy and flourishing environment in the long term.

The environmental movement is beginning to see some success in its contribution to global civil society. The activities of environmental organizations are contributing to the growth of public awareness and some consideration has been given to environmental issues on the part of international political institutions. There is now a system of international laws, conventions, and treaties covering such cases as protection of the North Sea, the elimination of CFC gases, and so on. Furthermore, most over-developed countries have accepted that they must reduce or stabilize carbon emissions to some extent, even when, as in the US, they did not sign the Kyoto Protocol. However, compared to the seriousness of environmental destruction, and the importance of changes needed to deal with it adequately, such measures are extremely limited.

Note

1   There are different definitions of cultural citizenship. For some commentators, multiculturalism includes the claims of all minorities (including gay men, for example, as well as cultural minorities) to be included in society as full citizens whose "cultural difference" is respected (e.g., Pakulski, 1997). For others, the most important aspect of cultural citizenship is communication and dialogue (Turner, 2001). I discuss communication and dialogue in chapter 5 on democracy and limit the discussion of multiculturalism to Kymlicka's definition of rights to live and choose within "societal cultures." One more caveat: the commonsense understandings of culture as "national," "high," "low," "difference," and so on are obviously different from the more technical way in which I am using "culture" throughout this book to understand "signifying practices" that are crucial to how society is reproduced and transformed.

Chapter 5
Globalization and Democracy

Political sociology is concerned, above all, with the study of the empirical conditions within which power is exercised and constrained. It is a distinctive enterprise in this respect, different from political theory and political philosophy, which deal with conceptual analysis and normative justifications. Separation of the empirical, analytic, and normative dimensions of the study of democracy cannot be made neatly, however; analyzing democracy in practice necessarily involves normative questions. Democracy is not just an ideal of political theory; in practice, it should live up to at least some of the most significant elements of what we think it should be. Otherwise, use of the term "democracy" is nothing more than propaganda.

There are two main ways in which globalization calls existing forms of representative democracy into question. The first concerns state autonomy and sovereignty, which we explored in chapter 2. To be sure, state autonomy has always been compromised in relation to capitalism. It is not just Marxists who have been concerned that where states are responsible for economic management, business lobbyists have a built-in advantage beyond that of money: what is good for business is, almost by definition, what is good for the national economy and, therefore, for the government. With increased flows of finance capital, investment by multinational corporations, and global markets, however, the picture becomes even more complex: the very idea of states managing "national" economies starts to look outdated. What has to be managed is a *global* economy, which has different consequences for those living in different national territories, but which has its own dynamics beyond the control of any single state.

We also looked, in chapter 2, at how states are transforming in global governance, to the point where they are now better seen as "internationalizing" rather than as nation-states. But if states are internationalizing, what happens to democracy, which was formed, and fought for, in nation-states? State transformation in global governance is a problem for the modern ideal of democracy because it requires autonomous and sovereign states. The ideal of "actually existing" democracy is that "the people," identified as "the nation," are able to take charge, albeit indirectly through their representatives, of the conditions of their own lives. In effect, democracy involves attempting to influence governments to use the special privileges of the state (the threat of force and the regulation and redistribution of wealth) to act for "the people." Voting to elect governments is just one aspect of democracy, but it is the most clear-cut and obvious; it is what most people understand by democracy and, as democracy involves rule by the people, the common understanding certainly should not be ignored. If globalization means that processes previously managed by the state now escape its control or can only be managed with the cooperation of unelected agencies both inside and outside the state, what are the implications for democracy?

The second main limitation of existing representative democracy in globalization is rather the reverse of this problem: if processes of globalization which impact on peoples' lives are not, by definition, confined within national territories, why should definitions of "national interest" be all-important in international affairs? Many political theorists now argue that what is more important is that "all affected" by a particular issue are able to influence how it is dealt with in ways that are relevant to their lives. "All-affected" by an issue may, on occasion, live within the territorial borders of a state, but this was never necessarily the case, and processes of globalization make it rare today. Globalization raises the question, "who is the people?", which is no longer settled by the response, "the nation." The "all-affected" principle of democratic participation seems intuitively right: if democracy is about control over the conditions of people's lives, it is irrelevant that some people happen to live within the same territorial boundaries; what is important is that *all* those affected by an issue, within and across borders, must have some impact on how their difficulties are resolved. If it is immensely hard to see how it can be put into practice (How to decide precisely who is affected? Who is to decide each time?), the "all affected" principle is certainly a compelling criticism of the idea that democracy can be contained within national territories (Held, 1995a; Held, 2004: 98–102; Gould, 2004: 176–8; Fraser, 2008: 64–7).

In normative terms, democracy may be formal or substantive. Definitions of democracy as formal – which prevail in political science – concern the procedures by which governments are made accountable and legitimate. Joseph Schumpter's definition of democracy as exclusively concerned with competition between political parties to win votes is such a definition (Mair, 2008: 113). Wider considerations of procedural democracy also concern questions such as: the methods by which candidates are selected within parties; the independence of legislatures from corruption; separation of powers between the judiciary, the legislature, and the executive; and so on. Substantive democracy is much harder to pin down since it involves judgments about the quality and the extent of popular participation in democratic decision-making: "rule by the people" should ensure the equality of all voices in society; all should be properly represented, and all should be heard. Thinking about democracy substantively involves asking questions about whether "the people" have really been represented in government. One of the main ways to assess this is to consider the outcome of democratic deliberations: do some people systematically benefit from democratic procedures, while others systematically lose? Such questions are tricky because it is difficult to agree on what the outcome of democratic decision-making would be if it were not distorted; inevitably, they raise further questions about what an undistorted outcome *should* be. In this respect, analyses of substantive democracy link up with issues of citizenship explored in chapter 4. At the very least, governments should act in the interests of "ordinary" people, many of whom might reasonably be expected to rely on public provision of education, healthcare, and social insurance against illness, unemployment, and old-age at different points in their lives. In this respect, something like Marshall's model of citizenship provides a rough guide to expected outcomes. As we also saw in chapter 4, however, in a pluralist society, different outcomes are required for the equality of different groups of "ordinary" people, whilst the problem of how to balance equality and freedom is always controversial, as it is for social movements involved in extending the equality and diversity of citizenship rights. Although the distinction between procedural and substantive democracy may seem relatively straightforward, and procedural questions much easier to assess, in practice things are not so clear-cut. Questions of both procedural and substantive democracy are almost always involved in judging whether particular procedures are actually democratic, where they result in outcomes that are skewed towards particular perspectives and definitions of the "common good."

In section 5.1, we first look at what most people consider the defining procedures of representative democracy, multi-party electoral politics. It is political parties that make governments, and voting in national elections is commonly seen as the defining act by which citizens make their individual views count in liberal-democracies. As citizens become increasingly mistrustful of politicians, however, and voting rates decline, what becomes of the ideal of democracy as representative government? Are multi-party elections in which large numbers of citizens participate essential to democracy? If so, are democracies in which this is no longer a feature now tipping over into something else? Have we reached "post-democracy" (Crouch, 2004)?

In political institutions beyond the state, elections to official positions are practically non-existent. The exception is Members of the European Parliament, which all European citizens are entitled to elect. However, European citizens take even less interest in European elections than they do in national elections. Voter turnout for European elections is roughly 20 percent lower than in national elections; it is falling, and less than half now vote across the EU. In addition, most people who do participate in European elections actually vote on national issues, using their votes to punish unpopular governments rather than voting for parties to deal with Europe-wide concerns. The fact that, although parties have formed cohesive coalitions in the European Parliament, there are no large and influential European parties to mobilize specifically on European issues is telling in this respect (Hix, 2008: 596–7). The formal rights European citizens have to vote in European elections do not begin to solve the problem of the democratic deficit of the European Union.

In section 5.2, we look a little more widely at democratic ideals in international political and legal institutions: how might democracy work beyond the state? One of the most promising developments here is that of international human rights law which, at least in principle, assures the individual rights that are necessary for democratic participation and which is itself developing through relatively democratic procedures. However, the development of international human rights law has been aimed at ensuring rights to democratic participation *within* states. Democratic procedures *between* states are a good deal more difficult to imagine as we will see from a brief look at the existing voting procedures of Inter-Governmental Organizations.

The way in which global social movements tend to see themselves as contributing to democratization beyond the state is through global civil society. Social movement organizations and networks are not, however, themselves democratic in any straightforward sense. Some, by no means all, NGOs have large memberships, some are relatively transparent and accountable, but NGO leaders are not elected by popular vote, and neither are the causes they champion subjected to popular democratic approval. If electing governments in a multi-party system is the basis of democracy, how can global governance be democratized without changes to democratic procedures? In section 5.3, we explore alternative ways of thinking of the activities of global social movements as democratizing. Finally, in section 5.4, we conclude with a brief summary of the cultural politics in which global social movements are engaged, and their importance for democratization.

5.1 Democracy in Crisis: Political Parties and Elections

What is surely the defining feature of democracy for most people today is the ballot box: citizens vote periodically in national elections for the political party of their choice to form a government. It is by no means obvious that this is all that is required for democracy, and contemporary political sociologists have actually taken more interest in other aspects of political participation, especially the activities of social movements. In part, this is because the popularity and influence of political parties has been in decline in Western democracies for decades, as indicated by the steady fall in numbers of voters who participate in national elections in countries where voting is not obligatory. Moreover, according to polling data, confidence and trust in political parties is lower than in any other high-profile public organizations, including large companies, trade unions, the press, and the police (Mair, 2008: 128–9; The Power Enquiry, 2006; Singh, 2003: chapter 4). Decline in their popularity and influence has been accompanied by changes in political parties themselves, which tend to make them even less like the vehicles for the expression of popular will they are ideally supposed to be, and even more like the organizations that get professional politicians elected that they have always been in practice. Nevertheless, to think of reforming democracy for complex, large-scale societies without considering the role of multi-party elections to government would seem to involve something other than democracy.

Historically, most political parties in Western Europe developed to represent the preferences of voters for whom class divisions were most important to the organization and regulation of national economies. (The exceptions here concern those in consociational democracies, like Holland and Belgium, in which parties represent religious divisions). In the US, where the working-class movement has always been weak, a liberal/conservative divide developed somewhat later than the Left/Right distinction in Europe, with Democrats tending towards the Left and

Republicans towards the Right (Singh, 2003: chapter 3). Many of those who study political parties argue that there has been class dealignment over the last few decades, a fall in the support of working-class voters for Left-wing parties, and of those in middle- and upper-class occupations for parties on the Right (Manza, Hout, and Brooks, 2009). There is continued controversy on this issue, but in a situation in which the traditional working class itself has shrunk in absolute terms, with the decline of manufacturing and the growth of service industry jobs, the question of class loyalty to political parties has become less relevant today. What is more important is that the numbers of people actually involved in party politics has declined. It has declined in absolute terms across Europe, as party members leave and others do not join (Mair and van Biezen, 2001). In the US, political parties were never mass membership organizations as they were in Europe, but there has also been a well-charted decline in nationwide voluntary associations that were networked into state and federal government (Skocpol, 2003; Putnam, 2000, 2002). The result in Europe and the US has been the same: a growing distance between ordinary people and professional political elites.

At the same time, as parties across Europe have adapted to neo-liberal globalization in different ways, they have tended to move towards the center, advocating pragmatic policies that tend to converge on keeping taxes low, encouraging business, and cutting state costs. Exceptionally, in the US, where historically parties have often been virtually indistinguishable in terms of ideology and policy, the Left/Right gap between Democrats and Republicans has opened up in recent years around issues of "social liberalism" like abortion rights and gay marriages, and also the domestic and foreign policies associated with the neo-liberal and authoritarian "New Right" (McKay, 2005: 121–7). The desire to overcome party divisions that Barack Obama expressed during the 2008 election should be understood in this context.

Political parties now target voters as citizen-consumers rather than in terms of political ideologies. They market themselves, focusing on keeping core voters, trying to confuse those who intend to vote for other parties, and, above all, trying to capture "floating" voters, those who have not made up their minds which way to vote. Parties have become a good deal more professional in techniques of political communication, strengthening the role of professional media managers in party structures in the process. "Spin doctors" are employed as experts in dealing with the media; they frame news releases to be favorable to party policies and personalities, preempt or conceal bad news, and generally try to represent the party as working for those who support them, whilst avoiding alienating those who might possibly be persuaded to do so.

As a result, style, appearance, and presentation for the media have become ever more important to political parties. Indeed, critics of what has become known as "political marketing" argue that a politician's personality is now more important than party policies. The contemporary focus on style involves the careful cultivation of "star quality" combined with the appearance of sincerity and trustworthiness. Political parties aim to produce what John Street calls "celebrity politicians," like Bill Clinton and Tony Blair, who successfully use techniques of show business (including photo-opportunities with stars of entertainment, and appearing on chat shows) to build their charisma and to influence the public. They try to convey the impression that, although they are special, they are also ordinary: they are authorized to speak for us because they are like us (Street, 2004). Especially on TV, politicians address audiences intimately, seeking emotional engagement and identification in order to overcome the cynicism with which politicians are generally regarded (Corner and Pels, 2003; Washbourne, 2010).

As a consequence of the decline of networked links with citizens, political parties are seeking new ways to build popularity through the media. John Street suggests that it is too soon to judge the viability of such an approach. Critics of parties' use of public relations techniques tend to take a rationalist view of how politics should be conducted, and they misunderstand how it was conducted in the past. Democratic politics has never involved the rational calculation of interests and needs, and policy was never designed methodically in utilitarian terms for the best outcome for the greatest number of people. Politics is always cultural politics: the manipulation of symbols, the creation of emotional identification, and the rhetorical production of "us" against "them" have always been important. Marketing and style is not new to party politics, even if it is now addressed a good deal more systematically in relation to the media (Street, 2003).

In fact, Street argues, thinking seriously about questions of aesthetics, and the appearance and style of celebrity politicians should make us think again about what we understand by representative democracy. How precisely do politicians in government represent "we the people"? Critics of the personalization of politics suppose that representation involves "acting for" the represented; they are, therefore, concerned with the capacities and skills of politicians, including their capacities to respond to people's demands and needs. However, this understanding of representation cannot be entirely separated from the *appearance* of representation: it is always enacted symbolically. Questions of appearance cannot be eliminated, and judgments about politicians' appearances can be discussed and validated in a range of ways. Especially under conditions where policy choices and implications have become so complex and difficult to follow, trying to "read" personality and trustworthiness from a television interview may not be such an absurd way to get to grips with the politicians who are supposed to represent us in democratic government (Street, 2004).

There is no doubt, however, that the personalization of politics does have disadvantages for parties trying to build popularity. Castells argues that it contributes directly to voters' disaffection with politicians and alienation from party politics because it leads to obsessive "digging the dirt" on individual politicians, targeting them with revelations about their personal lives. "Digging the dirt" is built-in to party politics now, as members of opposition parties, or indeed opponents within the same party, can be effectively eliminated, especially during elections, with a well-placed media story about their personal inadequacies. Investigative journalism that reveals political scandals (uncovering links between financial donations to political parties and government policies that favor donors' interests, for example) is a very important aspect of democracy, crucial to making governments accountable once they are elected. However, democracy is not necessarily well-served where the media stories that gather the most interest concern the personal assassination of political rivals (Castells, 2009: 196–9).

As party politics has become more personalized, there has been relatively little attention given to making media coverage of party politics interesting to voters in other ways. Theda Skocpol argues that, without necessarily intending to, the mainstream media has tended to disparage group activities and representative politics, neglecting to stage the importance of differences, arguments, and decisions for ordinary people in favor of expert opinion. It is, of course, much more difficult to make party politics interesting when ideological differences between parties are negligible, or when politicians do their best to avoid making any commitment that may alienate "floating" voters. In addition to a greater role for the participation of members of the public in mediated political debate, Skocpol also recommends the celebration of voting on election days, building "drama, group efforts, and collective effervescence" into voting for government to encourage citizens to participate (Skocpol, 2003: 283–4). Election days in the past were much more carnivalesque – though they were also then much more corrupt (Schudson, 1998). Skocpol's point here is, however, an interesting one: perhaps what is needed is not less but *more* attention to the style and performance of engagement in formal politics, though it should encourage party politics to become more inclusive rather than ever more tightly focused on the personalities of party leaders.

It is in this context that the triumphant election of Barack Obama in 2008 seems to mark something of an exception to the decline of political parties. The election was, of course, very much focused on Obama's personality, his individual charisma, as well as on the fact that he was the first African-American to be nominated to run for president. In addition, Obama presented himself very emphatically as a politician building consensus "beyond Left and Right." What was exceptional about his campaign for presidency, however, was the grassroots support it drew in, especially amongst young and African-American first-time voters. There are two important aspects of Obama's campaign that mean it may mark a turning point for the legitimacy of political parties. First, in terms of political communication, his supporters brought the campaign to the Internet in an unprecedented way, micro-targeting American citizens through social networking sites, personal websites, and the use of YouTube, as well as using more conventional political marketing techniques. Second, the campaign raised most of its money from small donations, which meant that Obama was not beholden to large funders once he was in office (Castells, 2009). In mobilizing grassroots supporters from outside the traditional party structure, and finding new ways to communicate beyond political communication via public relations professionals and "spin doctors," the Obama campaigners may have found a way to revitalize political parties and government elections. It remains to be seen, however, how much their success depended on Obama's special appeal as a person and as a representative of the American dream, as well as to the fact that he was a relative newcomer to the elites of the Democratic Party, and therefore had to find ways to reach out beyond it.

Political parties still function procedurally in liberal-democracies as the means by which governments are elected and organized. Those who favor direct democracy have always criticized representative democracy as effectively undemocratic: how democratic is a political system in which citizens are governed by people they only vote for every few years? In recent years, the criticism that citizens have too little voice in government is becoming even more telling, as so few people are directly involved in government politics, or choose to vote at all. In addition, those who are concerned that liberal-democratic procedures make little contribution to substantive democracy see the loss of citizens' social rights over the last few decades as clearly indicative that we are now in an era of "post-democracy" (Crouch, 2004).

5.2   Democracy, Human Rights, and International Political Institutions

David Held argues that globalization requires democratization of global governance. The cosmopolitan democracy he advocates involves three main principles. First, cosmopolitan law must be developed as a kind of global constitution to guarantee rights for all. Second, Inter-Governmental Organizations must become more democratic and more effective. In the short-term, this involves reforming existing IGOs to make them more transparent and accountable, especially the UN system; but in the long-term Held envisages a global parliament, making law and policy. Law made democratically should, he argues, be enforced, by military means if necessary. Third, democratic participation should be organized in terms of "subsidiarity": governmental decisions should be made as locally as possible to maximize accountability and the participation of those affected by particular issues. This means establishing transnational regional political institutions like the EU in other parts of the world in order to deal with economic regulation more effectively. It also means supporting democratization at the sub-national level. Held's ideal of cosmopolitan democracy is that of political and legal institutions nested within each other, from local to global, with decisions being made through participation at the appropriate scale for "all affected" by a particular issue. Popular participation in decision-making is to be guaranteed by rights codified in cosmopolitan law. Although Held denies that cosmopolitan democracy requires a world state, as Nadia Urbinati points out, the cosmopolitical order he proposes nevertheless resembles a "state-like sovereign" (Urbinati, 2003: 73; Held, 1995a, 1995b, 1998, 2003, 2004; Held and McGrew, 2002). Moreover, Held does anticipate that eventually the nation-state will "wither away," absorbed into the structures that it helped establish to enable more opportunities for democratic participation around the world (Held, 1999: 106).

For critics of cosmopolitan democracy, on the other hand, it is still much more important to support democratic institutions that have been established at the national level. In the first place, this involves a commitment to the continuation of states, largely on the pragmatic grounds that they will not simply "wither away." McGrew, for example, argues that states are still the most important actors in global governance, and they cannot easily be displaced to make it more democratic. International political institutions like the UN themselves rely on states, especially on those with the greatest economic and military power. In the absence of a world state, there is no means even of raising taxes to fund international political institutions, and certainly no global peace-keeping force beyond that which states provide (McGrew, 1997: 254–7). Others argue that Held exaggerates the loss of control that states have over processes of globalization, especially economic processes and, therefore, the loss of democratic control at the national level (Hirst and Thompson, 1996; Kymlicka, 1999b; Axtmann, 2002). Critics are also skeptical about the possibilities of developing democracy beyond the nation-state. Democracy involves more than simply voting, and differences in language, national context, history, and political expectations will make dialogue and debate across borders very difficult (as in the European Union) (Kymlicka, 1999b). Consequently, given the lack of interest ordinary people already take in foreign issues, it is likely that the perspectives of political elites will become even more dominant in international organizations, and popular influence will decline still further. On this basis, Robert Dahl argues that international organizations cannot be democratic. This does not necessarily mean that they are illegitimate. They are important as bureaucratic bargaining systems. But democracy is only possible, however imperfectly, at the national and sub-national level (Dahl, 1999; see also Urbinati, 2003; Woods, 2002; Archibugi, 2004).

The alternative to cosmopolitan democracy for these critics appears to be national democracy supplemented by international coordination where issues affect constituencies beyond national borders. If democracy is the only legitimate form of rule, and the only really legitimate form of democracy must include multi-party elections, then it is only in national states that government is legitimate. This suggests that the political representatives who are given a mandate from their electorates to represent them in Inter-Governmental Organizations are supposed to act either in terms of explicit policy promises assessed by national electorates or (what is more likely), what politicians themselves are able to negotiate in the "national interest." On the other hand, the decisions in IGOs are all themselves based on voting procedures. This suggests that international bodies see their decisions as based on a different source of legitimacy to mandates from national electorates. In some respects, then, IGOs are already making law and policy for the world. As internationalizing states become more deeply entangled with each other and with other actors in global governance, it is not always possible to separate out what is being agreed in the name of "national interests" from wider considerations of international concern. Where states themselves are no longer as clearly distinct from each other at the international level as they once were, coordination *between* states turns into something else. In this respect, there is every reason to consider democracy beyond the state.

Democracy and human rights

Many sociologists and political theorists see the development of human rights as a kind of democratic bridge between the international and national levels. Jackie Smith, for example, writes:

> Democracy is a delivery system for human rights, and indeed, without human rights, we do not have democracy. Thus, a more democratic world order is one that is organized to ensure the highest level of protection of human rights. (Smith, 2008: 229)

In a similar way, David Held seems to suggest that extending human rights represents a means by which cosmopolitan democracy may be achieved, as public law provides the conditions that ensure democratic participation (Held, 1995a: 153–8).

The international human rights that most obviously promote democracy are civil and political rights, prominent in the Universal Declaration of Human Rights and later made binding on most states in the world as they were ratified in the International Convention on Civil and Political Rights. The rule of law is crucial to ensuring civil rights to freedom of speech and association that enable the full expression and discussion of political opinions, not just for participating in the electoral politics of political parties but also for wider debate and discussion, social movement mobilization, and demonstrations and protests. Besides civil rights to freedom of speech and association, and political rights to vote and stand for office that are equally uncontroversial in this respect, the UDHR also states: "Everyone, as a member of society, has the right to social security and is entitled to realization, through national effort and international cooperation and in accordance with the organization and resources of each State, of the economic, social and cultural rights indispensable for his dignity and the free development of his personality" (Article 22). The UDHR then goes on to spell out individuals' social, economic, and cultural entitlements in detail, and these were later made binding on states – the majority of those in the UN – that ratified the International Convention of Economic, Social and Cultural Rights. David Held argues that social, economic, and cultural rights are as important to individual autonomy as civil and political rights. It is only in conditions in which individuals are free and relatively equal that democratic participation will be genuinely effective (Held, 1995a: 153–6).

International commitments to human rights regime seem, then, to represent a version of citizenship that is close to Marshall's social democratic model, with the notable difference that it is a global citizenship, specifying and granting entitlements to every individual in the world. This raises obvious questions about differences between the national and the international level that we already touched on in chapter 2: how are human rights to be ensured and enforced in the absence of a world state? Is international human rights law imposed on non-Western states, and if so, does that matter if it then protects individuals against state infringement of their civil and political rights? And if there is no international enforcement of civil rights, what difference does having human rights "on paper" make to the individuals within repressive or neglectful states for whom they are intended?

Habermas argues that a minimal human rights law is legitimate for the whole world insofar as it is supported by global consensus. He sees international law as legitimately becoming a global constitution, as people express universal indignation at gross violations of human rights (Habermas, 2001: 108; 2006: 144). Cosmopolitan law specifies crimes against humanity through what is called *jus cogens*, or "strong law. *Jus cogens* concerns gross violations of fundamental human rights such as slavery, torture, genocide, and disappearances. Though technically "crimes against humanity" are the province of humanitarian law (or the laws of war), it is these kinds of violations that most people associate with human rights issues, and they certainly arouse widespread indignation (though not necessarily action on the part of the "international community") wherever they are revealed. As well as in Conventions ratified by states, gross violations of human rights are also covered by international customary law – under which such actions are illegal, regardless of whether or not a state has signed a particular treaty or human rights convention. If public outrage is the sign of legitimacy, this type of law is undoubtedly legitimate, though it is especially controversial as it encroaches furthest on conventional understandings of state sovereignty as the authority to "have the last word" within its territory.

In chapter 2, we looked at the controversies raised by questions of the military enforcement of cosmopolitan law in cases of humanitarian intervention. Especially concerning in this respect is the way wealthy, militarized states have used human rights as a justification for overriding state sovereignty for reasons of Realpolitick rather than to stop gross violations of human rights (most evidently in the case of war in Iraq). International customary law may also override law made by democratically elected governments where state leaders are accused of "crimes against humanity." For example, amnesties granted to former dictators as part of processes of peace-making and reconciliation are not accepted by the International Criminal Court, which may still proceed with prosecution for gross violations of human rights.

Most human rights law, however, is developed and enforced in a much less dramatic fashion than these examples suggest, through "statist" procedures that respect the ideals of state sovereignty and national self-determination governing the UN systems. The "statist" adoption of human rights agreements, however, raises different problems: how then can respect for individuals' human rights be assured given that it is states that violate human rights? It is by no means clear how the tension between the principle that individual rights must be respected everywhere that is the basis of global human rights, and the principle that states are equal and independent, the basis of state sovereignty in the UN system, will be resolved, if at all. In the meantime, virtually all the development and monitoring of human rights agreements concerns consensus-building between and within states.

Sally Engle Merry has made an in-depth ethnographic study of how a UN document concerning violence against women was created. In *Human Rights and Gender Violence,* she shows the extraordinary lengths participants in UN conferences and meetings went to over a number of years to ensure consensus between state representatives and members of NGOs (Merry, 2006). Once they have been drawn up, human rights agreements are signed and ratified by state representatives. States may ratify human rights agreements with reservations: that is, they are allowed to opt out of some points, as long as this does not destroy the spirit of the agreement itself. A notorious example is US ratification of the International Convention on Civil and Political Rights (ICCPR); state officials insisted on a reservation to allow capital punishment for juveniles that was expressly prohibited by Article 6 (Roth, 2000). By far the largest number of reservations to any human rights agreement is to the Convention for the Elimination of Discrimination Against Women, especially concerning "cultural practices," where women's roles are defined by religious or family law within that state (Bayefsky, 1994). Finally, human rights agreements are "self-executing" for some states: they immediately become domestic law. For many others, however, like the US and the UK, they must be incorporated into national law through legislatures.

The member states of the Council of Europe (which includes all those in the EU, and Turkey) are a partial exception to the "statist" adoption of human rights insofar as the European Convention of Human Rights (ECHR) is binding on all member states, whether or not they have incorporated it into domestic law, and the European Court of Human Rights works as a kind of Supreme Court to interpret the ECHR for all member states. Even here, however, rulings are made on the basis of what is called the "margin of appreciation": in most cases, the European Court will find a state in breach of the European Convention *only* where there is agreement across member states that individuals should enjoy particular rights. A striking example is the Court's decision in the case of children's rights in T *v* United Kingdom in 1999, where it was decided that, as there is no common standard across the EU for the age at which someone can be considered criminally responsible, the English court that tried a child of 10 on charges of murdering another child was not in breach of European human rights law (Dembour, 2006: 163–5).

The democratic legitimacy of the vast majority of human rights agreements comes, then, from the way in which the procedures by which they are created and adopted at international and national levels have built-in state sovereignty. It is states that are bound to ensure the human rights of individuals within their jurisdictions. One notable feature of this system is that, although most states have ratified the major human rights Conventions, human rights law differs somewhat between states. Variation in the practices of human rights raises difficult questions, however, given that they are supposed to be universal: each and every individual in the world should be treated equal according to human rights principles. How acceptable are national variations in this case, and who is to decide (McCarthy, 1999)? In fact, once human rights law is incorporated into national law, to a large extent it is judges who decide, in high-profile cases brought by advocacy organizations precisely to test the law and extend it in scope and detail. Human rights become a "higher law" to which the policies and laws that governments make must legally conform and judges decide whether they have done so in a particular case (Stone Sweet, 2008; Nash 2009a). Moreover, judges reviewing national law and policy increasingly do so in the light of international understandings of human rights as they have been judged in other national and international courts (Slaughter, 2004: 66–7). Test cases also offer, then, a further opportunity for the convergence of norms across different states that support what is, effectively, the development of a global constitution "from below." A striking example is the US Supreme Court decision in *Roper v Simmons* that, though allowed in US law (by the special reservation from the ICCPR), capital punishment for juveniles should no longer be carried out because it is counter to "evolving standards of decency," based partly on the fact that it had been abolished or disavowed in every other state in the world (Roper *v* Simmons, US, 551. 2005).

Human rights are democratic, then, insofar as the domestic procedures by which states make and judge law are followed in the way international human rights agreements come to be binding within their territories. Human rights activists try to get states to the point of ratifying (if they are resistant) and then genuinely respecting international human rights agreements by bringing pressure on them from within, supported by International Non-Governmental Organizations and Inter-Governmental Organizations, and often also by NGOs in other states, that put pressure on their own governments to put pressure on recalcitrant states. Occasionally using economic sanctions – as in the international pressure on South Africa to end apartheid – this constellation of actors generally tries to persuade state officials into accepting the validity and legitimacy of human rights norms, to shame them over their state's human rights record, and to try to get them to change it (Keck and Sikkink, 1998; Risse et al., 1999).

An interesting recent example of such pressure is the Poor People's Economic Human Rights Campaign, through which poor and homeless people in the US have been trying to make their government accountable for meeting their basic needs as citizens, raising issues of welfare reform nationally, through marches and petitions, and at the same time at the international level, at the UN Human Rights Commission and the Inter-American Commission of Organization for American States. This example is particularly interesting because it confirms Margaret Somers' view that human rights will become increasingly relevant in the West as citizens become more distant from states as the last guarantor of material security. She argues that the marketization of social insurance is now so advanced in the US that poor people are effectively stateless: excluded from the civil sphere, citizenship rights are meaningless to them (Somers, 2008). Poor people in the US are, in part, trying to get their state to ratify the International Convention on Economic, Social, and Cultural Rights so that they will have legal leverage in the US courts. They are also using the language of human rights to give their cause *moral* leverage where national citizenship no longer seems to mean much. Finally, they are seeking to build common cause with representatives of other grassroots organizations around the world, arguing that, given the US influence over global governance, welfare reforms introduced by President Clinton in 1996 could be a model for dismantling government's welfare obligations around the world (Smith, 2008: 160–7; Lister, 2004: 162).

In addition, commitment to human rights is emerging as the common language that non-state actors use to put pressure on Inter-Governmental Organizations. It can be difficult to decide whether such uses of "human rights" are legal or moral or both. Human rights are increasingly being "mainstreamed" across the UN and even to some extent beyond it. The WTO, for example, which is outside the UN system and concerned exclusively with setting the rules of international trade, has come under pressure to consider how these rules conform to human rights principles. NGOs are lobbying the WTO to look at how international regulation ensures or damages social and economic rights to which states have committed themselves in ratifying the International Convention on Economic, Social, and Cultural Rights through the UN (Oberleitner, 2007: 135–9). This might, for example, involve implementing rules of *fair* rather than *free* trade (for example, ending subsidies on agricultural goods produced in Europe and the US that result in "dumping" surpluses in developing countries (Tonkiss, 2005: 76)). Critics of the strategy argue that although formal rights are attributed to all individuals in human rights law, such policies are too abstract and distant from what matters, which is what people make of resources in practice. Insofar as the human rights movement is concerned with *outcome*, however, simply ensuring that human rights norms are referred to in bureaucratic documents will not satisfy demands for action to realize human rights (Gready and Ensor, 2005; Blau and Moncada, 2007; Stammers, 2009). We will look more closely at the strategies for democratization of social movement actors in global civil society in the following section.

Democracy between states

Although human rights are developed in international political institutions, they are not designed to contribute to their democratization. Except in the EU, there are no international political institutions that make provision for political parties to represent individuals in law and policy-making at this level. Where *individuals* are the subjects of democratic procedures within states – each with a vote – at the international level it is representatives of *states* who vote. It is nations who are the subjects of democratic procedures in international political institutions insofar as the officials who carry out state business at the international level are almost invariably either elected in national elections, or appointed by elected governments. However, although all Inter-Governmental Organizations use voting to make final decisions, it is doubtful that any of them could be considered democratic.

Different IGOs have different voting procedures. Here we will consider only a selection of the most important. The United Nations is the most inclusive IGO (virtually all states are members), and it probably enjoys the most legitimacy worldwide as a result. It is nominally democratic in that the UN Charter stipulates that all states are to be treated equally (unlike the League of Nations, which it replaced), though (unlike the EU) the UN does not require member states themselves to be democratic. Set up with the aim of keeping world peace after World War II, it has since grown to encompass a vast range of activities, from setting and monitoring human rights standards, to establishing programs to advance social and economic development, protecting refugees, and encouraging environmental sustainability. In the General Assembly – the main deliberative forum of the UN – all member states have one vote each. Similarly, in the Economic and Social Council (ECOSOC), the members of which are elected by the General Assembly on the basis of geographical representation for a three-year term, each member has one vote. This nominal equality between states itself raises difficult questions for democratic procedure: should all states have equal voting rights when some represent tiny numbers of people, while others are huge? Is Tuvala the same as India for these purposes? If, however, states were to have votes proportionate to their populations, the balance of power for any decision would be held permanently by just a few states. These issues do not become as important as we might expect, however, because the General Assembly and ECOSOC are largely seen as "talking shops," where international agreements are based on consensus between state representatives. Difficult decisions that result in the UN taking action as a political body take place in the Security Council. The Security Council is strikingly undemocratic. It consists of five permanent members (US, UK, and France, the states that founded the UN on the basis of their victory in World War II, and their closest allies, Russia and China) and ten others elected by the General Assembly for a two-year term. Each of the permanent members has the power to veto any decision, even if unanimously agreed upon by the other members. These decisions concern the core business of the UN, war and peace: the Security Council decides whether a country is justified in attacking another, and how to deal with it, whether by economic sanctions, sending peace-keeping forces, or by authorizing member states to take military action. As George Monbiot notes, the permanent members of the UN Security Council are also those who sell the most arms. In addition, the five permanent members have vetoes over any constitutional reform of the UN, the appointment of the UN Secretary-General, the election of judges to the International Court of Justice, and the admission of a new member to the UN (Monbiot, 2004: 68–72; Archibugi, 1995).

The procedures for reaching agreements in the institutions of economic global governance are similarly skewed to benefit the wealthiest states. The World Bank, set up to finance investment projects, and the IMF, which is supposed to provide a framework for international trade by lending money to countries with balance-of-payments problems, both adopt the procedures of share-holding companies, weighting votes according to the investment stakes of different states. This means that, even in terms of formal procedures, a small number of wealthy states (those that make up the G8) control most of the votes in these Organizations. In addition, the US appoints the President of the World Bank, and the European Union chooses the Managing Director of the IMF (Monbiot, 2004: 153–4; Tonkiss, 2005: 61–70). In comparison, the WTO traditionally reaches agreement by consensus, and where that is not possible, voting is organized on the basis of membership: one vote, one state. In practice, Susan George argues, consensus means that the US, Canada, Japan, and the European Union agree on a policy and the others fall into line (George, 2004: 60). The G8 is a different kind of organization: a forum for the leaders of Western states with the largest economies, it tries to build consensus on world economic policy. It has no standing organization and its decisions are not formally binding on its members in the same way as those of the UN, the World Bank, the IMF, and the WTO.

What emerges, then, from this brief look at the formal procedures of Inter-Governmental Organizations is that there is a strong weighting towards states with historically over-developed economies: the over-developed are also over-represented in IGOs. There have been many suggestions for democratizing the UN and institutions of economic governance, including rotating membership of the UN Security Council, making the General Assembly more representative, adding another assembly to the UN system where individuals would be represented rather than states, and giving developing countries special borrowing rights from the IMF (see Archibugi, 1995; Archibugi, Held, and Kohler, 1998; Monbiot, 2004).

Amongst the simplest of these suggestions is that NGOs should have more involvement in debating and in decision-making in international political institutions, on the grounds that they bring new perspectives, expertise, and advocacy for justice into otherwise state-centric discussions. Some NGOs have consultative status already in some IGOs; they have been involved in the Economic and Social Council in the UN, for example, since the 1940s, and more recently, some have been allowed to participate in meetings of the World Bank and World Trade Organization. The inclusion of NGOs in government business raises, however, difficult questions about how they represent "ordinary" people. They vary enormously in this respect: some (e.g., Amnesty International, Friends of the Earth) are membership organizations funded by, and quite closely connected with, grassroots organizers; others are much more hierarchical and professional, oriented towards getting grants from donors (like the Ford Foundation) and governments; some have well-established reputations while others are virtually unknown outside elite circles; the largest and most well-funded, with the greatest credibility for North American and European governments, are based within these states. Above all, then, it is not obvious how the most internationally prominent NGOs would redefine issues, set agendas, and mobilize arguments that would redress the balance of power towards people in the developing world who are clearly under-represented in existing IGOs (Woods, 2002; Monbiot, 2004: 63).

The existing inequalities between states in Inter-Governmental Organizations make it hard to see how the procedures by which decisions are made might be reformed. What could possibly persuade any of the permanent members of the UN Security Council to give up or to share their veto power, for example? And where the states of the G8 are providing the majority of funding to the IMF and World Bank, how might they be encouraged to take the lead in introducing policies against what they perceive as their national interests? On the other hand, it is also clear that democratizing procedures would not lead to democratic outcomes where the agenda is set by wealthy states. As we saw in chapter 2, the "Washington consensus," which committed the IMF and the World Bank to neo-liberalism, has been especially damaging to developing countries. As a result of the global financial crisis of the 1990s, which suggested that global capitalism had not been rationalized, "good governance" and "accountability" are now seen as necessary to the successful implementation of Structural Adjustment Programmes. These are, however, relatively minor adjustments to what remains a neo-liberal project to free markets and minimize states (Chandhoke, 2002: 43–4). Besides inequalities between states in setting the agenda for discussions in IGOs, in more crude terms, it is also difficult for smaller states to resist the enticements and threats of those that are over-developed, over-represented, and have a larger military capacity. It is reported, for example, that when the US wanted to invade Iraq in 1999, it bought the votes of Zaire, Ethiopia, and Columbia by persuading Saudi Arabia to offer them free oil, and after the Yemeni representative on the UN Security Council voted against the resolution that would have legalized the invasion, the US cancelled its $70 million of annual aid to Yemen (Monbiot, 2004: 78).

Of course, in some respects, the problem that democratic procedures do not lead to substantively democratic outcomes is not peculiar to international institutions. On the contrary, backroom dealing, and outright bribery and threats go on everywhere in the lobbying of governments by wealthy interest groups, and policies that work for the benefit of some often do not work for the good of all. Nevertheless, the differences in state capacities are so great that to make IGOs genuinely democratic would surely require more than institutional reform. If gross social and economic inequalities between *individuals* within states inevitably lead to substantive failures in democracy, even if democratic procedures were developed and adhered to in IGOs, given the immense inequalities between states, much more than institutional reform would seem to be needed. In addition to this problem, moreover, the question of whether the leaders of states, elected on national issues, are able to represent citizens adequately in international political institutions exacerbates the "democratic deficit" of IGOs. This is especially the case because – as we have seen in the European Union – voters generally take very little interest in what is still perceived as "foreign policy." It is because IGOs are widely perceived as unrepresentative and unjust on all these counts that they have become the targets of different strategies of democratization by the organizations, groups, and individuals organized into social movements that make up global civil society.

5.3   Global Civil Society

"Global civil society" is a complex and controversial concept. It is intended to be simply descriptive in some respects. John Keane defines global civil society as "a dynamic non-governmental system of interconnected social-economic institutions that straddle the whole earth, and that have complex effects that are felt in its four corners" (Keane, 2003: 8). "Non-governmental" includes a huge range and variety of participants, from religious groups, sports clubs, debating societies, academies, and trades unions, through to groups of concerned citizens (Habermas, 1992: 453). Besides its non-governmental character, what characterizes civil society, above all, is *civility*, the peaceful negotiation of shared social meanings. From the point of view of the democratization of globalization, the most important participants in global civil society are individuals, groups, and

NGOs networked into social movements. In the absence of democracy between states, global civil society represents attempts to democratize "from below." Although global civil society is certainly unevenly developed geographically, there are very few places in the world that are untouched either by globalization or by movements that peacefully resist and contest its dominant forms.

What is important to global social movement networks is substantive democracy: they mobilize, draw in, and represent the marginalized and disenfranchised to each other as well as to those not directly involved in participation in movement communications and protest activities. They do so by making issues and causes visible: matters for public concern. Global social movements aim to influence the formation of ways of life by means of persuasion, to draw in wider and wider numbers of people to question how globalization affects themselves and others, and to think differently about how global issues might be addressed and "turbo-capitalism" contained. Although the effects of global social movements are intended to be quantitative, in that they aim to persuade everyone that "another world is possible," it is above all by the *quality* of their interventions that the democratic legitimacy of global social movements is to be judged.

Besides an analytic description, then, "civil society" also carries a normative weight: democracy *should* involve vibrant civil societies. Although "civil society" originated with the philosophers of the Enlightenment in the seventeenth century, for whom it indicated the capacity of society to organize itself without a state, its current popularity owes much more to the way it was used in relation to totalitarian regimes in Eastern Europe and Latin America in the 1970s and '80s (Kaldor, 2003; Calhoun, 2007: 81). What was emphasized in these cases was withdrawal from states, to engage in creating civilized ways of life in the face of their unrelenting repression and lies. Putting pressure on states to bring down repressive regimes, in part by building international solidarity, was a secondary consideration, especially in Eastern Europe, where even meeting to discuss ideas was dangerous as the state used spies and informants to penetrate every aspect of life. However, the influence of civil society on democratizing states has been very important to the subsequent popularity of the idea as a way of democratizing globalization. Following the success of the "Velvet Revolution" in Eastern Europe, as state after state collapsed in the face of peaceful, but extremely persistent, demonstrations, global civil society came to be seen as valuable for its orientation towards ending the domination of undemocratic international political institutions and neo-imperial "turbo-capitalism."

The question of what "civil society" should include as a normative concept is closely related to debates over what it is, and should become in reality. One of the main areas of contention here is the question of whether capitalist markets should be considered part of civil society or not. Political theorists tend to define civil society as existing between the state and the market, on the grounds that the market is as much of a danger to the peaceful solidarity of civil society as are repressive states. However, there is a danger that excluding capitalism altogether may lead to an understanding of civil society that is compelling normatively, but so narrow descriptively that it does not help sociological analysis of what potential for "actually existing" for global democratization. For example, Cohen's and Arato's influential work (concerned with national civil societies) defines civil society as consisting of "associations (especially voluntary associations), social movements, and forms of public communication ... created through forms of self-constitution and self-mobilisation" (Cohen and Arato, 1994: ix). There are, however, relatively few non-professional associations compared to the huge number and variety of NGOs active at the global level who employ professional staff; and it is virtually impossible to imagine how transnational mediated communication might be disentangled from markets. If we adopt such a stringent definition, we can only conclude that global civil society is practically non-existent.

At the other end of the spectrum, John Keane argues for a very inclusive definition of global civil society as including profit-seeking businesses. Although "turbo-capitalism" certainly produces immense and very damaging inequalities – and we should add that some transnational corporations have colluded with repressive states (for example, Unocal in Burma, and Shell in Nigeria) – he argues that, in general, business is much more difficult to carry on where there is the threat of violence because predictability and security are required in order to calculate profitability. Keane argues further that transnational corporations are contributing to the integration of a global society, "thickening" communications networks (by investing in and developing innovative new technologies), and generating income, goods, and services across the world. Indeed, it is where there is continual civil unrest and no investment, as in sub-Saharan Africa, that people are most impoverished and marginalized. It is important to note that Keane is not arguing *for* "turbo-capitalism." On the contrary, he sees the activities of other civil society actors as vital in altering transnational corporations to ameliorate the inequalities they produce and to prevent destructive effects on the environment. Nevertheless, he argues that complex societies need markets to provide goods and services. Active engagement in creating "best practice" for businesses is, therefore, crucial (Keane, 2003: 75–88).

Including capitalist markets within definitions of "global civil society," however, brings it uncomfortably close to neo-liberal ideals of economic globalization for many analysts and social movement activists. Neo-liberal globalization is entirely compatible with Keane's version of "civil society" insofar as both are concerned to enlarge social space *outside* states. Civil society actors may then be associated with neo-liberal projects to minimize the regulation of flows of capital and goods in order to promote global markets. Indeed, it becomes much more difficult to ignore those right-wing think tanks and lobbying organizations that explicitly seek to do so: they are also NGOs. Corporations are not inert, passive participants in globalization; they actively engage in trying to shape its conditions in ways that are beneficial to their shareholders (Tonkiss, 2005: 71). In this respect, they are engaged in a project that is very similar to that of other NGOs, though with very different aims and for different beneficiaries.

Global civil society has been formed quite differently from civil societies in Latin America and Eastern Europe. Although there is no world state, the formation of global civil society has been actively encouraged in relation to state-like international political institutions. In fact, it has, in large part, been fostered by the United Nations. Richard Falk argues that, since the environmental summit in Stockholm in 1972, which was planned as a dialogue exclusively between representatives of governments, but at which the unexpected presence of environmentalist groups became the main attraction for the media and for delegates, the UN has actively encouraged global civil society in the form of NGO participation in world conferences on human rights, environmental sustainability and development (Falk, 1998). Other international political institutions have *inadvertently* stimulated the growth of civil society precisely because they lack transparency and accountability. The most spectacular example here is the meetings of the IGOs of economic governance which have provided a focus for social movement politics. As well as the regular demonstrations of "anti-globalization" protestors, which became most dramatically visible around the world with the "Battle of Seattle" in 1999, these institutions are also now the target of concerted campaigns for their reform. Indeed, as Neera Chandhoke points out, NGOs now attend the meetings of the World Bank and the IMF as special guests, where they are actively involved in decision-making and implementing projects (Chandhoke, 2002: 44).

How does global civil society further democracy? Critics argue that, as global civil society is NGO-led, it is intrinsically undemocratic. Since no one has elected NGOs, they cannot claim to represent anyone but their members. Their direct input into international political institutions, and any influence they may have over the direction of global governance, is not democratic because they have not tested their policy commitments by putting them to a popular vote. In fact, NGOs tend to claim moral author-ity for their causes rather than democratic legitimacy: they aim at univer-sal justice (at fostering human rights or global standards for workers, for example) or at increasing access to public goods for everyone (global environmental sustainability or ensuring freedom of information). However, it is argued that even the moral authority that the majority of NGOs might legitimately claim on the basis of the validity of their aims is tainted because of the close involvement of many with projects of globalization led by undemocratic international political institutions. Chandhoke argues that, as the Washington Consensus comes under increased pressure, IGOs are now committed to building civil society inside developing countries, by channeling funds through NGOs to realize development projects, to build democratic capacity and further human rights. They aim to secure the trust and participation of local citizens, she argues, in order to facilitate the expansion of global markets. In this way, NGOs are being used to legitimate the policies of the IMF, the World Bank, and the UN, none of whom have a democratic mandate to interfere in the affairs of sovereign states (Chandhoke, 2002: Anderson and Reiff, 2005). According to these critics, then, "global civil society" is a not much more than a new word for Western imperialism.

These are very telling criticisms and should give pause for thought to those who effectively consider the aims they strive for as in and of them-selves democratic, regardless of popular consultation or public opinion. As Chandhoke argues, it is not enough to reply, as Lori Wallach, whose organization Public Citizen organized the Battle for Seattle, to the ques-tion "Who elected you?" simply to reply, "Who elected them?" (Chandhoke, 2002: 48). It is important rather to reflect on alternative views of democracy to those of the political party and the ballot box. In order to understand the democratic claims of social movements we need to understand how activists use "global civil society," not as a descriptive or normative term, but strategically. For global social movements, "global civil society" denotes how globalization can be prevented from destroying civilized ways of life between the state and the market by resisting com-modification, ensuring the environment is valued and cared for, and making injustices into matters for public concern.

Here I will analyze the democratic legitimacy of global civil society actors as of three different types. The first I call "alternative globalization": it involves a turning away altogether from formal politics at state and international level to the democratization of everyday life. The second I call "deliberative globalization": the strategy to democratize international political institutions and to establish popular consultation and dialogue over the content of their policy agendas. The third strategy for democratizing globalization I call "conditional globalization": it involves working through internationalizing states to alter conditions of democratic engagement within and across state borders. In practice, different parts of social movement networks, and even the same people in some cases, may be engaged in more than one of these strategies even though, in their purest forms, they are contradictory. It is useful to separate them out here for analytic purposes, in order to consider the way each is grounded in quite different claims for democratic legitimacy.

Alternative globalization

Alternative globalization is summed up in the slogan "Another world is possible!" Quite simply, it involves the creation of a range of alternatives to global capitalism. These include ways of living as far as possible outside the capitalist economy: living on little money by living communally and/ or squatting, setting up Local Economic Trading Schemes to exchange goods and services outside capitalist markets, working in cooperatives, or finding jobs in small businesses or political organizations that promote alternative ideals and practices (see Gibson-Graham, 2002). It also involves finding ways to communicate and network transnationally outside the commercial media. For example, the invention of Indymedia, a grassroots forum for reporting news from around the world that would not be reported by the mainstream news agencies, or (in the case of protests against neo-liberal globalization) that is consistently misreported, draws together a volunteer force of journalists, photographers, and video-makers and operates on a shoestring budget to preserve its independence (Allan, 2006; Castells, 2009). The World Social Forum (WSF) is an example of alternative political organization. Although, as a "movement of movements," the WSF also includes groups engaged in "deliberative globalization" within it, the WSF itself is an innovative space for activists of all kinds to meet face-to-face to exchange knowledge, learn practical skills, network with other activists and develop strategies that are relevant in their own situations (De Sousa Santos, 2006: 122). Finally, alternative globalization is associated with innovative forms of protest that graphically demonstrate different ways of living at the same time as drawing attention to global issues. Invariably involving the occupation of spaces in different ways – from environmentalists literally living in trees to prevent them being pulled down, to encampments at airports to prevent the building of more runways, to taking over the streets of major cities in protest against a society built around cars – the protest actions of alternative globalization are festive, carnivalesque, and actually enact ways of living outside the mainstream (McKay, 1998; Notes from Nowhere, 2003).

The first principle of democratic legitimacy underlying alternative globalization is that by demonstrating that attractive alternatives to global capitalism are possible, global social movements are bringing "another world" closer. In the West, the spirit of these endeavors is largely, though not exclusively, anarchist. In their purist forms, they seem to demand a great deal of those who practice them, in terms of living completely outside the comforts and conventions of mainstream society. However, alternatives originally invented or popularized by radicals may become mainstream in some cases, whilst still fostering global justice. It is possible for people who are employed in mainstream occupations to engage in a range of activities that contribute to alternative globalization, by growing their own organic food, buying fair-trade goods, making efforts to reduce their ecological footprint, and generally trying to live in such a way as to minimize their personal involvement in neo-liberal globalization. Furthermore, in other parts of the world, many people, especially in rural areas, still live in social settings where markets have not penetrated to anything like the same extent as they have in the West. In such cases, alternative globalization involves finding ways to improve the conditions of people's lives without "market fundamentalism," by land reform and subsidies to help small farmers, for example, by resisting large-scale infrastructure projects (like the notorious Narmada Dam in India) that will destroy the ancestral lands of indigenous peoples and the livelihoods of subsistence farmers, or through grassroots coalitions of peasants and of shanty-town dwellers who know very precisely what is needed to make their lives more secure and to help feed and educate their children (see Kumar et al., 2009). Alternative globalization is democratic, then, as a strategy to civilize neo-liberal globalization because it creates, develops, and makes public possibilities that would not otherwise be available or apparent. It attempts to persuade people that "another world is possible" in practice, by presenting alternatives which they may adopt, to their own benefit and to the benefit of those whose dignity and self-respect, livelihood, and social and physical environment is threatened by expanding global capitalism.

The second principle of democratic legitimation underlying alternative globalization is explicitly anarchist. The alternatives it offers are not intended simply to parallel mainstream ways of life, but to challenge them. As such, alternative globalization resists not just the hegemony of neoliberal globalization, but also any political program and state or international regulation as such. It is important to distinguish here between different kinds of consensus-building and organization. Activists of the anti-globalization movement have developed a range of ways of reaching consensus in order to strategize and organize protest events and discussions (Graeber, 2002; Notes from Nowhere, 2003). Consensus oriented towards developing and realizing a political program or to bring about state or international regulation is, however, antithetical to alternative globalization: it is only valid in relation to a particular course of action (Graeber, 2002: 6). Alternative globalization continually challenges authority and calls settled structures into question; anarchists organize precisely on the basis that they are resistant to any authority beyond that which they are personally free to create, revise, or leave.

In this respect, alternative globalization involves a form of democracy called "agonistic," in which a central place is given to the view that conflict between opposing viewpoints is inherent to social life and that there are no universal grounds that could be used to establish the definitive validity of one perspective over another. As there are no certainties to which those opposed may appeal, neither scientific nor moral, conflict is only ever ended through the exercise of power. Furthermore, in the absence of any legitimate authority or justification for preferring one perspective over another, power can only ever be exercised illegitimately; it is effectively the same as force. Any justifications for deciding between opposing viewpoints that might enable binding regulation for large numbers of people must always be treated with suspicion as effects of illegitimate, hierarchical authority (Benhabib, 1996: 8). There should be no agreements on general rules, and attempt to build lasting or large-scale consensus must be challenged. Democracy must be participatory and direct, engaging us in continually challenging established assumptions and ways of doing things.

The legitimation of alternative globalization as radical participatory democracy can be seen in the ongoing dispute over whether the World Social Forum should coordinate a political program. For many, the search for consensus that such coordination would require is inherently problematic because, in settling on a course of action, the equality of diversity of existing alternatives would be lost: some would be marginalized and even repressed. In contrast, a number of the founders of the WSF have argued that the major points of agreement amongst the movements participating in the WSF should be made publicly visible in order to provide a focus for worldwide action against neo-liberal globalization without which the creativity it generates will be wasted. They created the "Manifesto of Porte Alegre" on this basis in 2005, outlining twelve basic proposals for change to economic and state structures, and presented it to the media as an interpretation of the political will of the WSF. The vast majority of the participants at the meeting of the WSF that year, and in subsequent discussions, however, agree that a manifesto is fundamentally at odds with the spirit of the WSF as an open space where any number of different political projects may be formulated (De Sousa Santos, 2006: 120–4; Castells, 2009: 340–1).

As a strategy for *resisting* capitalist globalization, alternative globalization does not appear to require justification, as it makes no attempt to forestall or to repress any particular possibility. It is, in fact, based on a valid claim to democratic legitimacy insofar as it attempts to treat all voices with equal respect, to allow all points of view to flourish, and never to close down debate prematurely. But avoiding political program and resisting regulation of all kinds has its limitations. Alternative globalization tends to flourish in local and translocal spaces, and the alternatives it offers are created outside the framework of mainstream politics and markets. These spaces, too, are affected by policies, laws, and agreements at the formal political level, and whilst demolishing alternative spaces and ways of living is resisted at the local level, such a strenuous way of life is not for everyone. As many, if not most, of those involved in global social movements would agree, then, although alternative globalization makes a very important contribution, it can only ever be *part* of what is needed to democratize neo-liberal globalization.

Deliberative globalization

The principles of deliberative democracy are another important legitimation for the democratic potential of global civil society. The principles of democratic globalization underlie the activities of NGOs with consultative status in IGOs, as well as all the many more who try to influence their agendas and the content of what is discussed and agreed in IGO forums by direct lobbying and publicity. They underpin NGO attempts to represent "the public," even as they simultaneously try to persuade individuals and groups in their networks and outside that the ideas they advocate *should* be accepted by everyone. That is, they both claim and, at the same time they try to create a public mandate to influence the policy-making of international political institutions. Castells, for example, shows how the environmental movement put climate change on the international political agenda through a variety of interventions including popularizing scientific findings, UN conferences, widespread publicity in the mass media and on the Internet, and global demonstrations, including the Live Earth concert in 2007. He sees the way in which climate change has now become a major policy issue for governments across the world as "policy changes as a result of changes in the public mind" (Castells, 2009: 334). Although the democratic principles of deliberative globalization are rarely spelled out except by political theorists, they clearly underpin claims of this kind: democratizing globalization involves global social movements stimulating public debate across global civil society, and then NGOs translate principles agreed upon there into pressure on IGOs.

Deliberative democracy involves the justification of decisions taken by citizens together with their representatives. Decisions should be universalizable; they can be justified only by reasons that could not reasonably be refused by anyone seeking fair terms of cooperation. It is not acceptable that elites should themselves *invent* justifications for their decisions, as this might well involve nothing more than the rationalization of injustice. Deliberative democracy must be dialogical: "all affected" by a particular decision should be involved in the discussion of whether laws and policies truly do recognize the issues that are at stake for everyone. In this sense, deliberative democracy is both procedural and substantive. It is procedural in that it specifies how legitimate decisions are to be reached: in addition to aggregative dimensions of democracy (principally the adding up of individuals who are in favor of a particular program or policy that characterizes voting for political parties), "all affected" must be able to engage in discussion of universalizable decisions as free and equal individuals. Deliberative democracy is also substantive in that conditions must be created so that individuals can genuinely participate and reach consensus in this way. To some extent, deliberative democrats share agonists' suspicion of consensus: it is only where the better argument has prevailed, rather than the formation of public opinion by bribery or threats, that agreement is genuinely democratic (see Benhabib, 1996; Gutman and Thompson, 2004; Bohman, 2007).

The organizational form through which deliberative democracy is institutionalized is the public sphere. Habermas's work on the public sphere in the seventeenth and eighteenth centuries is the inspiration for ideals of deliberative democracy. In *The Structural Transformation of the Public Sphere*, he argued that the societies and clubs set up in London and elsewhere in Western Europe at that time provided social spaces for the rational criticism of state practices by informed outsiders. They nurtured the ideal of the public sphere – never fully realized – that free and equal

individuals should be able to debate the fundamental principles on which
society should be based for the common good, accepting only the reasons
put forward by the better argument as justification of the validity of their
conclusions. Habermas's main concern in this work is with the degenera-
tion of the public sphere as a result of modernization: the growth of
large-scale bureaucratic organizations, like political parties, replaced the
role of critical individuals; public life became more a matter of negotiating
interests between parties, administration, and special interest groups than
attempting to reach agreement about the objective common good; and
the growth of mass communications made citizens into the passive recipients of products of "the culture industry" and worked to manufacture
consent without genuine deliberation (Habermas, 1989). Nevertheless, in
his subsequent work, Habermas tried to develop the normative consequences of the ideal of the public sphere to inform critical social theory.
Using what is sometimes called the "ideal speech theory," it should be
possible to investigate the democratic legitimacy of structures and policies
by asking whether all those who *should* have been able to participate in
deciding on them would have been able to agree that they were justified
(Outhwaite, 1994).

As a result of criticisms, Habermas has now revised his understanding
of the public sphere to understand how deliberative democracy might be
engaged in practice. Feminist critics argued that his initial understanding
was too rationalist and too individualist: the most important contributions to democratic deliberation over the last two hundred years have
actually come from social movements, which have mobilized counter-
public spheres using a range of styles of communication, including story-
telling, graphic art, demonstrations, and political rhetoric aimed at stirring
emotions (Young, 1996; Fraser, 1997). In addition, Habermas has accepted
criticisms by theorists of popular culture that audiences of the mass media
are not simply cultural "dopes." He now understands the mass media to
be crucial to the functioning of any public spheres in contemporary societies. Media representations, whilst always susceptible to the influence of
money and power, are not wholly determined by economic and political
interests. Indeed, they are embedded in strategies of interpretation and
re-interpretation and are, therefore, subject to criticism and to redefinition
on the part of media audiences, who are not passive consumers of media
products. In his more recent work, then, rather than the ideal of rational
deliberation between members of a face-to-face, singular, and unified
public, Habermas sees "popular sovereignty [as] no longer embodied in
a visibly identified gathering of autonomous citizens. It pulls back into
the as it were 'subjectless' forms of communication circulating through

forums and legislative bodies" (Habermas, 1996: 136). He sees social movements in civil society which distil and transmit problems in an amplified form to the public sphere as especially important in these forms of communication.

Habermas's original understanding of the public sphere, and its subsequent development, was based on "methodological nationalism": it was developed entirely within the framework of the nation-state. Can deliberative democracy be scaled up to make sense of the democratizing activities of social movements in global civil society? Nancy Fraser has suggested that if deliberative democracy is to make a contribution to democratizing globalization, a global sphere must be institutionalized in such a way that it fulfils two main conditions. First, it must enable democratic discussion between "all affected" by a particular issue. Second, it must have political efficacy. At the national level, the public sphere is effective to the extent that it communicates the issues and principles agreed upon in wide-ranging discussion across different sites in the media into formal, procedural political channels. The practical work of translation is done, according to Habermas, by the media, but also by national elections, opinion polls, and referenda. In this way, principles agreed upon by "all affected" are translated into concrete policies and laws (Fraser, 2007).

Although talk of a global public sphere is quite common now in discussions of globalization and democracy, it is extremely difficult to imagine either of these conditions becoming a reality at the global level. First, there is the difficulty of unifying discussion across territorial borders. In fact, *within* territorial borders, media audiences are increasingly dispersed and fragmented in comparison with nation-wide audiences previously formed in relation to a handful of newspapers and TV and radio broadcasters, which were often dominated by a single national public broadcasting system. Satellite broadcasting does make it possible for the world to see and hear the same events at the same time. Global media events, like the release of Nelson Mandela from Robbens Island and the terrorist attacks on the World Trade Center in New York, are broadcast live on news channels around the world, interrupting mainstream programming and creating, for a brief period, a unity amongst TV and radio audiences (see Dayan and Katz, 1992; Couldry, 2003). There are surely also debates going on at various times about the same events around the world; there is no doubt that the legitimacy of the invasion of Iraq by the US and its allies has been talked about everywhere. There is even some interest in the media in translating how events are interpreted in different ways across different settings; the meaning of the election of Barack Obama for Americans, and also for people in Britain and around the world was widely discussed in the UK media, for example. Nevertheless, as we saw in chapter 2, the way in which the global media is organized does not facilitate systematic and in-depth discussion across national borders, as news is selected and edited to appeal to the existing preferences of ever narrower audiences. Indeed, it would be difficult to imagine how commercial media might organize a global public sphere even if the executives of global media corporations aimed to do so. Given differences of language and political culture, including the ways people prefer to access news media, and conflicting interpretations of the history and uneven development of globalization, it is far from obvious how everyone in the world might become interested in discussing the same fundamental issues across borders.

Nevertheless, some see the Internet as offering new possibilities for the formation of a global public sphere. James Bohman argues that it could enable what he calls a "public of publics"; it need not enable online discussion by "all affected" all together as long as it linked overlapping and interacting "leaky" mediated publics in which free and fair discussion was taking place (Bohman, 2007: 77). The Internet does enable communication in ways that are promising for the development of a global public sphere as a "public of publics." It is certainly "deterritorialized," functioning largely without regard for state borders. Although governments everywhere supervise the Internet, and it is possible to block access to some websites, it is impossible to close it down completely. Nor, Castells argues, is it possible to regulate the Internet by prosecuting users who defy regulations: there are simply too many people now using it in too many different places for too many different purposes. In addition, the Internet offers possibilities for online participation that non-digital media do not, with the creation of virtual spaces in which people contribute blogs to discussion-mailing lists and website postings, and put up podcasts, photographs, and videos to communicate with each other, wherever they are in the world. The Internet facilitates what Castells calls mass self-communication: in comparison with mass media, which was one-way, produced by a few and broadcast to a mass audience who could only select what to watch or listen to from a narrow range digital technology enables self-generated communication for an audience of individuals who have control over what they select and how they respond interactively to the diversity of what is available (Castells, 2009: 55).

On the other hand, however, the Internet is still far more available to people living in some places than elsewhere. Even if the digital divide between those who have regular access to computers and those who do not is shrinking, as Castells argues, insofar as it maps onto the global

division between wealthy, educated, and urban, on one side, and impoverished, in need of education, and rural on the other, the value of the
Internet as a "public of publics" must be doubtful (Castells, 2009: 62).
There are questions, too, over how far communication extends, even
amongst those who do have access to the Internet. Most interaction on
the Internet is personal, and the sheer volume and diversity of what is
available means that most contributions are seen by a very small number
of people, and responded to by even fewer. Even on websites that explicitly stage political discussion, Cammaerts and van Audenhove found
that many contributions came from a small number of like-minded
participants, and even fewer were directly related to debate between participants in the forum. Where people did not agree, and participation
widened, conflicts could be very uncivil, certainly undeliberative, trading
insults more often than detailed discussion (Cammaerts and van
Audenhove, 2005).

The main problem with the ideal of the global public sphere, however,
is the existing structure of international political institutions. As Fraser
points out, according to Habermas's work in *The Structural Transformation
of the Public Sphere*, the national public sphere developed in a setting in
which relative state control over the capitalist economy came *before* social
movements aiming at democratization. In comparison with sovereign
states, international political institutions are weak, and legitimate public
spheres, which would enable the participation in principle of "all affected"
by a particular issue, must therefore establish *both* the capacity of effective institutions *and*, at the same time, translate public opinion into law
and administration, to bring effective pressure to bear on those institutions. In other words, in contrast to the national public sphere, the global
public sphere must both enable the conditions for open participation in
wide-ranging public debate and, at the same time, create effective, but
porous and responsive institutions at the global level (Fraser, 2007).

International political institutions are weak in that they must negotiate
between the continuing ideals of state sovereignty and the benefits of
international cooperation across borders. Constructions and interpretations of "national interests" dominate policy-making in international
political institutions, whether they result in small states cooperating with
larger, wealthier states for their own purposes, making policies that can
be adapted to suit different state capacities, or bribery and threats by
larger states in order to realize their aims. There is no doubt that the ideas
governing global governance can be challenged and changed, as they have
been in the past. Neo-liberalism itself is just such a change in the practice
of Keynesian economics to which the World Bank and the IMF adhered

until the 1970s. David Harvey argues that it is difficult to say precisely why neo-liberalism became dominant as a result of "gyrations and chaotic experiments that really only converged as a new orthodoxy with the articulation of what became known as the 'Washington Consensus' in the 1990s," but economic theories developed and spread by Right-wing think-tanks played a very important role (Harvey, 2005: 13–31). It is difficult to imagine, however, that the undemocratic procedures of global governance that were set up according to statist principles following World War II might be significantly changed without a similar global catastrophe.

Deliberative globalization is based on a valid claim to democratic legitimacy in attempting to consult widely and to create public consent to global policy-making. The problem is that, as an ideal, it is too far from current practice to provide a satisfactory basis for global politics. Indeed, critics of democratic deliberation argue that the gap between ideal and real is invariably a problem for this approach (Norval, 2008). Legitimation of the practices of global social movements in terms of deliberative globalization does not, therefore, answer the critics of NGOs as unrepresentative and undemocratic. Ironically, this is especially the case where they may be *successful* in altering international regulation, the primary aim of many NGOs.

Conditional globalization

As we noted earlier in this chapter, in the face of the difficulties of democratizing international political institutions, some have argued that it is more important to focus on democracy *within* national territories. In addition to the democratic deficit of existing international institutions, it is only the nation that gives enough of a sense of a broad political community amongst all types of people, not just those engaged in radical politics, to make democracy effective. Under these circumstances, substantive democracy has been achieved in the past, as exemplified by the redistributive policies of post-war welfare states, and the extension of citizenship rights to groups previously excluded from the civil sphere (Calhoun, 2007; Turner 2002). Allowing for the possibility that such a national community may be civic rather than ethnic, the main problem with such pragmatic arguments is that they do not address the unfairness of undemocratic procedures at the international level which, as we have also seen, impact far more on people living in some states than on others. Nor do they have anything to offer concerning how issues that do not stop at territorial borders might be addressed democratically. They seem to imply a form of economic protectionism at the very least, a closing of borders to free trade, especially financial exchanges and exchanges of products, labor, and research and development across borders within multinational corporations. But this leaves unaddressed the importance of globalization to developing economies, as well as issues of human rights violations and other injustices.

As a principle of democratic legitimacy, conditional globalization involves something like the precautionary principle of the environmental movement, which Anthony Giddens glosses as "better safe than sorry" (Giddens, 2009: 57). Although democracy at the national level is far from ideal, it is important to safeguard what already exists, and international policies that *undermine* it should be resisted or reversed. Processes of globalization are only to be encouraged, then, insofar as they improve the conditions for equality of voice within and across *all* states. This involves, at a minimum, building and strengthening state capacities in the developing world to improve the possibility that elected leaders may enact and extend citizens' rights. Focused in the West, conditional globalization justifies global social movement activity that tries to persuade people living within internationalizing states to give their consent to international policies that remove some of the benefits of living in large, wealthy states in favor of those – the vast majority of the world's population – who do not.

The principle of conditional globalization, although I have never seen it spelled out as such, underlies a couple of campaigns in recent years that have targeted politicians in internationalizing states that are over-developed and over-represented internationally. In these campaigns, activists use national media in order to put pressure on politicians to try to influence them to make international policy to minimize the undemocratic effects of international political institutions within developing countries. The main example is that of the ongoing Global Call to Action Against Poverty. In 2005, this campaign coordinated NGOs across Europe, the US and South Africa, to put pressure on the G8 and the UN to change the global regulation of debt, aid, and trade that keeps the most impoverished of the world in conditions of starvation and destitution. In specific terms, activists demanded that the governments of the G8 increase aid to meet promises broken since the 1970s, cancel the unfairly incurred and economically crippling debt of developing countries, and institutionalize trade justice: ending subsidies on agricultural goods in the EU and North America, the dumping of surpluses elsewhere that is the result of these subsidies, and also ending tariffs on importing manufactured goods from developing countries. The campaign was immensely popular in some countries, especially the UK, where it was known as "Make Poverty History," using celebrities to achieve the kind of blanket media coverage that more usually accompanies national elections or sporting events, and culminating in the Live8 concerts around the world (Nash, 2008). The long-standing campaign by ATTAC (Association for the Taxation of Financial Transactions for the Aid of Citizens) for the introduction of the Tobin Tax, which would levy a small amount on each foreign finance transaction to put a brake on flows of finance across borders and, at the same time raise money for the developing world, is another example of conditional globalization. It should make the democratic management of national economies easier everywhere, whilst benefiting those in developing countries to a greater extent through the income that is raised – depending, of course, on how it is distributed (see Cassen, 2003).

The strategy of conditional globalization is not always so uncontroversial. It can be difficult to assess the real effects of campaigns focused on internationalizing states in the West on the conditions of democracy elsewhere. An example of such controversy is the use of the Alien Tort Claims Act in US courts. Human rights activists have been able to sue multinational corporations for their involvement in human rights abuses committed elsewhere under this obscure US law dating from the eighteenth century. Activists aim in this way to discourage future abuses as, besides the shame and cost of what are always long, drawn-out court cases, the executive directors of multinational corporations may also fear that the goods they produce will be boycotted by outraged consumers. The strategy of conditional globalization underpins these activities in that the human rights movement is using the facilities of the US state in order to prevent corporations colluding with and supporting the repressive and undemocratic practices of other states. This strategy has been celebrated by the human rights movement around the world. For example, where Unocal, accused of colluding with the Burmese government to enslave, rape, and murder villagers living in the area of the Yadana pipeline it was building, finally settled out of court to prevent the case being heard by a federal jury in 2003 (Nash, 2009a). The case that is currently being brought in the US courts by the South African-based NGO Khulumani against companies like Coca-Cola, Barclays Bank, and the Bank of America that did business there during apartheid is, however, much more problematic. The South African government is opposing the case, arguing that processes of reconciliation and reconstruction when apartheid was ended and a new government elected were designed to draw a line under what happened during the previous regime. They claim that it effectively threatens rather than strengthens democracy in South Africa, by overruling decisions that reflected the people's will, and also by discouraging investment in impoverished states that may have less than perfect human rights records but which nevertheless need development (Joseph, 2004).

There is a danger that, precisely because campaigns underpinned by the principle of conditional globalization target over-represented and over-developed internationalizing states, they risk losing touch with those they are supposed to be helping to strengthen their democratic voices in developing countries. They may become insular, focused on their own activities, and neglect building strong transnational networks with people in the places they are targeting. In this way, there is always the risk that such campaigns may not improve, they may actually worsen, democratic conditions in other states. As the Make Poverty History campaign became more popular in the UK, for example, it certainly lost touch with transnational networks established largely through churches and unions in Africa on which GCAAP was building. Although the campaign did educate large numbers of people in issues of global political economy concerning aid, trade, and debt relief in Europe and North America, these voices were not heard at all in the mainstream media during the campaign. In fact, the representations of those the campaign was supposed to help were patronizing and self-absorbed (Stevenson, 1999, 2007).

Even more problematically, however, neither the GCAAP demands, nor those of ATTAC have made much progress at all as a result of these campaigns. Some argue that this is because it is naïve to expect wealthy, large states to give up the benefits of their over-representation in IGOs to smaller, poorer states (Monbiot, 2005). However, any campaign to democratize international structures would be faced with the same problem: how could some kind of international democracy possibly be achieved except by privileged states giving up at least some of their privileges? In this sense, Make Poverty History activists are correct to say that persuading those who profit from the misery of others to stop is like trying to abolish slavery or to end apartheid. Campaigns for global democratization can only ever be effective by putting pressure on the strongest and wealthiest states in international political institutions. The principle of conditional globalization involves working through the electorates of these states to prevent or reverse international policies that make postcolonial states less democratically accountable to their citizens. It is surely a promising strategy in terms of democratic legitimacy. How successful it may be in practice is another question.

5.4   Democracy and Cultural Politics

Beyond the study of face-to-face interactions, sociology requires what is sometimes referred to, unflatteringly, as "slab thinking": naming, and thus carving out distinctions between sections of social life in order to theorize and study how they are related. Although "slab thinking" is an important sociological tool, it is important not to mistake the slabs or slices of social reality we name for social reality itself. These are analytic distinctions, sometimes close to those used by members of society, at other times developed to summarize sets of social relationships that members of society would not refer to in such a way. Though in this book, and especially in this chapter, we have been dealing with a number of such slices, naming them as "states," "civil society," "social movements" and so on, it is important to remember that these are not the stuff of social reality as such. To remind the reader of the discussion in chapter 1, social reality is created and sustained in ongoing face-to-face or mediated inter-actions of social actors, using and modifying social meanings to structure, modify, and on occasion transform the routines of their lives. It is in order to distinguish some of these interactions as having features in common that make them different from others that sociologists, and indeed, other members of society, including social movement activists, carve out the kinds of distinctions we have been discussing in these pages. They provide a map, more or less accurate and always in need of revision, to guide understanding and action.

In other words, it is important here to recall the role of cultural politics. Throughout this book, we have been looking at the cultural politics of social movements, and especially their importance to opposing and remak-ing the ideas that structure existing forms of citizenship and globalization. Social movements are effective only by persuasion; they create far-reach-ing and deep-rooted changes in perspective, the redefining of interests, and, hence, the reconfiguration of hierarchical social relations. It is these radically new perspectives that eventually alter how we identify ourselves and others, how we build or break social relations, and how we organize our common life – even if changes take a long time, and have unexpected consequences such that they escape any intention or attempt to secure them definitively.

The cultural politics of social movements do not respect the boundaries between state and civil society, voluntary associations and the market, or national and international. Indeed, global social movement networks themselves cross these boundaries, as do the ideas and innovative ways of seeing the world that they circulate, and put into circulation. Social movements persuade by forming "publics," problematizing taken-for-granted ways in which social interactions have been routinized, and developing new knowledges and alternatives through discussion and debate. They are counter-publics in the sense that they formulate oppositional discourses and forms of organization, and they expand the space for certain kinds of thinking and discussion in the mainstream media. The counter-publics created by social movements never conform to the ideal requirements of deliberative democracy. They are always fragmented, they are often stimulated by unreasonable voices and immoderate emotions, and they are not contained by the spaces of civil society. Insofar as social movements almost invariably target states in at least some ways, to make use of their special privileges to make law backed by force and/ or to redistribute wealth, counter-publics may be thought of, along the lines suggested by Nancy Fraser, as "strong" where their networks extend into state offices, in comparison with "weak" counter-publics that are networked only in civil society (Fraser, 1997). In respect of their "strong" networks, social movements always risk cooption by professional political parties and NGOs, and indeed, this is regularly their trajectory: beginning with grassroots mobilizations, they develop through a cycle of protest, and leave behind them a legacy of organizations that have taken on some of the movement tasks of agitating for reform through policy and legislation (Tarrow, 1998). Invariably, however, past the high point of a cycle of protest, social movements also leave behind less visible social movement networks that maintain a counter-public sphere outside mainstream political institutions. Perhaps most importantly, they transform social life and leave behind a significantly changed cultural context in which new issues are raised, debated, and addressed.

This continuing legacy is nowhere more evident than in the effects of the women's movement. Feminism has had comparatively little *direct* effect on state policies in Western liberal democracies (with the notable exception of Scandinavia), though it has resulted in a plethora of NGOs and made inroads into all the major political parties. The various waves of the women's movement have left legacies of organizations in mainstream politics that try to keep reform of those institutions "live." But it is in terms of altering identities and routines of daily life that the movement has been most effective. Although it is hard to pin down precisely what effects the women's movement has had, as distinct from the other changes in society that have impacted on our lives, it is only necessary to look at films, books, and TV programs from the 1960s – and to remember that the presentation of relations between the sexes there is generally not intended to be ironic – to realize that the definition of what it is to be a woman in contemporary society has completely changed. It is no longer simply assumed that all women will sacrifice their individual desires in the name of being a good wife and mother, living vicariously through their husbands and children; or that they will defer to men in public in exchange for men's protection and chivalry. Such changes are almost imperceptible over the long term, but they are, nevertheless, very real. It is incontrovertible that the way in which representations of women, and also men, gendered subjectivity, and the details of relations between the sexes contested as a result of the women's movement has resulted in profound changes in all these aspects of our lives. The expression "I'm not a feminist, but ..." followed by a statement which would have been unthinkable before the emergence of the women's movement in the 1960s is a well-documented feature of contemporary life.

Other social movements have also been very effective. Now represented by a multitude of scientific and political organizations, as well as putting climate change on the agenda of political parties and governments everywhere, the environmental movement has also had a more intangible, but more far-reaching impact on our very sense that we live on a planet with finite resources and to which we may do irreparable damage out of carelessness. Reflections on the causes and consequences of climate change have entered into the ways in which we work and enjoy ourselves; it is difficult to *avoid* knowing about the range of ways in which we could, or should, change our daily routines, think about what we consume or what modes of transport we use, the extent to which we support how national economies are oriented toward growth, our relationship with animals and the countryside, and so on. Although, as in the case of the women's movement, there are no uncontroversial answers to any of the problems raised by the environmental movement, the very fact that they are now widely understood to be issues that require urgent attention is in itself of political importance. They are not problems that can simply be solved by states, by national or even international regulation, or by markets appealing to self-interest. They require a complete transformation in our understanding of how life should be lived and who we are. Environmental problems can only be addressed if our self-image becomes tied in to routines of daily life that protect rather than damage the planet. In this respect, politics at the level of the state will only succeed if they are related to fundamental transformations in all social relations.

Finally, the global justice movement, which is much newer than either the feminist or the environmentalist movement and which has yet to make the same degree of popular impact, nevertheless requires a similar transformation in perspectives. As well as addressing possibilities of extending human rights through regulation in different ways, we must also come to see ourselves differently as members of local, national, *and* global political communities with obligations to other members of those communities as well as rights. Again, even if many of us become less mobile, more local, with the growth of environmental awareness, this will involve a shift in personal identity, in how we relate to "distant suffering" and to those who do move across borders for work or to escape war and persecution. It will also require the fundamental re-evaluation of priorities in the West as, like the environmental movement, the global justice movement surely requires far less consumer-oriented ways of life. If citizenship is to become more equal within states, while at the same time the exploitation in which Western states are involved that raises the standard of living of people here is ended, serious questions will need to be addressed about the sustainability of the ways of life most of us take for granted.

In this book, we have been concerned only with the cultural politics of egalitarian, "progressive" movements. These movements are inherently democratizing insofar as they open up questions concerning how to live that were previously settled or taken for granted, and make discussion of the issues possible, and necessary, across different groups and in different social contexts. They raise issues on which everyone must make decisions for themselves, and, insofar as this is the case, everyone participates in the ongoing consideration of how fundamental questions might be resolved. In this respect, the questions raised by cultural politics are democratically contested, even if some individuals and groups are more articulate, better organized, or better placed to make their definitions of the issues acceptable to the majority.

The cultural politics of progressive movements tends, then, to lead to a greater degree of pluralism. Their effect in liberal-democracies has been to open up sites of contestation and to keep them open. In large part, this is because these movements were formed through resistance to hegemonic interpretations of how society should be organized, encoded in policies and laws that have been unjust or negligent in their consequences. Again, the women's movement is exemplary. Despite fears of "political correctness," a wide range of personal and professional life choices are now acceptable for both men and women. At the same time, the issue of equality between the sexes is a recurring one in the media, in daily life, and in relation to policy-making and the law. The cultural politics of the women's movement has been broadly democratizing, then, as it has tended to be identified with claims that individuals should have the right to choose their own way of life, and that women should enjoy the same conditions and rewards as men.

It is important to note, however, that cultural politics is not necessarily democratizing in this respect. Right-wing social movements have not been as much studied in political sociology as those to which sociologists are sympathetic, and I have followed this tendency in this book. They include nationalist, racist movements like the National Front in Britain, and the White Supremacy movement in the US. All those movements that militate for a return to the pre-1960s morality of the "permissive society," like the "moral majority" in the US, and fundamentalist movements of all kinds are also to be included in this category. Such movements engage in cultural politics, though they attempt to close down rather than to open up the contestation of fundamental questions, trying to end personal decision-making and pluralism. The paradox, of course, is that, in order to do so, they have to engage in constructing new identities and transforming ongoing social practices. Arguably, it is for this reason that such movements cannot ultimately succeed. The fact that they have to engage in cultural politics to bring about a re-traditionalization of society makes their very project self-defeating (Giddens, 1994). Nevertheless, the way in which right-wing social movements engage in cultural politics to limit individual freedom and equality makes it evident that, although cultural politics is inherently democratic in promoting contestation, it is not necessarily democratic in terms of aims, nor, possibly, of effects.

In general, the emphasis of global social movements tends to be on the democratization of civil society, but I have argued in this chapter that the internationalizing state is also vital. Tolerance of diversity and respect for participation in the contestation of fundamental issues depend, in part, on a rule of law properly and impartially enforced by states; and urgent problems raised by global social movements concerning violence, environmental damage, and injustice require regulation. On the other hand, it is important to understand that state formations are as much a product of cultural politics as any other slice of social reality. Study of the accelerating development of the internationalizing state of global governance over the last few decades makes the contingency of state formations very evident. In fact, it is this sense of the fundamental contingency of social life that is perhaps the most important contribution of contemporary political sociology. Another world is not only possible; *some* other world is always in the making.

Glossary

cosmopolitanism: In social and political debates today, cosmopolitanism generally means detachment from the nation in favor of a commitment to universal values of humanity. It is useful to distinguish political from cultural cosmopolitanism. Political cosmopolitanism is concerned with the institutions necessary for global democracy, justice, and peace. Cultural cosmopolitanism is concerned with the experience of oneself as a person who is at home anywhere in the world.

cultural politics: There are at least four ways in which the term is used:

1   The politics of cultural representations: for example, Stuart Hall charts the shift from a politics of "the relations of representation" to a politics of "representation itself" (Hall, 1992b: 253).
2   The politics of cultural production: the way in which it is organized, promoted, or suppressed in, for example, education, broadcasting, and trade policy (Street, 1997b).
3   The politics of what counts as culture and who is marginalized or excluded from its production (Jordan and Weedon, 1995: 7).
4   The politics of signifying practices through which identities, social relations, and rules are contested, subverted, and may be transformed. This is the sense with which this book is predominantly concerned.

culture: The best analysis of the term is still that of Raymond Williams. It is used in at least four different ways:

1   "A general process of intellectual, spiritual, and aesthetic development" as in, "She is a cultured person."

2   "A particular way of life, whether of a people, a period or a group" as used by anthropologists to describe different cultures.
3   "The works and practices of intellectual and especially artistic activity" such as music, literature, painting, and sculpture, sometimes including works of popular culture, too.
4   "The signifying order through which necessarily...a social order is communicated, reproduced, experienced and explored," as in the post-structuralist understanding of culture as material practices in which identities, objects, and social rules are constituted (quoted in Jordan and Weedon, 1995: 6–8).

essentialism: Diana Fuss (1989) gives a very subtle analysis of essentialism in contemporary debates in *Essentially Speaking*. Following Locke, she distinguishes between:

1   "Real essences:" "the Aristotelian understanding of essence as that which is most irreducible and unchanging about a thing." It is discovered in nature by close observation.
2   "Nominal essence:" "merely a linguistic convenience, a classificatory fiction we need to categorize and label." It is assigned or produced in language through the arbitrary naming of objects.

To use an example Fuss gives to sum up the difference between them: for a real essentialist, a rose by any other name would still be a rose; for a nominal essentialist, it would be something quite different (Fuss, 1989: 4–5). Challenges to essentialism have been particularly important in feminist and queer theory, and also in debates on racism and cultural differences. "Essentialism" is invariably used as a pejorative term in such debates.

governance: the effective regulation of social activity without the formal authority of government

Inter-Governmental Organization (IGO): an organization made up of official representatives of states and/or other IGOs

international: referring to the relations between nation-states. See also *transnational*.

International Non-Governmental Organization (INGO): legally constituted organization that is independent of governments and oriented towards action in regions larger than that of the territory of a single state. See also *Non-Governmental Organization*.

internationalizing state: the form of the state currently developing as an aspect of global governance which involves its restructuring within and across borders. See also *nation- state*.

imperialism: political control by a state over external territories or nationalities. Imperialism can be formal, when imperial powers govern territories or subjugated peoples directly—as in the British Empire of the nineteenth century. Or it can be informal, when a state's military, economic, and political power is used to control other territories and peoples without formally creating colonies.

nation-state: a historically specific form of the state, developed initially in Europe and the US from the seventeenth to the nineteenth centuries and spread to the rest of the world with decolonization in the twentieth century, which attempts to integrate people according to shared cultural norms. It is also a political ideal: the modern state should be sovereign over a nation, the members of which are supposed to form a political community through their belonging to a state and common cultural norms. See also *internationalized state*; *state*.

neo-liberalism: David Harvey describes it as a set of economic ideas and practices, the core of which is that "human well-being can best be advanced by liberating individual entrepreneurial freedoms and skills within an institutional framework characterized by strong private property rights, free markets, and free trade" (Harvey, 2005: 2). It also involves the political ideal that "[t]he role of the state is to create and preserve an institutional framework appropriate to such practices" (Harvey, 2005: 2).

Non-Governmental Organization (NGO): legally constituted organization that is independent from government. See also *International Non-Governmental Organization*, with which it is often used interchangeably, though strictly speaking, NGOs only act within states.

state: Hall and Ikenberry (1989: 1–2) give the following definition:

1 It is a set of institutions, the most important of which are those of violence and coercion.
2 It is at the center of a geographically bounded territory, a society.

3   It monopolizes rule-making within its territory, which tends to create a common political culture shared by its citizens.

See also *internationalizing state*.

supranational: above the state; a political institution with powers that have been transferred from the state and with which it is now committed to sharing sovereignty. The European Parliament is the classic example.

transnational: referring to relations or processes which cross national boundaries, by-passing the nation-state. See also *international*.

References

Agamben, G. (1995). *Homo Sacer: Sovereign Power and Bare Life*. Stanford: Stanford University Press.

Agamben, G. (2005). *State of Exception*. Chicago: Chicago University Press.

Agyeman, J., and Evans, B. (2006). "Justice, Governance, and Sustainability: Perspectives on Environmental Citizenship from North America and Europe." In A. Dobson and D. Bell (eds.), *Environmental Citizenship*. Cambridge, MA: MIT Press.

Albrow, M. (1996). *The Global Age: State and Society beyond Modernity*. Cambridge: Polity Press.

Alexander, J. (1998). "Introduction: Durkheimian Sociology and Cultural Studies Today." In J. Alexander (ed.), *Durkheimian Sociology: Cultural Studies*. Cambridge: Cambridge University Press.

Alexander, J. (2003). *The Meanings of Social Life: A Cultural Sociology*. Oxford: Oxford University Press.

Alexander, J. (2006). *The Civil Sphere*. Oxford: Oxford University Press.

Alexander, J., and Smith, P. (1993). "The Discourse of American Civil Society: A New Proposal for Cultural Studies." *Theory and Society*. 22: 157–202.

Alexander, J., Giesen, B., and Mast, H. (2006). *Social Performance: Symbolic Action, Cultural Pragmatics and Ritual*. Cambridge: Cambridge University Press.

Allan, S. (2006). *Online News: Journalism and the Internet*. Maidenhead: Open University Press.

Althusser, L. (1971). "Ideology and Ideological State Apparatuses." In *Lenin and Philosophy and Other Essays*, trans. B. Brewster. London: New Left Books.

Amir, S. (2007). *Empire of Chaos*. New York: Monthly Review Press.

Anderson, B. (1983). *Imagined Communities: Reflections on the Origin and Spread of Nationalism*. London: Verso.

Anderson, K., and Rieff, D. (2005). "Global Civil Society: a Sceptical View." In H. Anheier, M. Glasius and M. Kaldor (eds.), *Global Civil Society 2005/6*. London: Sage.

Anheier, H., Glasius, M., and Kaldor, M. (2004). "Introducing Global Civil Society." In H. Anheier, M. Glasius, and M. Kaldor (eds.), *Global Civil Society 2004/5*. London: Sage.

An'Naim, A. (2002). "The Legal Protection of Human Rights in Africa: How to Do More with Less." In A. Sarat and T. Kearns (eds.), *Human Rights: Concepts, Contests, Contingencies*. Ann Arbor: University of Michigan Press.

Archibugi, D. (1995). "From the United Nations to Cosmopolitan Democracy." In D. Archibugi and D. Held (eds.), *Cosmopolitan Democracy: An Agenda for a New World Order*. Cambridge: Polity.

Archibugi, D., Held, D., and Kohler, M. (eds.) (1998). *Re-Imagining Political Community: Studies in Cosmopolitan Democracy*. Stanford, CA: Stanford University Press.

Archibugi, R. (2004). "Cosmopolitan Democracy and Its Critics: A Review." *European Journal of International Relations*, 10/3: 937–473.

Arendt, H. (1968). *The Origins of Totalitarianism*. San Diego: Harvest.

Axtmann, R. (2002). "What's Wrong with Cosmopolitan Democracy?" In N. Dower and N. Williams (eds.), *Global Citizenship: A Critical Reader*. Oxford: Blackwell.

Bacchi, C. (1990). *Same Difference: Feminism and Sexual Difference*. London: Allen and Unwin.

Bafesky, A. (1994). "General Approaches to Domestic Application of Women's International Human Rights Law." In R. Cook (ed.), *Human Rights of Women*. Philadelphia: University of Pennsylvania Press.

Balakrishnan, G. (1996). "The National Imagination." In G. Balakrishnan (ed.), *Mapping the Nation*. London: Verso.

Balibar, E. (2004). *We, the People of Europe? Reflections on Transnational Citizenship*. Princeton, NJ: Princeton University Press.

Barbalet, J. (1988). *Citizenship*. Milton Keynes: Open University Press.

Barker, M. (1981). *The New Racism*. London: Junction Books.

Barrett, M. (1991). *The Politics of Truth*. Cambridge: Polity Press.

Barthes, R. (1972). *Mythologies*. London: Paladin.

Baubock, R. (2002). "Political Community Beyond the Sovereign State, Supranational Federalism, and Transnational Minorities." In S. Vertovec and R. Cohen (eds.), *Conceiving Cosmopolitanism: Theory, Context and Practice*. Oxford: Oxford University Press.

Bauman, Z. (1998). *Work, Consumerism and the New Poor*. Buckingham: Open University.

Beck, U. (1992). *Risk Society: Towards a New Modernity*. London: Sage.

Beck, U. (1998). *Democracy without Enemies*. Cambridge: Polity Press.

Beck, U. (2000). *What Is Globalization?* Cambridge: Polity.

Beck, U., and Grande, E. (2007). *Cosmopolitan Europe*. Cambridge: Polity.

Beck, U., and Sznaider N. (2006). "Unpacking Cosmopolitanism for the Social Sciences: A Research Agenda." *British Journal of Sociology*, 57/1: 1–23.

Benhabib, S. (1996). "Introduction." In *Democracy and Difference: Contesting the Boundaries of the Political*. Princeton, NJ: Princeton University Press.

Benhabib, S. (2004). *The Rights of Others: Aliens, Residents and Citizens*. Cambridge: Cambridge University Press.

Bennet, W. L. (2004). "Branded Political Communication: Lifestyle Politics, Logo Campaigns, and the Rise of Global Citizenship." In M. Micheletti, A. Follesdal, and D. Stolle (eds.), *Politics, Products and Markets: Exploring Political Consumerism Past and Present*. New Brunswick, NJ: Transaction.

Bennet, W. L. (2005). "Social Movements beyond Borders: Understanding Two Eras of Transnational Activism." In D. Della Porta and S. Tarrow (eds.), *Transnational Protest and Global Activism: People, Passions, Power*. Lanham, MD: Rowman and Littlefield.

Benton, T. (1994). *The Rise and Fall of Structural Marxism*. London: Macmillan.

Bhambra, G. K. (2007). *Rethinking Modernity: Postcolonialism and the Sociological Imagination*. Basingstoke, Palgrave: Macmillan.

Billig, M. (1995). *Banal Nationalism*. London: Sage.

Blau, J., and Moncada, A. (2007). *Freedoms and Solidarities: In Pursuit of Human Rights*. Lanham, MD: Rowman and Littlefield.

Blau, J., and Moncada, A. (2009). "Sociological Theory and Human Rights." In B. Turner (ed.), *The New Blackwell Companion to Social Theory*. Malden, MA: Wiley-Blackwell.

Bohman, J. (2007). *Democracy across Borders: From Demos to Demoi*. Cambridge, MA: MIT Press.

Boli, J. (1987). "Human Rights or State Expansion? Cross-National Definitions of Constitutional Rights." In G. Thomas, J. Meyer, F. Ramirez, and J. Boli (eds.), *Institutional Structure: Constituting State, Society and the Individual*. Newbury Park, CA: Sage.

Boli, J., and Thomas, G. (1997). "World Culture in the World Polity." *American Sociological Review*, 62/2: 171–90.

Boli, J., and Thomas, G. (eds.) (1999). *Constructing World Culture: International Nongovernmental Organizations since 1875*. Stanford, CA: Stanford University Press.

Boltanski, L. (1999). *Distant Suffering: Morality, Media and Politics*. Cambridge: Cambridge University Press.

Boltanski, L., and Thevenot, L. (2006). *On Justification: Economies of Worth*. Princeton, NJ: Princeton University Press.

Bosniak, L. (2006). *The Citizen and the Alien: Dilemmas of Contemporary Membership*. Princeton, NJ: Princeton University Press.

Bottomore, T. (1964). *Elites and Society*. Harmondsworth: Penguin.

Bottomore, T. (1993). *Political Sociology*, second edition. London: Pluto Press.

Brubaker, R. (1992). *Citizenship and Nationhood in France and Germany*. Cambridge, MA: Harvard University Press.

Brubaker, R. (2002). "The Return of Assimilation? Changing Perspectives on Immigration and Its Sequels in France, Germany, and the United States." *Ethnic and Racial Studies*, 24/4: 531–548.

Butler, J. (1990). *Gender Trouble: Feminism and the Subversion of Identity*. Routledge: London.

Butler, J. (1993). *Bodies That Matter: On the Discursive Limits of Sex*. London: Routledge.

Butler, J. (1997). *The Psychic Life of Power: Theories in Subjection*. Stanford, CA: Stanford University Press.

Butler, J. (2004). *Precarious Life: The Power of Mourning and Violence*. London: Verso.

Calhoun, C. (1995). " 'New Social Movements' of the Early Nineteenth Century." In M. Traugott (ed.), *Repertoires and Cycles of Collective Action*. Durham, NC: Duke University Press.

Calhoun, C. (2002). "The Class Consciousness of Frequent Travellers: Towards a Critique of Actually Existing Cosmopolitanism." In S. Vertovec and R. Cohen (eds.), *Conceiving Cosmopolitanism: Theory, Context and Practice*. Oxford: Oxford University Press.

Calhoun, C. (2007). *Nations Matter: Culture, History, and the Cosmopolitan Dream*. London and New York: Routledge.

Cammaerts, B., and Van Audenhove, L. (2005). "Online Political Debate, Unbounded Citizenship, and the Problematic Nature of a Transnational Public Sphere." *Political Communication*, 22/2: 147–62

Cassen, B. (2003). "On the Attack." *New Left Review*, 19.

Castles, S., and Miller, M. (2005). *The Age of Migration*, third edition. New York: Guilford Press.

Castells, M. (2000a). *The Rise of the Network Society*, vol. 1: *The Information Age: Economy, Society and Culture*, second edition. Oxford: Wiley-Blackwell.

Castells, M. (2000b). *End of Millennium*, vol. 3: *The Information Age: Economy, Society and Culture*, second edition. Oxford: Wiley-Blackwell.

Castells, M. (2003). *The Power of Identity*, vol. 2: *The Information Age: Economy, Society and Culture*, second edition. Oxford: Wiley-Blackwell.

Castells, M. (2009). *Communication Power*. Oxford: Oxford University Press.

Chandhoke, N. (2002). "The Limits of Civil Society." In M. Glasius, M. Kaldor, and A. Helmut (eds.), *Global Civil Society Yearbook 2002*. Oxford: Oxford University Press.

Chandler, D. (2006). *From Kosovo and Beyond: Human Rights and International Intervention*. London: Pluto.

Chasek, P., Downie, D., and Brown, J. (2005). *Global Environmental Politics*. Boulder, CO: Westview Press.

Cheah, P., and Robbins, B. (eds.) (1998). *Cosmopolitics: Thinking and Feeling beyond the Nation*. Minneapolis: University of Minnesota Press.

Christoff, P. (1996). "Ecological Citizens and Ecologically Guided Democracy." In B. Doherty and M. de Geus (eds.), *Democracy and Green Political Thought: Sustainability, Rights and Citizenship*. London: Routledge.

Chomsky, N. (2000). *Rogue States: The Rule of Force in World Affairs*. London: Pluto.

Chouliaraki, L. (2006). *The Spectatorship of Suffering*. London: Sage.

Cladis, M. (2005). "Beyond Solidarity? Durkheim and Twenty-First Century Democracy in a Global Age." In J. Alexander and P. Smith (eds.), *The Cambridge Companion to Durkheim*. Cambridge: Cambridge University Press.

Cochrane, A., Clarke, J., and Gewirtz, S. (eds.) (2001). *Comparing Welfare States*. London: Sage.

Corner, J., and Pels, D. (eds.) (2003). *Media and the Restyling of Politics*. Sage: London.

Couldry, N. (2003). *Media Rituals: A Critical Approach*. London: Routledge.

Cohen, J., and Arato, A. (1994). *Civil Society and Political Theory*. Cambridge, MA: MIT Press.

Crook, S., Pakulski, J., and Waters, M. (1992). *Postmodernization: Change in Advanced Society*. London: Sage.

Crouch, C. (2001). "Markets and States." In K. Nash and A. Scott (eds.), *The Blackwell Companion to Political Sociology*. Oxford: Blackwell 2001.

Crouch, C. (2004). *Post-Democracy*. Cambridge: Polity.

Culler, J. (1976). *Saussure*. Brighton: Harvester Press.

Curtis, B. (1995). "Taking the State Back Out: Rose and Miller on Political Power." *British Journal of Sociology*, 46/4: 575–97.

Dahl, R. (1956). *A Preface to Democratic Theory*. Chicago: University of Chicago Press.

Dahl, R. (1999). "Can International Organizations Be Democratic? A Sceptic's View." I. Shapiro and C. Hacker-Cordon (eds.), *Democracy's Edges*. Cambridge: Cambridge University Press.

Dayan, D., and Katz, E. (1992). *Media Events: The Live Broadcasting of History*. Cambridge, MA: Harvard University Press.

De Sousa Santos, B. (2006). *The Rise of the Global Left: The World Social Forum and Beyond*. London: Zed Books.

Dean, M. (1994). *Critical and Effective Histories: Foucault's Methods and Historical Sociology*. London: Routledge.

Della Porta, D. (2005). "Multiple Belongings, Tolerant Identities, and the Construction of Another Politics: Between the European Social Forum and the Local Social Fora." In D. Della Porta and S. Tarrow (eds.), *Transnational Protest and Global Activism: People, Passions, Power*. Lanham, MD: Rowman and Littlefield.

246   *References*

Della Porta, D. (ed.) (2007). *The Global Justice Movement: Cross-National and Transnational Perspectives*. Boulder, CO, and London: Paradigm.

Della Porta, D., and Tarrow, S. (eds.) (2005). *Transnational Protest and Global Activism: People, Passions, Power*. Lanham, MD: Rowman and Littlefield.

Dembour, M.-B. (2001). "Following the Movement of a Pendulum: Between Universalism and Relativism." In J. Cowan, M. Dembour, and R. Wilson (eds.), *Culture and Rights: Anthropological Perspectives*. Cambridge: Cambridge University Press.

Dembour, M.-B. (2006). *Who Believes in Human Rights? Reflections on the European Convention*. Cambridge: Cambridge University Press.

Denzin, N. (1992). *Symbolic Interactionism and Cultural Studies*. Cambridge, MA: Blackwell.

Derrida, J. (1978). "Structure, Sign, Play." In *Writing and Difference*, trans. A. Bass. Routledge and Kegan Paul: London.

Dews, P. (1984). "Power and Subjectivity in Foucault." *New Left Review*, 144: 72–95.

Diani, M. (1992). "The Concept of Social Movement." *Sociological Review*, 40(1).

Dobson, A. (2003). *Citizenship and the Environment*. Oxford: Oxford University Press.

Dobson, A. (2006). "Thick Cosmopolitanism." *Political Studies*, 54: 165–84.

Dobson, A., and Bell, D. (2006). *Environmental Citizenship*. Cambridge, MA: MIT Press.

Douzinas, C. (2007). *Human Rights and Empire: The Political Philosophy of Cosmopolitanism*. Abingdon, Oxford: Routledge-Cavendish.

Dowse, R., and Hughes, J. (1972). *Political Sociology*. London: John Wiley and Sons.

Dunleavy, P., and O'Leary, B. (1987). *Theories of the State: The Politics of Liberal Democracy*. London: Macmillan.

Durkheim, E. (1992). *Professional Ethics and Civic Morals*. London and New York: Routledge.

Edwards, T. (1994). *Erotics and Politics: Gay Male Sexuality, Masculinity and Feminism*. London: Routledge.

Eschle, C. (2001). *Global Democracy, Social Movements, and Feminism*. Boulder, CO: Westview Press.

Evans, D. (1993). *Sexual Citizenship: The Material Construction of Sexualities*. London, Routledge.

Eyerman, R., and Jamison, A. (1991). *Social Movements: A Cognitive Approach*. Cambridge: Polity.

Fainstein, N. (1996). "A Note on Interpreting American Poverty." In E. Mingione (ed.), *Urban Poverty and the Underclass*. Oxford: Blackwell.

Falk, R. (1998). "The United Nations and Cosmopolitan Democracy: Bad Dream, Utopian Fantasy, Political Project." In D. Archibugi, D. Held, and M. Kohler (eds.), *Re-Imagining Political Community: Studies in Cosmopolitan Democracy*. Cambridge: Polity.

Favell, A. (2001). *Philosophies of Integration: Immigration and the Idea of Citizenship in France and Britain*. Basingstoke: Palgrave.

Feree, M., and Tripp, A. (eds.) (2006). *Global Feminism: Transnational Women's Activism: Organizing, and Human Rights*. New York: New York University Press.

Ferguson, N. (2008). *Colossus: The Price of America's Empire*. Harmondsworth: Penguin.

Fine, B., Lapavitsas, C., and Pincus, J. (eds.) (2001). *Development Policy in the Twenty-First Century: Beyond the Post-Washington Consensus*. London: Routledge.

Fortier, A.-M. (2008). *Multicultural Horizons: Diversity and the Limits of the Civil Nation*. London: Routledge.

Foucault, M. (1979). *Discipline and Punish: The Birth of the Prison*, trans. A. Sheridan. Harmondsworth: Penguin.

Foucault, M. (1980a). "Two Lectures." In C. Gordon (ed.), *Power/Knowledge: Selected Interviews and Other Writings 1972–1977*. Brighton: Harvester.

Foucault, M. (1980b). "Truth and Power." In C. Gordon (ed.), *Power/Knowledge: Selected Interviews and Other Writings 1972–1977*. Brighton: Harvester.

Foucault, M. (1982). "The Subject and Power." In H. Dreyfus and P. Rabinow (eds.), *Michel Foucault: Beyond Structuralism and Hermeneutics*. Brighton: Harvester Wheatsheaf.

Foucault, M. (1984a). "Politics and Ethics: An Interview." In P. Rabinow (ed.), *The Foucault Reader*. Harmondsworth: Penguin.

Foucault, M. (1984b). *The History of Sexuality: An Introduction*, trans. R. Hurley. Harmondsworth: Penguin.

Foucault, M. (1991). "Governmentality." In G. Burchell, C. Gordon, and P. Miller (eds.), *The Foucault Effect: Studies in Governmentality*: London: Harvester Wheatsheaf.

Foucault, M. (1997). "The Birth of Biopolitics." In P. Rabinow (ed.), *Ethics, Subjectivity and Truth*. London: Allen Lane.

Fraser, N. (1989). "Foucault on Modern Power: Empirical Insights and Normative Confusions." In *Unruly Practices: Power, Discourse and Gender in Contemporary Social Theory*. Cambridge: Polity Press.

Fraser, N. (1997). "From Redistribution to Recognition? Dilemmas of Justice in a 'Postsocialist Age.'" In *Justice Interruptus: Critical Reflections on the Postsocialist Condition*. New York and London: Routledge.

Fraser, N. (2007). "Transnationalizing the Public Sphere: On the Legitimacy and Efficacy of Public Opinion in a Post-Westphalian World." *Theory, Culture and Society*, 24/4: 7–30.

Fraser, N. (2008). *Scales of Justice: Reimagining Political Space in a Globalizing World*. Cambridge: Polity.

Frazer, E., and Lacey, N. (1993). *The Politics of Community: A Feminist Critique of the Liberal-Communitarian Debate.* London: Harvester Wheatsheaf.

Fuss, D. (1989). *Essentially Speaking: Feminism, Nature and Difference.* London: Routledge.

Gamson, J. (1996). "Must Identity Movements Self-Destruct?" In S. Seidman (ed.), *Queer Theory/Sociology.* Blackwell: Oxford.

Gamson, W. (1992). "The Social Psychology of Collective Action." In A. Morris and C. Mueller (eds.), *Frontiers in Social Movement Theory.* New Haven, CT, and London: Yale University Press.

Gamson, W., and Meyer, D. (1996). "Framing Political Opportunity." In D. McAdam, J. McCarthy, and M. Zald, (eds.), *Comparative Perspectives on Social Movements: Political Opportunities, Mobilizing Structures, and Cultural Framings.* Cambridge: Cambridge University Press.

Gellner, E. (1983). *Nations and Nationalism: New Perspectives on the Past.* Oxford: Blackwell.

George, S. (2004). *Another World Is Possible If...* London: Verso.

Gibson-Graham, J.-K. (2002). "Beyond Global vs Local: Economic Politics Outside the Binary Frame." In A. Herod and M. Wright (eds.), *Geographies of Power: Placing Scale.* Oxford: Blackwell.

Giddens, A. (1971). *Capitalism and Modern Social Theory: An Analysis of the Writings of Marx, Durkheim and Max Weber.* Cambridge: Cambridge University Press.

Giddens, A. (1972). *Politics and Sociology in the Thought of Max Weber.* Houndmills, Basingstoke: Macmillan.

Giddens, A. (1979). *Central Problems in Social Theory: Action, Structure and Contradiction in Social Analysis.* Basingstoke, Hampshire: Macmillan.

Giddens, A. (1982). "Class Division, Class Conflict and Citizenship Rights." In *Profiles and Critiques in Social Theory.* Basingstoke, Hampshire: Macmillan.

Giddens, A. (1984). *The Constitution of Society: Outline of the Theory of Structuration.* Cambridge: Polity Press.

Giddens, A. (1990). *The Consequences of Modernity.* Cambridge: Polity Press.

Giddens, A. (1991). *Modernity and Self-Identity: Self and Society in the Late Modern Age.* Cambridge: Polity Press.

Giddens, A. (1994). *Beyond Left and Right: The Future of Radical Politics.* Cambridge: Polity Press.

Giddens, A. (2009). *The Politics of Climate Change.* Cambridge: Polity.

Gilligan, C. (1993). *In a Different Voice: Psychological Theory and Women's Development.* Cambridge, MA, and London: Harvard University Press.

Gilroy, P. (1992). *There Ain't No Black in the Union Jack: The Cultural Politics of Race and Nation.* London: Routledge.

Gilroy, P. (1993). *The Black Atlantic: Modernity and Double Consciousness.* London: Verso.

Gilroy, P. (2004). *After Empire: Melancholia or Convivial Culture*. London: Routledge.

Goodhart, D. (2006). *Progressive Nationalism: Citizenship and the Left*. London: Demos.

Gould, C. (2004). *Globalizing Democracy and Human Rights*. Cambridge: Cambridge University Press.

Graeber, D. (2002). "The New Anarchists." *New Left Review*.

Gramsci, A. (1971). *Selections from Prison Notebooks*, ed. Q. Hoare and G. Nowell Smith. London: Lawrence and Wishart.

Gready, P. (ed.) (2004). *Fighting for Human Rights*. London: Routledge.

Gready, P., and Ensor, J. (eds.) (2005). *Reinventing Development: Translating Rights-Based Approaches into Practice*. London: Zed Books.

Greene, O. (2005). "Environmental Issues." In J. Baylis and S. Smith (eds.), *The Globalization of World Politics*, third edition. Oxford: Oxford University Press.

Guild, E. (1996). "The Legal Framework of Citizenship of the European Union." In D. Cesarani and M. Fullbrook (eds.), *Citizenship, Nationality and Migration in Europe*. London: Routledge.

Gunning, I. (2002). "Global Feminism at the Local Level: The Criminalization of Female Genital Surgeries." In F. Valdes, J. McCristal Culp, and A. Harris (eds.), *Crossroads, Directions and a New Critical Race Theory*. Chicago: Temple University Press.

Gutting, G. (1994). "Michel Foucault: A User's Manual." In G. Gutting (ed.), *The Cambridge Companion to Foucault*. Cambridge: Cambridge University Press.

Gutman, A., and Thompson, D. (2004). *Why Deliberative Democracy?* Princeton, NJ: Princeton University Press.

Habermas, J. (1989). *The Structural Transformation of the Public Sphere*, trans. T. Burger. Cambridge: Polity Press.

Habermas, J. (1992). "Citizenship and National Identity: Some Reflections on the Future of Europe." *Praxis International*, 12(1).

Habermas, J. (1996). *Between Facts and Norms*. Cambridge: Polity Press.

Habermas, J. (1999). "Bestiality and Humanity: A War on the Border between Legality and Morality." *Constellations* 6/3: 263–72.

Habermas, J. (2001). *The Postnational Constellation*. Cambridge: Polity.

Habermas, J. (2006). *The Divided West*. Cambridge: Polity.

Habermas, J., and Derrida, J. (2005). "February 15, or, What Binds Europe Together." In D. Levy, M. Pensky, and J. Torpey (eds.), *Old Europe, New Europe, Core Europe: Transatlantic Relations after the Iraq War*. London: Verso.

Hadden, J., and Tarrow, S. (2007). "The Global Justice Movement in the United States since Seattle." In D. Della Porta (ed.), *The Global Justice Movement: Cross-National and Transnational Perspectives*. Boulder, CO, and London: Paradigm.

Hafez, K. (2007). *The Myth of Media Globalization*. Cambridge: Polity.

Hall, S. (1990). "Cultural Identity and Diaspora." In J. Rutherford (ed.), *Identity: Community, Culture, Difference*. London: Lawrence and Wishart.

Hall, S. (1991a). "Old and New Identities, Old and New Ethnicities." In A. D. King (ed.), *Culture, Globalisation and the World System: Contemporary Conditions for the Representation of Identity*. London: Macmillan.

Hall, S. (1991b). "The Local and the Global: Globalisation and Ethnicity." In A. D. King (ed.), *Culture, Globalisation and the World System: Contemporary Conditions for the Representation of Identity*. London: Macmillan.

Hall, S., and du Gay, P. (1996). *Questions of Cultural Identity*. London: Sage.

Hammar, T. (1990). *Democracy and the Nation-State: Aliens, Denizens and Citizens*. Aldershot, Hants: Avebury Press.

Hardt, M., and Negri, A. (2000). *Empire*. Cambridge, MA: Harvard University Press.

Harvey, D. (1989). *The Condition of Postmodernity*. Oxford: Blackwell.

Harvey, D. (2003). *The New Imperialism*. Oxford: Oxford University Press.

Harvey, D. (2005). *A Brief History of Neo-Liberalism*. Oxford: Oxford University Press.

Held, D. (1987). *Models of Democracy*. Cambridge: Polity Press.

Held, D. (1995a). *Democracy and Global Order: From the Modern State to Cosmopolitan Governance*. Cambridge: Polity Press.

Held, D. (1995b). "Democracy and the New International Order." In D. Archibugi and D. Held (eds.), *Cosmopolitan Democracy: An Agenda for a New World Order*. Cambridge: Polity Press.

Held, D. (1998). "Democracy and Globalization." In D. Archibugi, D. Held, and M. Kohler (eds.), *Re-Imagining Political Community*. Stanford, CA: Stanford University Press.

Held, D. (1999). "The Transformation of Political Community: Rethinking Democracy in the Context of Globalization." In I. Shapiro and C. Hacker-Cordon (eds.), *Democracy's Edges*. Cambridge: Cambridge University Press.

Held, D. (2002). "Law of States, Law of Peoples: Three Models of Sovereignty." *Legal Theory* 8/1: 1–44.

Held, D. (2003). "Global Social Democracy." In A. Giddens (ed.), *The Progressive Manifesto*. Cambridge: Polity.

Held, D. (2004). *Global Covenant: The Social Democratic Alternative to the Washington Consensus*. Cambridge: Polity.

Held, D., and McGrew, A. (2002). *Globalization/Anti-Globalization*. Cambridge: Polity.

Herman, D. (1993). "The Politics of Law Reform: Lesbian and Gay Rights Struggles into the 1990s." In J. Bristow and A. Wilson (eds.), *Activating Theory: Lesbian, Gay, Bisexual Politics*. London: Lawrence and Wishart.

Hernes, H. (1984). "Women and the Welfare State: The Transition from Private to Public Dependence." In H. Holter (ed.), *Patriarchy in a Welfare State.* Oslo: Universitetsforlaget.

Hindess, B. (1996). *Discourses of Power: From Hobbes to Foucault.* Oxford: Blackwell.

Hirsh, D. (2003), *Law against Genocide: Cosmopolitan Trials.* London: Glasshouse Press.

Hirst, P. (1979). *On Law and Ideology.* London: Macmillan.

Hirst, P., and Thompson, G. (1996). *Globalization in Question: The International Economy and the Possibilities of Governance.* Cambridge: Polity Press.

Hix, S. (2008). "The EU as a New Political System." In D. Caramani (ed.), *Comparative Politics.* Oxford: Oxford University Press.

Hollinger, D. (2000). *Postethnic America.* New York: Basic Books.

Ignatieff, M. (1994). *Blood and Belonging.* London: Vintage.

Ignatieff, M. (2001). *Human Rights as Politics and Idolatry.* Princeton, NJ: Princeton University Press.

Ignatieff, M. (2003). *Empire-Lite: Nation-Building in Bosnia, Kosovo and Afghanistan.* London: Vintage.

Imrig, D., and Tarrow, S. (eds.) (2001). *Contentious Europeans: Protest and Politics in an Emerging Polity.* Lanham, MD: Rowman and Littlefield.

Jacobson, D. (1996). *Rights across Borders: Immigration and the Decline of Citizenship.* Baltimore, MD, and London: Johns Hopkins University Press.

Jacobson, D., and Ruffer, G. (2003). "Courts across Borders: The Implications of Judicial Agency for Human Rights and Democracy." *Human Rights Quarterly,* 25/1: 74–93.

Jameson, F. (1984). "Postmodernism, or the Cultural Logic of Late Capitalism." *New Left Review,* 146.

Jessop, B. (1997). "Capitalism and Its Future: Remarks on Regulation, Government and Governance." *Review of International Political Economy,* 4(3).

Johns, F. (2005). "Guantanamo Bay and the Annihilation of the Exception." *European Journal of International Law* 16/4: 613–35.

Johnston, H., and Klandermans, B. (eds.) (1995). *Social Movements and Culture.* London: UCL Press.

Joppke, C. (2004). "The Retreat of Multiculturalism in the Liberal State: Theory and Practice." *British Journal of Sociology,* 55/2: 237–57.

Jordan, G., and Weedon, C. (1995). *Cultural Politics: Class, Gender, Race and the Postmodern World.* Oxford: Blackwell.

Joseph, S. (2004). *Corporations and Transnational Human Rights Litigation.* Portland, Oregon: Hart.

Kaldor, M. (2003). "The Idea of Global Civil Society." *International Affairs,* 79/3: 583–93.

Keane, J. (2003). *Global Civil Society?* Cambridge: Cambridge University Press.

Keck, M., and Sikkink, K. (1998). *Activists beyond Borders: Advocacy Networks in International Politics*. Ithaca, NY: Cornell University Press.

King, D. (1991). "Citizenship as Obligation in the United States: Title II of the Family Support Act of 1988." In U. Vogel and M. Moran (eds.), *The Frontiers of Citizenship*. London: Macmillan.

Kivisto, P. (ed.) (2005). *Incorporating Diversity: Rethinking Assimilation in a Multicultural Age*. Boulder, CO: Paradigm Publishers.

Kivisto, P., and Faist, T. (2007). *Citizenship: Discourse, Theory, and Transnational Prospects*. Oxford: Blackwell.

Klandermans, B., Kriesi, H., and Tarrow, S. (eds.) (1988). *From Structure to Action: Social Movement Research across Different Cultures*. Greenwich, CT, and London: JAI Press.

Klein, N. (2000). *No Logo*. London: Flamingo.

Kuhn, T. (1970). *The Structure of Scientific Revolution*. Chicago: University of Chicago Press.

Kumar, A., Scholte, J., Kaldor, M., Glasuis, M., Seckinelgin, H., and Anheier, H. (2009). *Global Civil Society 2009: Poverty and Activism*. London: Sage.

Kumar, K. (1995). *From Post-Industrial to Postmodern Society: New Theories of the Contemporary World*. Oxford: Blackwell.

Kymlicka, W. (1995). *Multi-Cultural Citizenship: A Liberal Theory of Minority Rights*. Oxford: Oxford University Press.

Kymlicka, W. (1999a). "Liberal Complacenicies." In J. Cohen, M. Howard, and M. Nussbaum (eds.), *Is Multiculturalism Bad for Women?* Princeton, NJ: Princeton University Press.

Kymlicka, W. (1999b). "Citizenship in an Era of Globalization: Commentary on Held." In I. Shapiro and C. Hacker-Cordon (eds.), *Democracy's Edges*. Cambridge: Cambridge University Press.

Laclau, E., and Mouffe, C. (1985). *Hegemony and Socialist Strategy: Towards a Radical Democratic Politics*. London: Verso.

Lamont, M., and Thevenot, L. (2000). *Rethinking Comparative Cultural Sociology: Repertoires of Evaluation in France and the United States*. Cambridge: Cambridge University Press.

Lash, S., and Urry, J. (1987). *The End of Organized Capitalism*. Cambridge: Polity Press.

Lash, S., and Urry, J. (1994). *Economies of Signs and Space*. London: Sage.

Lechner, J., and Boli, J. (2005). *World Culture: Origins and Consequences*. Malden, MA: Blackwell.

Lipschutz, R. D. (2004). *Global Environmental Politics: Power, Perspectives, and Practice*. Washington, DC: CQ Press.

Lieven, A. (2004). *America Right or Wrong: An Anatomy of American Nationalism*, Hammersmith: HarperCollins.

Lister, R. (1996). *Charles Murray and the Underclass: The Developing Debate*. London: IEA Health and Welfare Unit.

Lister, R. (2004). *Poverty*. Cambridge: Polity.

Long, E. (1997). *Sociology and Cultural Studies*. Maiden, MA: Blackwell.

Lukes, S. (1973). *Emile Durkheim: His Life and Work*. Harmondsworth, Middlesex: Penguin.

Lukes, S. (1974). *Power: A Radical View*. London: Macmillan.

Lury, C. (2004). *Brands: The Logos of the Global Economy*. London: Routledge.

McAdam, D. (1996). "Conceptual Origins, Current Problems, Future Directions." In D. McAdam, J. McCarthy, and M. Zald (eds.), *Comparative Perspectives on Social Movements: Political Opportunities, Mobilizing Structures, and Cultural Framings*. Cambridge: Cambridge University Press.

McAdam, D., McCarthy, J., and Zald, M. (eds.) (1996). *Comparative Perspectives on Social Movements: Political Opportunities, Mobilizing Structures, and Cultural Framings*. Cambridge: Cambridge University Press.

McCarthy, T. (1999). "On Reconciling Cosmopolitan Unity and National Diversity." *Public Culture*. (1999), 11/1:175–208.

McKay, D. (2005). *American Politics and Society*, sixth edition. Oxford: Blackwell.

McClure, K. (1992). "On the Subject of Rights: Pluralism, Plurality and Political Identity." In C. Mouffe (ed.), *Dimensions of Radical Democracy: Pluralism, Citizenship, Community*. London: Verso.

McDonald, K. (2002). "*L'Intervention sociologique* after Twenty-Five Years: Can It Translate into English?" *Qualitative Sociology*, 25/2: 247–60.

McDonald, K. (2006). *Global Movements: Action and Culture*. Oxford: Blackwell.

McGrew, A. (1992). "A Global Society?" In S. Hall, D. Held, and A. McGrew (eds.) *Modernity and Its Futures*. Cambridge: Polity Press.

McGrew, A. (1995). "World Order and Political Space." In J. Anderson, C. Brook, and A. Cochrane (eds.), *A Global World? Re-Ordering Political Space*. Oxford: Oxford University Press.

McGrew, A. (1997). "Democracy beyond Borders." In A. McGrew (ed.), *The Transformation of Democracy? Globalization and Territorial Democracy*. Cambridge: Polity Press.

McKay, G. (1998). *DIY Culture: Party and Protest in Nineties Britain*. London: Verso.

McKay, D. (2005). *American Politics and Society*, sixth edition. Oxford: Blackwell.

McNay, L. (1994). *Foucault: A Critical Introduction*. Cambridge: Polity Press.

Mair, P. (2008). "Democracies." In D. Caramani (ed.), *Comparative Politics*. Oxford: Oxford University Press.

Mair, P., and van Biezen, I. (2001). "Party Membership in Twenty European Democracies, 1980–2000." *Party Politics*, 7/1: 5–21.

Mann, M. (1996). "Ruling Class Strategies and Citizenship." In M. Bulmer and A. Rees (eds.), *Citizenship Today: The Contemporary Relevance of T. H. Marshall*. London: UCL Press.

Mann, M. (2003). *Incoherent Empire*. London: Verso.

Manza, J., Hout, M., and Brooks, C. (2009). "Class Voting in Capitalist Democracies since World War II: Dealignment, Realignment, or Trendless Fluctuation?" In K. Nash, A. M. Smith, and A. Scott (eds.), *Contentious and Conventional Politics*, vol. 2: *New Critical Writings in Political Sociology*, Aldershot, Hampshire, and Burlington, VT: Ashgate.

Marsh, D. (1995). "The Convergence between Theories of the State." In D. Marsh and G. Stoker (eds.), *Theory and Methods in Political Science*. London, Macmillan.

Marshall, T. H. (1992). *Citizenship and Social Class*, ed. T. Bottomore. London: Pluto Press.

Marx, K. (1977). *Selected Writings*, ed. D. McLellan. Oxford: Oxford University Press.

Marx, K. (1992). "The Eighteenth Brumaire of Louis Bonaparte." In *Surveys from Exile: Political Writings*, vol. 2, D. Fernbach (ed.). London: Penguin.

Mason, D. (1995). *Race and Ethnicity in Modern Britain*. Oxford: Oxford University Press.

Meehan, E. (1997). "Political Pluralism and European Citizenship." In P. Lehning and A. Weale (eds.), *Citizenship, Democracy and Justice in the New Europe*. London: Routledge.

Melucci, A. (1988). "Getting Involved: Identity and Mobilization in Social Movements." In B. Klandermans, H. Kriesi, and S. Tarrow (eds.), *From Structure to Action: Comparing Social Movement Research across Cultures*. Greenwich, Connecticut: JAI Press.

Melucci, A. (1989). *Nomads of the Present: Social Movements and Individual Needs in Contemporary Society*, ed. J. Keane and P. Mier. London: Hutchinson Radius.

Melucci, A. (1995a). "The New Social Movements Revisited: Reflections on a Sociological Misunderstanding." In L. Maheu (ed.), *Social Movements and Social Classes: The Future of Collective Action*. London: Sage.

Melucci, A. (1995b). "The Process of Collective Action." In H. Johnston and B. Klandermans (eds.), *Social Movements and Culture*. London: UCL Press.

Melucci, A. (1996). *The Playing Self: Person and Meaning in the Planetary Society*. Cambridge: Cambridge University Press.

Merry, S. (2006). *Human Rights and Gender Violence: Translating International Law into Local Justice*. Chicago: University of Chicago Press.

Meyer, J., Boli, J., Thomas, G., and Ramirez, F. (1997). "World Society and the Nation-State." *American Journal of Sociology*, 103(1): 144–81.

Meyer, J. (1999). "The Changing Cultural Content of the Nation-State: A World Society Perspective." In G. Steinmetz (ed.), *State/Culture: State-Formation after the Cultural Turn*. Ithaca, NY: Cornell University Press.

Meyer J., and Jepperson, R. (2000). "The Actors of Modern Society: The Cultural Construction of Social Agency." *Sociological Theory*, 18/1: 100–20.

Meyer, J., Ramirez, F., and Soysal, Y. (1992). "World Expansion of Mass Education 1870–1980." *Sociology of Education*, 65/2: 128–49.

Micheletti, M., Follesdal, A., and Stolle, D. (eds.) (2004). *Politics, Products and Markets: Exploring Political Consumerism Past and Present*. New Brunswick, NJ: Transaction.

Michels, R. (1962). *Political Parties*. New York: Free Press.

Miliband, R. (1969). *The State in Capitalist Society*. London: Weidenfeld and Nicolson.

Mills, C. W. (1956). *The Power Elite*. Oxford: Oxford University Press.

Mitchell, M., and Russell, R. (1996). "Immigration, Citizenship and the Nation-State in the New Europe." In B. Jenkins and S. Sofos (eds.), *Nation and Identity in Contemporary Europe*. London: Routledge.

Modood, T. (2007). *Multiculturalism*. Cambridge: Polity.

Moghadam, V. (2005). *Globalizing Women: Transnational Feminist Networks*. Baltimore, MD: Johns Hopkins University Press.

Moghadam, V. (2008). *Globalization and Social Movements: Islamicism, Feminism, and the Global Justice Movement*. Lanham, MD: Rowman and Littlefield.

Monbiot, G. (2004). *The Age of Consent: A Manifesto for a New World Order*. London: Harper Perennial.

Monbiot, G. (2005). "Africa's New Best Friends." *The Guardian*, 5 July.

Montgomery, J. (2002). "Sovereignty in Transition." In J. Montgomery and N. Glazer (eds.), *Sovereignty under Challenge*. New Brunswick, NJ: Transaction.

Morley, D., and Chen, K.-H. (1996). *Stuart Hall: Critical Dialogues in Cultural Studies*. London: Routledge.

Morris, A. (1993). "Cultures of Black Protest: Its Significance for America and the World." In H. Hill and J. E. Jones Jr. (eds.), *Race in America: the Struggle for Equality*. Madison: University of Wisconsin Press.

Morris, A., and Mueller, C. (eds.) (1992). *Frontiers in Social Movement Theory*. London: Yale University Press.

Morris, L. (1996). "Dangerous Classes: Neglected Aspects of the Underclass Debate." In E. Mingione (ed.), *Urban Poverty and the Underclass*. Oxford, Blackwell.

Morris, M. (1992). "The Man in the Mirror: David Harvey's 'Condition of Postmodernity.'" In M. Featherstone (ed.), *Cultural Theory and Cultural Change*. London: Sage.

Morrison, T. (1992). *Playing in the Dark: Whiteness and the Literary Imagination*. London: Picador.

Mort, F. (1994). "Essentialism Revisited? Identity Politics and Late Twentieth Century Discourse of Homosexuality." In J. Weeks (ed.), *The Lesser Evil and the Greater Good: The Theory and Politics of Social Diversity*. London: Rivers Oram Press.

Muller, H.-P. (1993). "Durkheim's Political Sociology." In S. P. Turner (ed.), *Emile Durkheim: Sociologist and Moralist*. London and New York: Routledge.

Naples, N., and Desai, M. (eds.) (2002). *Women's Activism and Globalization: Linking Local Struggles and Transnational Politics*. New York and London: Routledge.

Nash, K. (1997). "A 'Politics of Ideas' and Women's Citizenship." *Acta Philosophica*, 2.

Nash, K. (1998). "Beyond Liberalism: Feminist Theories of Democracy." In V. Randall and G. Waylen (eds.), *Gender, Politics and the State*. London: Routledge.

Nash, K. (2008). "Global Citizenship as Show Business: The Cultural Politics of Make Poverty History." *Media, Culture and Society*, 30/2.

Nash, K. (2009a). *The Cultural Politics of Human Rights: Comparing the US and UK*. Cambridge: Cambridge University Press.

Nash, K. (2009b). "Between Citizenship and Human Rights." *Sociology*, 43/6.

Newman, M. (1996). *Democracy, Sovereignty and the European Union*. London: Hurst and Co.

Nicholson, L. (1983). "Women, Morality and History." *Social Research*, 50(3).

Norval, A. (2008). *Aversive Democracy: Inheritance and Originality in the Democratic Tradition*. Cambridge: Cambridge University Press.

Notes from Nowhere. (2003). *We Are Everywhere: The Irresistible Rise of Global Anti-Capitalism*. London: Verso.

Nye, J. (2005). *Soft Power: The Means to Success in World Politics*. New York: Public Affairs.

Nyer, P. (2006). "The Accidental Citizen: Acts of Sovereignty and (Un)making Citizenship." *Economy and Society*, 35/1: 22–41.

Oberleitner, G. (2007). *Global Human Rights Institutions: Between Remedy and Ritual*. Cambridge: Polity.

Oberschall, A. (1973). *Social Conflict and Social Movements*. Englewood Cliffs, NJ: Prentice-Hall.

Offe, C. (1987). "Challenging the Boundaries of Institutional Politics: Social Movements since the 1960s." In C. S. Maier (ed.), *Changing Boundaries of the Political: Essays on the Evolving Balance between the State and Society, Public and Private in Europe*. Cambridge: Cambridge University Press.

Ohmae, K. (1995). *The End of the Nation State: The Rise of Regional Economies*. London: Harper Collins.

Okin, S. (1999). "Is Multiculturalism Bad for Women?" In J. Cohen, M. Howard, and M. Nussbaum (eds.), *Is Multiculturalism Bad for Women?* Princeton, NJ: Princeton University Press.

O'Leary, S. (1995). "The Social Dimension of Community Citizenship." In A. Rosas and E. Antola (eds.), *A Citizens' Europe: In Search of a New Order*. London: Sage.

Olson, M. (1968). *The Logic of Collective Action: Public Goods and the Theory of Groups*. New York: Schocken Books.

Omi, M., and Winant, H. (1987). *Racial Formation in the United States: From the Sixties to the Eighties*. London: Routledge.

Oommen, T. (1997). *Citizenship, Nationality and Ethnicity*. Cambridge: Polity Press.

Ortener, S. (2006). *Anthropology and Social Theory: Culture, Power, and the Acting Subject*. Durham, NC, and London: Duke University Press.

Orum, A. (1983). *Introduction to Political Sociology: The Political Anatomy of the Body Politic*, second edition. Englewood Cliffs, NJ: Prentice-Hall.

Oswell, D. (2006). *Culture and Society: An Introduction to Cultural Studies*. London: Sage.

Outhwaite, W. (1994). *Habermas: A Critical Introduction*. Cambridge: Polity Press.

Pakulski, J. (1997). "Cultural Citizenship." *Citizenship Studies*, 1/1: 73–86.

Parekh, B. (1993). "The Cultural Particularity of Liberal Democracy." In D. Held (ed.), *Prospects for Democracy: North, South, East, West*. Cambridge: Polity Press.

Parkin, F. (1992). *Durkheim*. Oxford: Oxford University Press.

Parry, G. (1969). *Political Elites*. London: George Allen and Unwin.

Peretti, J., with Micheletti, M. (2004). "The Nike Sweatshop Email: Political Consumerism, Internet, and Culture Jamming." In M. Micheletti, A. Follesdal, and D. Stolle (eds.), *Politics, Products and Markets: Exploring Political Consumerism Past and Present*. New Brunswick, NJ: Transaction.

Phillips, A. (1991). *Engendering Democracy*. Cambridge: Polity Press.

Phillips, A. (1995). *The Politics of Presence*. Oxford: Clarendon Press.

Phillips, A. (2007). *Multiculturalism without Culture*. Princeton, NJ: Princeton University Press.

Pickvance, C. (1995). "Social Movements in the Transition from State Socialism." In L. Maheu (ed.), *Social Movements and Social Classes: The Future of Collective Action*. London: Sage.

Poguntke, T., and Webb, P. (2005). *The Presidentialization of Politics: A Comparative Study of Modern Democracies*. Oxford: Oxford University Press.

Potužáková, Z. (2007). "Current Situation of the EU Labour Market." Central and East European International Studies Association 6th Convention, Wroclaw, 24–26 May.

Procacci, G. (1996). "A New Social Contract? Against Exclusion: The Poor and the Social Sciences." European University Institute Working Paper, RSC, no. 96/41.

Przeworski, A. (1990). *The State and the Economy under Capitalism*. London: Harwood Academic Publishers.

Pugh, M. (1992). *Women and the Women's Movement in Britain 1914–59*. London: Macmillan.

Putnam, R. (2000). *Bowling Alone: The Collapse and Revival of American Community*. New York: Simon and Schuster.

Putnam, R. (ed.) (2002). *Democracies in Flux: The Evolution of Social Capital in Contemporary Society*. Oxford: Oxford University Press.

Ratner, S., and Abrams, J. (2001). *Accountability for Human Rights Atrocities in International Law: Beyond the Nuremberg Legacy*. Oxford: Oxford University Press.

Rees, A. (1996). "T. H. Marshall and the Progress of Citizenship." In M. Bulmer and A. Rees (eds.), *Citizenship Today: The Contemporary Relevance of T. H. Marshall*. London: UCL Press.

Richmond, A. (1994). *Global Apartheid: Refugees, Racism and the New World Order*. Oxford: Oxford University Press.

Riley, D. (1988). *Am I That Name?: Feminism and the Category of "Women" in History*. London: Macmillan.

Risse, T., Ropp, S., and Sikkink, K. (1999). *The Power of Human Rights: Institutional Norms and Domestic Change*. Cambridge: Cambridge University Press.

Robbins, B. (1998). "Actually Existing Cosmopolitanism." In P. Cheah and B. Robbins (eds.), *Cosmopolitics: Thinking and Feeling beyond the Nation*. Minneapolis: University of Minnesota Press.

Robertson, R. (1992). *Globalization: Social Theory and Global Culture*. London: Sage.

Roche, M. (1995). "Rethinking Citizenship and Social Movements: Themes in Contemporary Sociology and Neoconservative Ideology." In L. Maheu (ed.), *Social Movements and Social Classes: The Future of Collective Action*. London: Sage.

Rochon, T. (1998). *Culture Moves: Ideas, Activism, and Changing Values*. Princeton, NJ: Princeton University Press.

Rootes, C. (2005). "A Limited Transnationalization? The British Environmental Movement." In D. Della Porta and S. Tarrow (ed.), *Transnational Protest and Global Activism*. Lanham, MD: Rowman and Littlefield.

Rosaldo, R. (1999). "Cultural Citizenship, Inequality and Multiculturalism." In R. Torres, L. Miron, and J. India (eds.), *Race, Identity and Citizenship*. Oxford: Blackwell.

Rose, N. (1990) *Governing the Soul: The Shaping of the Private Self*. London: Routledge.

Rose, N. (1999). *Powers of Freedom: Reframing Political Thought*. Cambridge: Cambridge University Press.

Rose, N., and Miller, P. (1992). "Political Power beyond the State: Problematics of Government." *British Journal of Sociology*, 43/2: 173–205.

Rose, N., and Miller, P. (1995). "Political Thought and the Limits of Orthodoxy: A Response to Curtis." *British Journal of Sociology*, 46/4: 590–7.

Roth, K. (2000). "The Charade of US Ratification of International Human Rights Treaties." *Chicago Journal of International Law*, 1/2: 347–54.

Rumford, C. (2007). *Cosmopolitanism and Europe*. Liverpool: Liverpool University Press.

Sassatelli, R. (2007). *Consumer Culture: History, Theory and Politics*. London: Sage.

Sassen, S. (2006). *Territory, Authority, Rights: From Medieval to Global Assemblages*. Princeton, NJ: Princeton University Press.

Saussure, F. de (1966). *Course in General Linguistics*. New York, London: McGraw-Hill.

Schachar, A. (2001). *Multicultural Jurisdictions: Cultural Differences and Women's Rights*. Cambridge: Cambridge University Press.

Schlosberg, S., Shulman, S., and Zavestoski, S. (2006). "Virtual Environmental Citizenship: Web-Based Public Participation in Rule Making in the United States." In A. Dobson and D. Bell (eds.), *Environmental Citizenship*. Cambridge, MA: MIT Press.

Scholte, J. (2005). *Globalization: A Critical Introduction*. Basingstoke: Palgrave Macmillan.

Schudson, M. (1998). *The Good Citizen: A History of American Civic Life*. Cambridge, MA: Harvard University Press.

Schumpeter, J. (1943). *Capitalism, Socialism and Democracy*. London: Unwin University Books.

Schwarz, J. (2005). *Freedom Reclaimed: Rediscovering the American Vision*. Baltimore, MD: Johns Hopkins University Press.

Scott, A. (1990). *Ideology and the New Social Movements*. London: Unwin Hyman.

Scott, A. (1996a). "Weber and Michels on Bureaucracy." In R. Bellamy and A. Ross (eds.), *A Textual Introduction to Social and Political Theory*. Manchester: Manchester University Press.

Scott, A. (1996b). "Movements of Modernity: Some Questions of Theory, Method and Interpretation." In J. Clark and M. Diani (eds.), *Alain Touraine*. London: Falmer Press.

Scott, A. (1997a). "Modernity's Machine Metaphor." *British Journal of Sociology*, 48(4).

Scott, A. (1997b). "Introduction – Globalization: Social Process or Political Rhetoric." In A. Scott (ed.), *The Limits of Globalization: Cases and Arguments*. London: Routledge.

Scott, A., and Street, J. A. (2001). "From Media Politics to E-protest? The Use of Popular Culture and New Media in Parties and Social Movements." In F. Webster (ed.), *Culture and Politics in the Information Age*. London: Routledge.

Scott, J. (1994). *Poverty and Wealth: Citizenship, Deprivation and Privilege*. Longman: Harlow, Essex.

Seidman, S. (1993). "Identity Politics in a 'Postmodern' Gay Culture: Some Historical and Conceptual Notes." In M. Warner (ed.), *Fear of a Queer Planet*. Minneapolis: University of Minnesota Press.

Sen, A. (1999). *Development as Freedom*. Oxford: Oxford University Press

Sewell, W. (1992). "A Theory of Structure: Duality, Agency, and Transformation." *American Journal of Sociology*, 98/1: 1–29.

Siim, B. (1988). "Towards a Feminist Rethinking of the Welfare State." In K. Jones and A. Jonasdottir (eds.), *The Political Interests of Gender: Developing Theory and Research with a Feminist Face*. London: Sage.

Silver, H. (1996). "Culture, Politics and National Discourses of the New Urban Poverty." In E. Mingione (ed.), *Urban Poverty and the Underclass*. Oxford: Blackwell.

Simon, R. (1982). *Gramsci's Political Thought: An Introduction*. London: Lawrence and Wishart.

Singh, R. (2003). *American Government and Politics: A Concise Introduction*. London: Sage.

Sklair, L. (2002). *Globalization: Capitalism and Its Alternatives*, third edition. Oxford: Oxford University Press.

Skocpol, T. (2003). *Diminished Democracy: From Membership to Management in American Civic Life*. Norman: University of Oklahoma Press.

Slaughter, A.-M. (2004). *A New World Order*. Princeton, NJ: Princeton University Press.

Smith, J. (2008). *Social Movements for Global Democracy*. Baltimore, MD: Johns Hopkins University Press.

Smith, M. (1995). "Pluralism." In D. Marsh and G. Stoker (eds.), *Theory and Methods in Political Science*. London: Macmillan.

Smith, P. (2005). *Why War? The Cultural Logic of Iraq, the Gulf War and Suez*. Chicago: University of Chicago Press.

Snow, D., and Benford, R. (1988). "Ideology, Frame Resonance, and Participant Mobilization." In B. Klandermans, H. Kriesi, and S. Tarrow (eds.), *From Structure to Action: Social Movement Research across Different Cultures*. Greenwich, CT, and London: JAI Press.

Snow, D., and Benford, R. (1992). "Master Frames and Cycles of Protest." In A. Morris and C. Mueller (eds.), *Frontiers in Social Movement Theory*. New Haven, CT, and London: Yale University Press.

Snow, D., Rocheford, E., Worden, S., and Benford, R. (1986). "Frame Alignment Processes, Micromobilization and Movement Participation." *American Sociological Review*, 51: 464–81.

Snow, D., Zurchner, L., and Ekland-Olson, S. (1980). "Social Networks and Social Movements." *American Sociological Review*, 45(5).

Solomos, J. (1993). *Race and Racism in Britain*, second edition. London: Macmillan.

Somers, M. (2008). *Genealogies of Citizenship: Markets, Statelessness, and the Right to Have Rights*. Cambridge: Cambridge University Press.

Soysal, Y. (1994). *Limits of Citizenship: Migrants and Postnational Membership in Europe*. Chicago: University of Chicago Press.

Spivak, G. (1999). *A Critique of Postcolonial Reason: Toward a History of the Vanishing Present*. Cambridge, MA: Harvard University Press.

Stammers, N. (2009). *Human Rights and Social Movements*. London: Pluto Press.

Stephens, J. (1996). "The Scandinavian Welfare States: Achievements, Crisis and Prospects." In G. Epsing-Andersen (ed.), *Welfare States in Transition: National Adaptations in Global Economies*. London: Sage.

Stevenson, N. (1999). *The Transformation of the Media: Globalisation, Morality and Ethics*. Harlow, Essex: Pearson Education.

Stevenson, N. (ed.) (2001). *Cultural Citizenship*. London: Sage

Stevenson, N. (2003). *Cultural Citizenship: Cosmopolitan Questions*. Buckingham: Open University.

Stevenson, N. (2007). "Cosmopolitanism and Europe: Post-Colonialism and the Politics of Imperialism." In C. Rumford (ed.), *Cosmopolitanism and Europe*. Liverpool: Liverpool University Press.

Steward, F. (1991). "Citizens of Planet Earth." In G. Andrews (ed.), *Citizenship*. London: Lawrence and Wishart.

Stone Sweet, A. (2008). "Constitutions and Judicial Power." In D. Caramani (ed.), *Comparative Politics*. Oxford: Oxford University Press.

Street, J. (2003). "The Celebrity Politician: Political Style and Popular Culture." In J. Corner and D. Pels (eds.), *Media and the Restyling of Politics*. London: Sage.

Street, J. (2004). "Celebrity Politicians: Popular Culture and Political Representation." *British Journal of Politics and International Relations*, 6/4: 435–52.

Sullivan, A. (1995). *Virtually Normal: An Argument about Homosexuality*. London: Picador.

Tarrow, S. (1989). "Struggle, Politics and Reform: Collective Action, Social Movements and Cycles of Protest." Western Societies paper no. 21. Ithaca, NY: Cornell University Press.

Tarrow, S. (1992). "Mentalities, Political Cultures, and Collective Action Frames: Constructing Meanings Through Action." In A. Morris and C. Mueller (eds.), *Frontiers in Social Movement Theory*. New Haven, CT, and London: Yale University Press.

Tarrow, S. (1998). *Power in Movement: Social Movements and Contentious Politics*, second edition. Cambridge: Cambridge University Press.

Tarrow, S. (2005). *The New Transnational Activism*. Cambridge: Cambridge University Press.

Taylor, B. (1983). *Eve and the New Jerusalem: Socialism and Feminism in the Nineteenth Century*. London: Virago.

Taylor, G. (1995). "Marxism." In D. Marsh and G. Stoker (eds.), *Theory and Methods in Political Science*. London: Macmillan.

Thompson, J. B. (1996). *The Media and Modernity: A Social Theory of the Media*. Cambridge: Polity.

Tilly, C. (1978). *From Mobilization to Revolution*. Reading, MA: Addison-Wesley.

Tilly, C. (1984). "Social Movements and National Politics." In C. Bright and S. Harding (eds.), *Statemaking and Social Movements: Essays in History and Theory*. Ann Arbor: University of Michigan Press.

Tonkiss, F. (2001). "Markets against States: Neo-liberalism." In K. Nash and A. Scott (eds.), *The Blackwell Companion to Political Sociology*. Oxford: Blackwell.

Tonkiss, F. (2005). *Contemporary Economic Sociology: Globalisation, Production, Inequality*. London: Routledge.

Touraine, A. (1981). *The Voice and the Eye: An Analysis of Social Movements*. Cambridge: Cambridge University Press.

Touraine, A. (1983). *Anti-Nuclear Protest: The Opposition to Nuclear Energy in France*. Cambridge: Cambridge University Press.

Turner, B. (1986). *Citizenship and Capitalism: The Debate over Reformism*. London: Allen and Unwin.

Turner, B. (1990). "Outline of a Theory of Citizenship." *Sociology*, 24/2: 189–217.

Turner, B. (1992). "Preface to the Second Edition." In E. Durkheim, *Professional Ethics and Civic Morals*. London and New York: Routledge.

Turner, B. (1996). *The Body and Society: Explorations in Social Theory*, second edition. London: Sage.

Turner, B. (2001). "Outline of a General Theory of Cultural Citizenship." In N. Stevenson (ed.), *Cultural Citizenship*. London: Sage.

Turner, B. (2002). "Cosmopolitan Virtue, Globalization and Patriotism." *Theory, Culture and Society*, 19/1–2: 45–63.

Urbinati, N. (2003). "Can Cosmopolitan Democracy Be Democratic?" In D. Archibugi (ed.), *Debating Cosmopolitics*. London: Verso.

Urry, J. (2000). *Sociology beyond Societies: Mobilities for the Twenty-First Century*. London: Routledge

Van de Donk, W., Loader, B., Nixon, P., and Rucht, D. (eds.) (2004). *Cyberprotest: New Media, Citizens and Social Movements*. London: Routledge.

Van Steenbergen, B. (1994). "Towards a Global Ecological Citizenship." In B. van Steenbergen (ed.), *The Condition of Citizenship*. London: Sage.

Vertovec, S., and Cohen, R. (eds.) (2002). *Conceiving Cosmopolitanism: Theory, Context and Practice*. Oxford: Oxford University Press

Vogt, W. P. (1993). "Durkheim's Sociology of Law: Morality and the Cult of the Individual." In S. P. Turner (ed.), *Emile Durkheim: Sociologist and Moralist*. London and New York: Routledge.

Volpp, L. (2001). "Feminism and Multiculturalism." *Columbia Law Review*, 101: 1181–218.

Walby, S. (1994). "Is Citizenship Gendered?" *Sociology*, 28(2).

Wallerstein, I. (1979). *The Capitalist World Economy*. Cambridge: Cambridge University Press.

Wallerstein, I. (1990). "Culture as the Ideological Battleground." In M. Featherstone (ed.), *Global Culture: Nationalism, Globalization and Modernity*. London: Sage.

Wallerstein, I. (1991). "The National and the Universal: Can There Be Such a Thing as World Culture?" In A. King (ed.), *Culture, Globalization and the World-System*. London: Macmillan.

Washbourne, N. (2010). *Mediating Politics*. Maidenhead, Berkshire: Open University Press.

Waters, M. (1995). *Globalization*. London: Routledge.

Weber, M. (1948a). "Class, Status and Party." In H. H. Gerth and C. Wright Mills (eds.), *From Max Weber: Essays in Sociology*. London: Routledge and Kegan Paul.

Weber, M. (1948b). "Science as a Vocation." In H. H. Gerth and C. Wright Mills (eds.), *From Max Weber: Essays in Sociology*. London: Routledge and Kegan Paul.

Weeks, J. (1986). *Sexuality*. London: Routledge.

Weeks, J. (1993). *Sexuality and Its Discontents*. London: Routledge.

Wilkinson, R., and Pickett, K. (2009). *The Spirit Level: Why More Equal Societies Almost Always Do Better*. London: Allen Lane.

Williams, R. (1976). *Keywords*. London: Fontana.

Williams, R. (1981). *Culture*. Glasgow: Fontana.

Wilson, W. J. (1987). *The Truly Disadvantaged: The Inner City, the Underclass and Public Policy*. Chicago: University of Chicago Press.

Woods, N. (2002). "Global Governance and the Role of Institutions." In D. Held and A. McGrew (eds.), *Governing Globalization: Power, Authority and Global Governance*. Cambridge: Polity.

Young, I. (1996). "Communication and the Other: Beyond Deliberative Democracy." In S. Benhabib (ed.), *Democracy and Difference: Contesting the Boundaries of the Political*. Princeton, NJ: Princeton University Press.

Zald, M., and McCarthy, J. (eds.) (1987). *Social Movements in an Organizational Society: Collected Essays*. New Brunswick, NJ: Transaction Books.

Zald, M., and McCarthy, J. (eds.) (1988). *The Dynamics of Social Movements: Resource Mobilization, Social Control, and Tactics*. Lanham, MD, Boston, and London: University Press of America.

Index

Banal nationalism, 81–82
Bank of America, 229
Barbalet, Jack, 137
Barclays Bank, 229
Battle of Seattle, 216, 217
Baubock, Rainer, 180
Bay Times, 158
BBC, 83
Beck, Ulrich, 38–39, 55, 57–59
Belgium, political parties in, 197
Bellow, Saul, 163
Belmarsh Prison, 67
Benford, Rob, 101–102, 104
Blair, Tony, 199
Bohman, James, 225
Boltanski, Luc, 83
Bosniak, Linda, 180
Bottomore, Thomas, 11
Brands, *vs.* products, 54
Britain. *See* United Kingdom (UK)
Bureaucracy, in Weberian thought, 10–11
Butler, Judith, 82, 154, 158

C
Calhoun, Craig, 79, 88–89
Calvin Klein, 54
Cammaerts, Bart, 226
Canada
  multicultural ideal in, 165
  Shari'a law in, 167
Capitalism
  alternative globalization and, 218, 219, 221
  citizenship and, 136, 140
  civil society and, 215–216
  disorganized, 51–53
  environmentalism and, 188
  flexible post-modernity, 50
  footloose, 44
  globalization as consequence of, 46, 47–55
  Marxism tradition of political sociology and, 4–9
  turbo-, 44, 214, 215

Capital (Marx), 5
Castells, Manuel, 30, 35–37, 200, 221, 225–226
Castles, Stephen, 178
Celebrity politicians, 199
Chandhoke, Neera, 217
Chandler, David, 72
Child Poverty Action Group, 122–123
Chouliaraki, Lilie, 83–84
Citizens
  as consumers, 54, 141, 142, 198
  role in politics, 13–15
Citizenship
  attributing at birth, 161–162
  civil rights and, 135
  civil sphere and, 132, 133
  commitments to human rights and, 205
  criteria for, 187
  cultural politics of, 132–133
  ecological, 189–190
  effect of neo-liberal policies on, 134, 141–143, 146–147
  environment and, 186–191
  European, 182–186
  gay and lesbian movement/queer politics and, 155–159
  historical development of, 131, 136
  immigration, assimilation, "new racism" and, 161–165
  Marshall model of, 131–140
  migration and rights across borders, 177–182
  multiculturalism, group-differentiated rights, "new assimilationism" and, 165–176, 191n1
  national borders and, 133–134
  nationality and, 183
  political rights and, 135
  post-national (*see* Post-national citizenship)
  proliferation of statuses, 181
  racialization, ethnicity and, 159–176

expert systems and, 55
of modernity, 55–56, 58
Refugees, 176, 181–182
Religious minorities, rights granted to
in Britain, 167
Representative democracy, criticism
of, 201
Resident aliens, in U.S., 179–180
Resistance, power, domination, and,
24–25
Resource Mobilization Theory
(RMT), 91–106
cultural turn in, 99–106
national context, 129–130n1
New Social Movement Theory and,
112, 113, 118–123
premises, 93–99
rational choice theory and, 91, 92,
93–95
social movement analysis and,
130n2
Reverse discrimination, 169
Richmond, Anthony, 179, 180
Right-wing social movements, 235
Risk society, 57–59
RMT. *See* Resource Mobilization
Theory (RMT)
Robbins, Bruce, 82
Robertson, Roland, 48–49
Roosevelt, Eleanor, 77
Roper v Simmons, 207–208
Rose, Nikolas, 28
Rosenau, James, 64
Roth, Phillip, 163

S
"Salad bowl," 163–164
Sameness-difference dilemma,
women's movement and, 149–150
Same-sex partner rights, 156–157
Sarkozy, Nicolas, 81
Sassen, Saskia, 65, 66, 67
Satellite TV, creation of global
political community and, 82

Saussure, Ferdinand de, 20, 32
Scandinavia, citizenship rights in, 138
Schumpeter, Joseph, 11, 12, 13, 195
Schwarz, John, 144
Scientists
as members of world society, 60
role in sub-politics, 58
Scott, Alan, 41n3, 111
Scott, John, 147–148
Security state, 67
Seidman, Steven, 159
Self
formation through consumption,
52
life politics and transformation of,
56
Self-government, in federal systems,
154–155
Semiotics, 20
Sex, age of consent, 156
Sexual identity
modification of social structure
and, 35
queer activism and, 158–159
Sexuality, 22–23
Sexual orientation, discrimination for.
See Gay and lesbian movement
Shari'a law, 167
Signifying order, culture as, 238
Signifying practices, politics of, 237
Signs, post-industrial societies and,
114
Sikkink, Kathryn, 128, 129
Skocpol, Theda, 200
Slab thinking, 231
Slaughter, Anne-Marie, 65
Smelser, Neil, 92
Smith, Jackie, 129, 204
Snow, David, 100–102, 104
Social cohesion
multiculturalism and, 171–173
new assimilationists and, 175–176
Social constructionists, nominal
essentialism and, 153

Somers, Margaret, 133, 208
Soysal, Yasemin, 179, 180, 182
"Special rights," 169–171
"Spin doctors," 198–199
State autonomy
  globalization and, 193
  state sovereignty *vs.*, 68–69, 71
State censorship, information
  technology and, 45, 69
State(s). *See also* Nation-state
  as actors in global governance,
    202–203
  arbiter model of, 5, 6
  citizenship and, 132, 134
  conditional globalization and,
    227–230
  convergence of Weberians and
    Marxists on relative autonomy
    of, 13
  cultural politics and, x
  democracy between, 209–213
  in Durkheimian thought, 15–16
  economic power of, 36–37
  effect of society on, 3
  Foucault and governmentality,
    26–29
  functionalist model of, 5, 7–8
  globalization and, 44, 45, 46, 48,
    69–70
  human rights and, 74
  human rights law and, 206–208
  imperialism and transformation of,
    63–78
  inequalities between, in IGOs,
    210–213
  instrumental model of, 5
  internationalizing, 38, 53, 64–66,
    239
  labor movement and modern, 89
  markets and, 44–45
  Marxist theory of, 4–6
  neo-Marxist theories of, 6–9
  new social movements and, 90–91
  NGOs and INGOs and, 64

  old social movements and, 88, 89,
    90
  in pluralist theory, 14
  privatization of functions, 65–66
  Resource Mobilization Theory and,
    92–93, 97
  rights of non-citizens and, 180,
    181–182
  security, 67
  as site of cultural politics, 36
  United Nations and, 210–211
  use of force and, 36, 37
  vertical and horizontal networks
    and, 65
  Weberian theory of, 9–10
State sovereignty
  cosmopolitan law and, 73–74
  globalization and, 193
  modern international state system
    and, 71–72
  restructuring of in global
    governance, 67–68
  state autonomy *vs.*, 68–69, 71
  terrorism and, 66–67
Steel-hard housing, of bureaucratic
  power, 10, 41n3
Street, John, 199
Structural Adjustment Programs, 71,
  212
*Structural Transformation of the
  Public Sphere, The* (Habermas),
  222–223, 226
Structuration theory, 34
Student movement of 1960s, 88, 98–99
"Subject and Power, The" (Foucault),
  24–25
Subjectivity
  disorganized capitalism and, 52
  global social movements and, 126
  as means of social control, 8
  politicizing of, 152
  power and, 23
  Resource Mobilization Theory and,
    92, 100